How to Trade Stocks for a Living

4 Books in 1

How to Start Day Trading, Dominate the Forex Market, Reduce Risk, and Increase Profit Fast with Swing Trading Options

PUBLISHED BY: Mark Lowe

Table Of Contents

Book#1

Day Trading for Beginners

Proven Strategies to Succeed and Create Passive Income in the Stock Market - Introduction to Forex Swing Trading, Options, Futures & ETFs

Introduction

Thank you for purchasing this beginner's guide to day trading.

In this book, you will learn the fundamentals of day trading and how it is different from other investment opportunities. You will also learn important trading strategies that many profitable day traders are using today.

This book is written in a simple and straightforward style so even people with no prior background in the stock market can easily learn the 'secrets of the trade'. If you are a newbie in day trading, this book can equip you with a basic understanding of where to begin, how to start, what to expect, and how you can create your own strategy.

However, merely reading this book will not make you a profitable day trader. Making money in the stock market hardly comes from reading a book. As you will learn later, revenue comes from actually doing it. Knowing is not enough. You need to practice, use the right tools, and continuously invest in your own education.

Even those with some years of experience in day trading can still benefit from this book's discussion of traditional strategies that most day traders are using effectively. Even if you are not a novice reader, I still encourage you to read the whole book as you may still find valuable lessons in these pages.

Day trading can help you make money, but it is not a sure way to get rich fast. This is not similar to playing the lottery. This is the biggest misconception that people have about day trading, and hopefully, you will dispel this notion after you read this book.

In fact, around 95% of people who start day trading end up in net loss.[1] It is easy to be part of the 95%. It is easy to lose money in day trading. So remember this number one rule in day trading:

Rule No. 1 - Day Trading Is Not a Get-Rich-Quick Scheme

A lot of people think that it is easy to make money in day trading. After all, you just need to buy some stocks, wait for them to go higher a bit, and then you sell them for a good price, right? Unfortunately, this is not true. If that is the case, then everyone would be rich by now.

You should always remember that day trading is not easy and it will not make you a millionaire overnight.

If you have this misconception, and you want to get rich fast, you must stop reading this book and invest your money somewhere else. If you are not ready to lose money in day trading, then forget day trading.

Day trading is a highly competitive market. Day traders are always trying to make a profit by outsmarting other day traders. The primary goal of day trading is to grab money from other day traders while they are also trying to take your money.

This is the reason why this is an intellectually intense financial activity. Basically, you can't make money in the stock market. The only reason there's money in the stock market is that other traders have invested it there. The money that you want to take belongs to other traders and they will do everything to hold on to their money.

Day trading is not easy peasy. And in light of this, you should remember rule number two.

Rule No. 2 - Day Trading Is Hard

Day trading is a serious business, and you must treat it as such. You can be profitable in day trading only if you have the capacity and the perseverance to pursue this opportunity. Trading on high emotions is the number one reason why day traders fail.

You have to practice self-discipline and manage your money well. Decent day traders take care of their capital as carefully as astronauts monitor their oxygen supply. In day trading, you can't be weak. You need to be above average if not excellent in order to win the game.

Sadly, day trading usually attracts gamblers or impulsive people who feel they are entitled. If you have this sense of entitlement, then this book is not for you. Day trading is not fit for you. You must have the mindset of a winner. You need to think like a winner. Feel like a winner. Act like a winner.

Changing your mindset is not easy. But if you wish to be profitable in this business, you must work on changing and developing your personality. In order to succeed in day trading, you need discipline, knowledge, and motivation. These elements, in fact, will make you successful in any profession you choose.

Remember, day trading is a profession. People who are serious in this financial activity treat it like they would treat work in medicine, engineering, or law. Day trading requires the right education, discipline, and practice.

You need to dedicate countless hours reading about different trading styles, observing how successful traders are doing the job, and practicing using simulation programs so you can learn how to trade in the real arena.

Many successful day traders are now making $500 to $1,000 every day. This is equivalent to $10,000 to $20,000 each month or roughly $120,000 to $240,000 per year.

Day trading can pay you well. However, it is not easy money. Similar to engineers, lawyers, or doctors who are required to study long years and dedicate their talents in their profession, day traders also have to spend time studying the industry and perform well.

Many people are enticed to try day trading mainly because of their lifestyle. It is possible to work from home, spend only a few hours every day, and go wherever you want to go whenever you want.

You can easily spend more time with your family and friends without waiting for your scheduled vacation or requesting from your manager or boss. In day trading, you are your own boss. Because day trading is a business, you are the executive of your own business, so you make your own decisions.

Ultimately, once you master day trading skills, you can easily make thousands of dollars every day, which is a lot more than most other careers pay. There even are traders who make $2,000 every day or more.

Regardless of your location, $2,000 per day is a significant amount of money that can change your life. If you want to control how you want and how much you make, day trading is an easy way to begin.

Let's compare day trading with opening a restaurant. If you want to go into the food business, you need to spend a huge amount of money on inventory, rent, equipment, people, training, licenses, insurance, marketing, and a whole lot more. And you still won't be guaranteed to earn money from this business. Many businesses are like this.

On the other hand, day trading is quite easy to set up and start. You can sign up for a trading account today, usually at no cost, then begin trading tomorrow. Of course, you need to understand the fundamentals of day trading, at least, before you start. However, the logistics of starting day trading are quite easy if you compare it to other businesses and professions.

Another advantage of day trading is the ease of managing the cash flow. You can purchase a stock, and if things don't turn out well, you can easily sell it. Compare this to people who have to manage inventory from different suppliers.

There are many things that can go wrong when you are getting your supplies so you can sell food in your restaurant. You may need to deal with different problems with customer satisfaction, quality, marketing, distribution, shipping, and vendors. Plus, your money is locked in for the whole process. Unless everything goes well, you can hardly do anything about it. There are instances that you may not even accept a small loss and you just want to go out of business.

If things are not going well with day trading, you can easily come out as quickly as clicking a simple button. It is easy to start over in day trading, and this is a highly attractive element of any business.

Closing your day trading business is also quite easy. If you realize that day trading is not for you, or if you have not succeeded in making money from it, you can easily stop the business, close your accounts, and withdraw your balances. Apart from the money and the time that you have already spent, there are or other charges or fees that you have to pay.

Closing other forms of business is not nearly as easy, It will take a lot of requirements before you can close your store, lay off your people, or walk away from your rental contract.

Why then are people losing money in day trading? Later in this book, we will explain the specific reasons behind this critical question. But more often than not, the most common reason why people fail in day trading is that they don't consider it as a serious business.

Instead, they consider it as a form of gambling, which will quickly and easily make them rich. Some people begin to day trade as a hobby or for fun because they consider it as cool. They trade for the adventure and excitement of short-term gambling in the stock market. They play around in the market, but they don't commit to learning the fundamentals of day trading.

They may be fortunate a few times and make some money, but in the end, the market will punish them. If you are new in day trading, you should never lose sight of the fact that you are actually competing with professionals and experienced traders around the world. Many of these seasoned traders are masters of the trade, and they are equipped with the tools that help them make profitable trading decisions.

You must always remember the second rule - day trading is a business, and you must take it seriously. You must wake up early each day, prepare yourself on the stocks that you want to trade, and make sure that your tools are ready before the market opens.

If you have a restaurant business, can you open your shop three hours late? You can't close the restaurant just because you are not in the mood, you are not feeling well, or you didn't have the time to restock ingredients for your crew to prepare meals. You should always be ready.

This should also be the case with day trading. You need to be educated, you need to use the right tools, and you must hustle every day.

Day trading can be a lucrative business if you are willing to do whatever it takes to succeed.

Chapter 1 - How Day Trading Works

In this chapter, we will take a look at the fundamentals of day trading so you will understand what day trading is, and how it works.

We will also cover some of the basic tools and strategies that you can use to be profitable in the business. As with any profession, tools are useless if you don't know how to properly use them. This book is written to guide you on the proper use of these tools.

Day Trading Vs. Swing Trading

A basic question to start with is this one - what are you looking for as a day trader? The answer here is quite easy.

First, you must look for stocks that are following a predictable trend. Then, you need to trade them in one single day. You don't need to keep them longer than a day. If you purchase stocks of Amazon (AMZN) today, you should not hold the stocks overnight and sell them tomorrow. It is no longer day trading if you hold on to your position. That one is called swing trading.

As a day trader, you need to understand the difference between day trading and swing trading. The latter is a type of trading in which you hold the stocks over a certain period of time, usually from one day to several weeks. This is a different style of trading, and you must not use these tools and strategies that are ideal for day trading if you want to follow the swing trading style.

Remember, day trading is a business (Rule 2). Swing trading is also a business, albeit a totally different type of business. The differences between day trading and swing trading are similar to the differences between owning a meat processing plant and a hamburger chain.

Both businesses involve food, but these are not similar. They operate with different revenue models, market segments, regulations, and time frames. You must not confuse day trading with other trading styles just because the trades are performed in the stock market.

Professional day traders close their positions before the stock market closes. Many traders perform both swing trading and day trading. They are aware that they are running two different businesses, and they are trained to manage the risks of these two types of trading.

One of the main differences between swing trading and day trading is the style of choosing stocks. Many traders do not day trade and swing trade the same stocks. Swing traders often look for stocks in established companies that they know will not lose their value in a few weeks.

But for day trading, you can trade any stock you want including companies that are predicted to go bankrupt. Day traders don't care what happens to the stocks after the market closes.

As a matter of fact, many of the companies that you day trade are quite risky to hold overnight because they may lose much of their value in a short period of time.

At this point, you are now ready to know the third rule of day trading:

Rule No. 3 - Do Not Hold Stocks Overnight

Even if you will sell at a loss, it is still ideal not to hold on to any position overnight.

Buy Long, Sell Short

In day trading, you buy stocks in the hope that their price will increase later in the day. This is known as buying long or just long. Whenever you hear a trader saying "I'm long 200 shares MSFT," it means that he bought 200 shares of Microsoft and would like to sell them at a higher price.

If the market is going higher, going long is good. But what will you do with the stocks if the prices are plummeting? In this case, you can sell the stocks short and still make some money.

Day traders may borrow shares from their broker and place them in the market, hoping that the price will go lower and that they can buy the shares at a lower price and make a profit. This is known as selling short, or just short.

When you hear a trader say "I am short Microsoft," it means he has sold short Microsoft stocks and he hopes that the price will drop. If the price is going lower, you owe 100 shares to your broker, which is usually deducted from your day trading account. This means you need to return the shares back to your broker. Most brokers want shares instead of money.

Therefore, if the price decreases, you can purchase them at an affordable rate than your purchase price and make some money. Let's say that you borrow 100 shares of Microsoft from your broker, and you sell them at $150 per share. Apple's price then plummets to $140, so you buy back the 100 shares at 140 and return them to the broker.

In this transaction, you have made $1,000 ($10 per share). What if the Microsoft stocks go up to $160? In this case, you need to buy 100 shares and give them back to your broker, because you owe them shares and not cash. Hence, you need to buy 100 shares at $160 so you can return 100 shares to your broker. This means you have lost $1000.

Short-sellers make money if the price of the stock they have borrowed and sold falls down. This type of trading is essential because the prices of the stocks normally drop much faster than they increase. Remember, fear is stronger than greed. Hence, short-sellers, when they trade right, can make a lot of money while other traders go into a panic mode and begin to sell their shares.

But just like anything in the market that has the potential for profit, short selling can be also risky. In buying company stocks for $10, the worst thing that can happen is that the company files for bankruptcy that same day and you lose $10. There's a limit to your loss, but if you short sell that company for $10 and then the price, instead of falling down, begins to go higher, then there's no limit to your loss.

Let's say the price increases from $10 to $100. Your broker will demand you to return the shares. You may lose all your money in your trading account, and your broker may even file a legal case against you to recover money if your funds are insufficient.

Short selling is considered legal and helpful in the stock market because of the following:

- ***It provides the stock market with valuable information*** - Day traders usually perform comprehensive due diligence to learn facts and flaws that support their assumption that a particular company is overvalued. Without short selling, the stock prices can go higher and higher, even if the company is not doing well.
- ***Short sellers balance the market*** - Short selling is necessary to keep the stock market alive. If the price is predicted to go lower, you might be wondering why the broker permitted you to short sell rather than selling the stocks themselves prior to the price drop. Remember, brokers, are usually interested in holding their position for the long-term. Through short-selling, investors will be able to generate extra profit by lending their shares.

Also, take note that long-term investors who make their shares available for short-selling are not afraid of short-term ups and downs. They usually have good reasons why they have invested in the company, and they are not usually interested in selling their stocks in a short period of time.

Therefore, they prefer to lend their stocks to traders who wish to make money from short-term market fluctuations. In exchange for lending their stocks, they will charge interest. So, by short selling, they will need to pay some interest to your broker as the cost of borrowing these shares.

Brokers don't usually charge interest if you short sell within the same day. On the other hand, swing traders who sell short typically have to pay daily interest on the stocks they borrowed.

In general, short selling is a risky practice in day trading. For example, some traders are long-biased because they are more interested in buying stocks that they want to sell for a higher rate.

Most profitable day traders don't have any bias. They will short sell when they think that the shares are ready. They will also buy whenever it fits their trade strategy. You need to be careful when you short stocks.

Many of the strategies that you will learn in this book are applicable for holding long positions. There are also strategies that are only recommended for short selling.

Institutional vs. Retail Traders

Retail traders are individuals who can be either part-time or full traders but don't work for a firm, and are not managing funds from other people. These traders hold a small percentage of the volume in the trade market.

On the other hand, institutional traders are composed of hedge funds, mutual funds, and investment banks who are often armed with advanced software, and are usually engaged in high-frequency trading.

Nowadays, human involvement is quite minimal in the operations of investment firms. Backed up by professional analysts and huge investments, institutional investors can be quite aggressive.

So at this point, you might be wondering how a beginner like you can compete against the big players?

Our advantage is the freedom and flexibility we enjoy. Institutional traders have the legal obligation to trade. Meanwhile, individual traders are free to trade or to take a break from trading if the market is currently unstable.

Institutional traders should be active in the market and trade huge volumes of stocks regardless of the stock price. Individual traders are free to sit out and trade if there are possible opportunities in the market.

But sadly, most retail traders do not possess the know-how in identifying the right time to be active and the best time to wait. If you want to be profitable in day trading, you need to eliminate greed and develop patience.

The biggest problem of losers in day trading is not the size of their accounts or the lack of access to technology, but their sheer lack of discipline. Many are prone to bad money management and over-trading.

Some retail traders are successful by following the guerilla strategy, which refers to the unconventional approach to trading derived from guerilla warfare. Guerilla combatants are skilled in using hit-and-run tactics like raids, sabotage, and ambushes to manipulate a bigger and less-mobile conventional opponent.

The US military is considered as one of the strongest armies in the modern world. But this mighty force suffered humiliation caused by the guerilla warfare used by North Vietnam during the Vietnam War.

Following this analogy, guerilla trading involves waiting or hiding until you are ready to grab an opportunity to win small battles in the financial warfare. This can help you gain fast revenue while minimizing your risk.

Remember, your mission is not to defeat institutional traders. Instead, you should focus on waiting for the right opportunity to earn your target income.

As a retail trader, you can make profits from market volatility. It can be impossible to make money if the markets are flat. Only institutional traders have the tools, expertise, and money to gamble in such circumstances.

You must learn how to choose stocks that can help you make fast decisions to the downside or upside in a predictable approach. On the other hand, institutional traders follow high frequency trading, which allows them to profit from very small price movements. Some savvy retail traders often stay away from stocks that are heavily traded by institutional traders.

As a retail trader, you should only work in the retail domain. It is usually a loss if you trade other stocks that other retail traders are not seeing or trading. The advantage of retail trading is that other retail traders also use them. The more traders use these strategies, the better they can work.

As more traders learn effective stock market strategies, more people will join the market so more stocks will move up faster. The more players in the market, the faster it will move. This is the reason why it is important for successful traders to share their strategies. This will not only help other traders to become more profitable, but it can also increase the number of traders who are using proven strategies.

There's no benefit in hiding these strategies or keeping them secret. In computer-aided trading, most of the stocks will follow the trend of the market, unless there's a good reason not to follow. Therefore, when the market is rising, most stocks will also move up. If the overall market is declining, the prices of the stocks will also decline.

But you should also bear in mind that there will be a handful of stocks that can go against the grain because they have a catalyst. These are known as Alpha Predators, which we will discuss in more detail in Chapter 4.

But for a brief overview, Alpha Predators are what retail traders are hunting for. These stocks usually tank when the markets are running, and they run when the markets are tanking.

It is generally okay if the market is running, and the stocks are running as well. Just be sure that you are trading stocks that are moving because they have a valid reason to move, and are not just moving with the general market conditions.

Probably, you are wondering what the basic catalyst for stocks is to make them ideal for day trading.

Here are some catalysts:

- Debt offerings
- Buybacks

- Stock splits
- Management changes
- Layoffs
- Restructuring
- Major contract wins / losses
- Partnerships / alliances
- Major product releases
- Mergers and / or acquisitions
- FDA approval / disapproval
- Earnings surprises
- Earnings reports

Retail traders who are engaged in reversal trades usually choose stocks that are selling off because there has been some bad press about the company. Whenever there's a fast sell-off because of bad press, many traders will notice and begin monitoring the stock for what is called a bottom reversal.

It can be difficult to perform a reversal trade if the stocks are trending down with the overall market like what happened to oil several years ago. The stock value increases by 20 cents and you may think it is a reversal. Then they are quickly sold off for another 60 cents. The sell-off is happening because the stocks are getting bad press.

For a while, oil was a weak sector and the majority of the energy and oil stocks were selling off. If a sector is weak, then it is not a good time for a reversal trade. This is where you need to identify the reason behind any significant movement in the market.

In order to do that, you need to remember the fourth rule in day trading:

Rule No. 4 - Always ask: is this stock moving because the general market is moving, or there's a unique catalyst behind this movement?

Research is crucial at this point. As you gain experience as a day trader, you will need to identify the difference between general market trends and catalyst-based movements. As a day trader, you need to be careful that you are not on the wrong side of the trade, and going against institutional traders.

How can you do that? Rather than trying to emulate institutional traders, you need to detect where the retail traders are hanging out on a particular day, and then place your bet with them.

Stay away from trading stocks that are not getting enough attention. You will be in a sandbox doing your own thing. Go where everyone else is going. Concentrate on the stocks that are moving every day and are getting attention from retail traders.

Are blue-chip stocks like IBM, Coca-Cola, or Apple ideal for retail traders? You can try, but you need to remember that these are slow-paced stocks, which are heavily dominated by algorithmic traders and institutional traders. Plus, they are often very hard to trade.

How can you identify the stocks that are alluring retail traders? There are some proven ways to do this.

First, you can use day trading stock scanners. Later in this book, we will discuss how you can set up your own day trading scanner. Basically, the stocks that are significantly moving up or down are the stocks that are being monitored by retail traders.

Second, find online community groups or social media groups where retail traders hang out. Twitter and StockTwits are often good places to learn what is currently trending. If you regularly follow successful traders, then you may see for yourself what everyone is following. There's a big advantage to being part of a community of day traders.

You can read the insights of traders and the specific stocks they are considering. If you are a lone trader, then you may be out of touch in the market. You will just make it difficult for yourself because you will not know where the action is.

A Day in the Life of a Day Trader

Steve is a day trader who lives in New York. His day usually starts at around 6 am with pre-market scanning. As early as 6 am, he already knows what stocks are gapping up or down. He scans the market to check if there's volume in the market.

Then Steve begins browsing the news for possible catalysts that might be behind the gap. He begins to set up an alert list. He rules out some stocks, and then chooses which ones he is interested to trade or not. By 9 am, he is chatting with his fellow day traders as they go over his list. By 9:30 AM, when the stock market opens, he is ready to execute his plan.

In the New York Stock Exchange (NYSW), the heaviest volumes happen between 9:30 am and 11:30 am, which is also the most volatile period in the market. This is the best window for trading and performing momentum trading, which you will later learn in this book.

Liquidity is the main advantage of having all that volume in the market. When the volume is high, it only means there are many buyers and sellers in the market. After lunch, you can have good trading patterns, but the volume starts to fade. Liquidity is also affected, so it can be difficult to get in and out of stocks. This is particularly crucial to consider when you want to take bigger shares.

Steve's focus is to always trade near the market's opening. He only trades within the first one or two hours of the market opening. He rarely trades during midday, and on a good day, he reaches his trading goal by 8 am.

After lunch, Steve has reached his goal and he would now be waiting out unless there's a significant movement in the market. By late afternoon, he reviews his trades for the day.

Today, Steve made $2,000 by 1 pm. What is he going to do? Will he walk away with that money or will he keep trading until he starts losing this money? He decided to call it a day and cash out.

Steve usually finishes his trading by lunchtime, and then he is off his way to doing whatever he likes. But whenever he loses money before lunch, he would continue fighting to stay in the market. He would keep on trading trying to regain his money.

As such, mid-day trading is often dominated by traders who have lost their money in the morning and are now trying to gain their losses.

This causes high volatility, which is not a good sign as it may cause stocks to become unpredictable because people are moving a lot of stocks. This is usually the time of the day that is often dominated by amateur traders.

Steve avoids pre-market trading because there's minimal liquidity as there is very few day traders during this period. This means stocks can increase a few points higher then suddenly drop. It is impossible to get in and out with these shares.

The great advantage for Steve is that he can be done trading before most of the people are even awake. Then he can spend the rest of his day at his own leisure or focusing on his other businesses. He tries to hit his daily goal early on and then relax. He is aware of the fact that it is quite easy to lose money in the stock market, so once he has made some money, he stops trading.

Chapter 2 - Managing Risk in Day Trading

There are three important components of day trading that you need to master so you can become successful in this business:

1. Sound Psychology
2. Effective Day Trading Strategies
3. Risk Management

These three are the pillars of day trading. If you are weak in one area, the whole business can collapse. It is a common beginner's mistake to concentrate only on trading strategies. An effective strategy delivers positive expectancy because it produces higher profits than losses over a certain period of time.

All the day trading strategies that you will learn in this book are used by profitable traders, but they should be properly executed. Bear in mind that even the most effective strategy cannot guarantee success in every trade.

No single strategy can guarantee you of never having a losing trade or even experiencing a series of losses. This is the reason risk control should be an important part of every trading strategy.

The number one reason new traders fail at day trading is their inability to manage risks. We have the tendency to accept revenue fast and we also like to wait around until losing trades return to even.

By the time some amateur traders learn how to manage their risks, their accounts are depleted. To become successful in this craft, you should learn risk management rules, and then properly execute them.

There must be a clear rule that can guide you when you should get out of the trade. It is okay to commit mistakes in your trade. In fact, even ultra-successful traders still make bad decisions despite their experience.

You will lose a lot of trades, but don't forget to be a good loser. You need to accept a loss. This is an important part of day trading. In the strategies outlined in this book, you will learn the entry points, the exit targets, and the stop loss.

As a beginner, you should follow the rules and plans of your trading strategy. And this is one of the challenges that you need to face whenever you are in a bad trade.

Many amateur day traders justify their decision to hold bad stocks by saying, "Well, it's Amazon, and it's a billion dollar company. Surely, they will not get out of business, so I think I will hold just a bit longer." You should not do this. You should follow the rules of your own day trading strategy. You can easily return to the trade, but it can be difficult to recover from a huge loss.

Get out once you are losing money, then promptly return once the market is showing stability. Each time you trade, you are exposing your money, so you need to minimize this risk exposure. You must find the ideal set-up, then manage the risk with the proper share size and stop loss.

Here's the fifth rule in day trading:

Rule No. 5 - Risk Management is important for successful day trading.

An ideal setup is an opportunity for you to get into a trade with minimal risk. This means you might risk $50 but you have the potential to make $150. This is a 3:10 profit-loss ratio.

Meanwhile, if you get into a setup where you are risking $50 to make $5, then you have a less than 1 risk-reward ratio, and this is a trade that you should avoid. Seasoned day traders will not take the trades with profit-to-loss ratio of less than 2:1.

This means if you buy $500 stocks and you are risking $50 on it, you should sell it for at least $600 to make at least $100. Certainly, if the price comes down to $400, you should accept the loss and exit the market with only $400 ($50 loss).

If you are not able to find a good setup with the ideal profit-to-loss ratio, then try to move on and keep looking for another trade. As a day trader, you should always look for opportunities to obtain low risk entries with huge win potential.

Part of the learning process in day trading is the ability to identify setups that have huge potential for winning. As a newbie in this area, you may find it difficult to identify different setups. It can be difficult for you to identify a false breakout from a home run. This is something that you can develop through experience and training. We will discuss this in more detail in the succeeding chapters.

Using a 2:1 win-loss ratio, there's a chance that you can be wrong 40% of the time, but you can still make money. Again, your job as a day trader is to manage risk, not merely to buy and sell stocks. Your chosen broker will handle the transaction of buying and selling. Your main responsibility is to manage the risks.

Whenever you buy stocks, you are exposing money to a risk. How can you manage this? Basically, there are three steps you need to remember in order to manage risk. You need to determine if you are trading the right stock.

Later in Chapter 4, we will learn how to find the right stocks for day trading. We will discuss in detail how to find stocks that are ideal for day traders, and what criteria you must look for in them.

Basically, you must remember the following:

- Avoid stocks that are mainly traded by institutional traders and algorithmic traders.
- Avoid stocks that have a small relative trading volume.
- Avoid penny stocks that are clearly manipulated.
- Avoid stocks that are moving without clear basic catalysts.

You will learn more about this in Chapter 4. Bear in mind that risk management begins from selecting the right type of stock to trade. You can have the best platform and tools, and become skilled in day trading strategies. But you will certainly lose money if you are trading the wrong stocks.

You also need to determine the ideal share size you should take. Are 10 shares enough? Is it recommended to take 100 shares? How about 1000 shares? This all depends on the size of your account as well as your daily target.

If you are targeting $1,000 per day, then 10 to 20 shares will suffice. You can either increase your account size or take more shares. You may need to lower your daily goal if you don't have enough money to trade for a $1,000 daily target.

I am holding around $25,000 in my trading account and I usually choose 800 shares to trade. My daily goal is $500 or $120,000/year. That is sufficient for my lifestyle.

What is your trading goal? What is your stop loss?

The absolute maximum a trader should risk on any trade is 2% of his or her account equity. For example, if you have a $30,000 account, you should not risk more than $600 per trade, and if you have a $10,000 account, you should not risk more than $200.

If you have a small account, it is best to trade fewer shares at first. When you see an attractive trade but you need to place a logical stop where higher than 2% of your capital is at risk, then you should pass on that trade, and move on to find another one.

Always know your risk tolerance, and many profitable traders don't risk more than 2% of their capital on a single trade.

Three Steps in Managing Risks

Here are the three steps you can take to effectively manage your risks:

Step 1 - Figure out the maximum dollar risk for the trade you are planning

Take note that this should not be higher than the 2% of your account. Make sure that you have calculated this before you start your trading day.

For example, let's say that you have a $20,000 account. With the 2% rule, you can only risk $400 for a single trade. If you want to be more conservative, you can limit yourself to trading $200 every trade or 1% of your account.

Step 2 - Estimate your max risk per share and stop-loss strategy

We will discuss this in more detail in Chapter 6, wherein for each strategy, we explore what the stop loss must be.

Let's say that you are looking at the stock of BBRY (Blackberry) using ABCD Pattern Strategy. You buy stocks at $8 and want to sell it at $11, with a stop loss at $6.50. You will be risking $1.50 / share.

Step 3 - Find the absolute maximum number of shares you should trade each time

You can do this by dividing 1 by 2. Following the examples above, you will be allowed to buy only 133 shares or rounded to 125 shares.

With the strategies explained in Chapter 6, you will learn where the stop loss should be based on your trade plan and technical analysis.

You can only consider max loss for your account depending on your account size. So you need to make that call for yourself. For instance, if your stop is higher than your moving average, you need to make some calculations and check if this stop is bigger than the maximum account size.

If the break of moving average will yield a $300 loss, and you have set a $200 max loss every trade, then you must cancel the trade or take a lower number of shares.

You may think that it can be difficult to compute share size or stop loss depending on a max loss on your account, while you are waiting for the right opportunity. It's true that you need to make fast decisions or you may lose the opportunity. It is also true that computing your stop loss and max loss in your account size in a live trade is not usually easy.

Let me take you back to Rule No. 2: Day Trading Is Hard.

You need to practice, and it is ideal for amateur traders to practice under supervision for at least three months in a simulated account. Through this, you can learn how to manage your account as well as your risk for every trade. Gradually, you can easily figure out the numbers by yourself.

Risk Management and Trading Psychology

Day trading is often difficult and a lot of new traders fail. It requires sound decision-making skills, as well as strong self-discipline.

When you learned that an investor has taken a stake in Tesla, your initial reaction might be to join the trend. However, you need to make a fast decision whether you must buy or sell or sell short Tesla stocks. You can effectively do this with discipline.

Your trading strategies will gradually improve over time. But as early as now, you should understand that the key to making money in day trading is to control yourself, and practice self-discipline.

It can be difficult to predict the stock market behavior, and if you don't know what you will do, you can lose the game.

You need to stand on your own feet as even the most advanced trading tools cannot help a trader who doesn't know what to do. You need to ask the following questions:

- Does this particular course of action fit into my trading strategy?
- What trading strategy will this action fit into?
- If this trade goes awry, where do I stop?
- How much money am I risking in the trade, and what is the potential reward?

This is what many day traders find difficult. The decision-making process in day trading is usually a tough multitasking call. On top of that, you may feel the pressure. Many day traders, even successful ones, still find themselves looking at their screens and can't even figure out what action to take.

This type of paralysis is not uncommon when you are under pressure. When this happens, you must understand that you might have pushed yourself a bit too far out of your comfort zone. It can happen even to the most experienced day trader, albeit only once in a while.

By trading regularly, you will gain some experience, and it's ideal to work on the edge of your comfort zone so you can push your boundaries. But if you find yourself too far outside of your comfort zone and beyond your risk tolerance, you may end up making some costly errors. It is always best to foster a self-awareness.

Learn how to be calm under pressure, so you can make decisions without losing your mind. Regularly assess your decisions and always review your performance.

Are you making profits in your trades? Are you getting winning streaks or losing streaks? If you are losing five trades in a row, are you checking your emotions and maintaining your composure? Or will you let your judgment cloud your mind?

Discipline is crucial to develop your trading muscles, which require exercise to grow. Once you have developed these muscles, you need to exercise regularly so you can maintain your physique.

Day trading can give you this opportunity. Regularly exercise your ability to demonstrate discipline and self-control. Some of these skills are also comparable to learning to drive a car. Once you have acquired this skill, no one can take it away.

When you've learned it, the skill of identifying a great stock chart will not fade away. However, discipline is something that you need to regularly work at to be a profitable trader.

You have chosen a venture in which constant learning is important. This profession can be invigorating. But take note that if you begin to gain too much confidence, and think you have outsmarted the market on trading know-how, or that there is no need to learn anymore, you will surely get a quick reminder from the stock market.

You may lose money, and you shall see that the market can rectify your overconfidence. The ability to make fast decisions and your ability to make and then follow your rules for day trading are important for success in this market.

As you read this guide, you can learn more about risk management. Everything that you do as a day trader comes back to managing risks because, at the end of the day, this is the most important concept for you to understand.

Visualize yourself as a risk manager. You need to effectively manage risks so that you can make good decisions even under extreme pressure. This leads us to Rule No. 6 in day trading:

Rule No. 6 - Your Broker Will Trade the Stocks for You

Your focus is to manage risk. It can be quite difficult to become a successful day trader without effective risk management skills, even if you are knowledgeable with many trading strategies.

Day traders are in the business of day trading. You must clearly define your risk as a business person. You must specifically know the amount of money you are willing to risk on any single trade.

As mentioned earlier in this chapter, the acceptable risk depends on the size of your trading account as well as your trading method, personality, as well as risk tolerance. But you should remember the 2% rule discussed above. This rule is very important that we need to highlight it again: the maximum amount that you can risk on any trade should not exceed 2% of your account size.

For instance, if you have a $60,000 account, you should not risk more than $1200 per trade. If you have a $20,000 account, you should never risk more than $400 per trade.

If your account is still small, you should limit yourself to trading fewer shares. If you think there's a good trade, but a logical step is to place where more than 2% of your equity is at risk, sit it out and move on. You may have minimal risk, but you should never risk more.

Again, never risk more than 2% of your day trading account.

Chapter 3 - Hunting for Stocks to Trade

After risk management, the next challenge for a day trader is looking for stocks to trade. You may spend a lot of time studying the mechanism behind day trading, but when it comes to choosing stocks, it can be quite difficult. You will certainly experience this as a new trader.

Apex Predators

Bear in mind that not all stocks are ideal for day trading as it only works on stocks with high relative volume. Some stocks such as AAPL will usually trade millions of shares every day, while other stocks may only trade a couple of hundreds of thousands.

So does this mean you should only trade Apple stocks? The volume for a stock is relative. And focusing on the total volume is not enough. There are some stocks that on average will trade with such high volume. You must look for what is above average for that particular stock.

For example, 35 million shares of Apple traded in a single day could be the average. Avoid trading this stock unless it hits double. If the volume is not higher than usual, it could mean that the market is dominated by institutional traders and algorithmic investors. Move on to the next.

Bear in mind that high relative volume stocks are independent of what their sector and overall market are following. If the market is weak, it only means that most stocks are selling off. It doesn't matter if the stocks are Amazon, Facebook, or Google. If the market is strong, the price of most stocks will rise. Likewise, if you learn that the market is bearish, the overall market is collapsing because the whole market is losing its value and not only certain stocks.

This is also true with particular sectors. For instance, if the energy sector is weak, it means all energy companies are losing their value as a group.

But how can you detect the market behavior? Index funds like S&P 500 or Dow Jones are often good indicators of what the overall market is doing. If the S&P and Dow Jones are weak, then the general market is collapsing.

The behavior of stocks with high relative volume is independent of the general market. Every day, only a few stocks are traded independently of their sector and the general market. Retail traders only trade those stocks that are known as Apex Predators.

In the Animal Kingdom, Apex Predators are predators located at the top of the food chain. No one preys upon them. In the world of day trading, Apex Predator stocks are those that are not dependent on the general market and their sector. They are not controlled by the market.

Therefore, the next rule is about Apex Predators:

Rule No. 7 - Day Traders Only Trade Apex Predators

Profitable day traders also trade high relative volume stocks that have fundamental catalysts and are traded regardless of the condition in the overall market.

What makes a stock an Apex Predator? Normally, it is the release of fundamental news about the stock either the day prior to or during the same trading day. Essential news or events for companies can have huge effects on their value in the market and thus serve as fundamental catalysts for the price action.

As enumerated in Chapter 1, some examples of basic catalysts for stocks that make them ideal for day trading include the following:

- Debt offerings
- Buybacks
- Stock splits
- Management changes
- Layoffs
- Restructuring
- Major contract wins / losses
- Partnerships / alliances
- Major product releases
- Mergers and / or acquisitions
- FDA approval / disapproval
- Earnings surprises
- Earnings reports

In Chapter 6, we will explore specific day trading strategies such as Moving Averages, VWAP Strategy, Reversal, and Momentum.

At this point, your only concern should be how you can find the stock for each strategy. Day traders usually categorize stocks for retail trading into three groups. Through this, you can gain some clarity on how you can hunt for stocks and what strategy you must use.

There are other methods of categorizing stocks for day trading, and even some day traders do not agree with this method of classification. Therefore, before I discuss the three categories, it is important to explain first the definition of market capitalization and “float”.

In day trading, when we say float, it means the number of shares available for trading.

Microsoft, for instance, as of November 2019, has 7.3 billion shares in the market that are available for trade. The company is deemed as a "Mega Cap" type of stock. Such stocks often don't move so much during the day because you need a huge sum of money to move the volume.

Hence, Microsoft shares usually move by a few dollars every day. Mega Cap stocks are not volatile, so retail traders don't like to trade them. As a day trader, you should always look for volatility.

Meanwhile, there are some stocks that have a very low float. For instance, Nortech Systems (ticker: NYSYS) has only 981,000 stocks available for trade. This means that the supply of stocks of NYSYS is low and so a big demand can easily move the share price.

Low float stocks are volatile and can move quite fast. Usually, low float stocks are priced under $10 because they are early IPO companies that are still not profitable. These companies are still growing, and by growing further, they issue more stocks and raise more money from the public, and gradually increase their market capitalization.

Low float stocks are called micro cap stocks or small cap stocks. Retail traders love low float stocks.

Now, let's go back to the three classes mentioned earlier.

Low Float Stocks

The first class is composed of low float stocks that are priced under $10. These stocks are quite volatile, moving from 10% to as high as 1,000% every day. With this extreme volatility, you should be cautious when dealing with these stocks.

Just as you can grow your $1,000 into $10,000 in one trade, you can also diminish your $1,000 to only 10 in a few minutes. Low float stocks under $10 are also usually manipulated and usually not easy to trade. And so, only experienced day traders must venture in these stocks.

Rare is the chance that amateur day traders can trade low float stocks with such efficiency and accuracy. If you try to trade low float stocks that are under $10, then the risk is high that you will turn your $1000 into nothing in a few days. For a low float stock, the Bull Flag Momentum Strategy (which you will learn in Chapter 6) is highly recommended. Other day trading strategies explored in this book are not recommended for low float stocks under $10.

In general, you cannot sell short low float stocks that are priced under $10. Bear in mind that in order to short sell, you must borrow shares from your stockbroker, which is highly unlikely for volatile stocks.

Even if your broker approves your loan, I highly implore you not to try short selling low float stocks. They are extremely volatile and you may end up losing all your money, and even come out negative because you have to pay your broker.

Remember, you can become a fulltime profitable day trader even without having to short-sell risky stocks. If you are just a beginner in this field, sit this one out and try it if you have gained some experience in the field.

Medium Float Stocks

The second category of stocks is called medium float stocks. It is in the range of $10 to $100. These stocks have medium floats between 5 million to 500 million shares.

Many of the strategies discussed in this book can work well on these stocks, especially the Resistance Strategies. These are Medium float stocks priced more than $100 and are not ideal for day traders.

More often than not, you can't buy many shares of medium float stocks because of their high price. Thus, it is fundamentally futile to day trade them.

Mega Cap Stocks

The third category of stocks for trading is mega cap stocks such as Home Depot, Microsoft, Yahoo, Ali Baba, and Apple. These are strong companies that usually have more than $500 million in outstanding shares available for buying and selling.

Mega stocks are traded in millions of shares each day, and they only move if huge institutional traders, hedge funds, and investment banks are trading large positions.

Day traders who usually trade between 100 and 1,000 shares cannot cause any significant movement in these stocks. Day traders must stay away from these stocks unless there's a good catalyst behind the move.

In the strategies described in Chapter 6, Moving Average and Reversal Strategies often work well on mega stocks.

But remember, unless there's a catalyst, these stocks are heavily traded by algorithms and high frequency traders, and are not ideal for day trading.

Chapter 4 - Day Trading Tools and Platforms

Just like starting any other business or profession, you need a few important tools to begin day trading. Basically, you need a broker and a platform to execute your orders. These are the tools that you will certainly need to function as a day trader.

As explained in Chapter 3, you also need a stock scanner to help you find a watch list, and look for potential setups in real time. On top of a stock scanner, it is ideal to be part of a trading community.

Day Trading Broker

You need a reliable broker for day trading. You don't need a popular broker; you need a reliable one. Remember, your broker is your vehicle to trade. Even if you are trading properly, you can lose money if you have a bad broker.

There are numerous brokers out there with different software and price schemes. Some are cheap but terrible, and some offer super service but expensive.

The following are the top brokers used by day traders around the world:

- E*Trade
- TD Ameritrade
- Tradestation
- Interactive Brokers
- Fidelity

To maintain the focus of this book, we will not review day trading brokers here. You can easily search for them online and read reviews about them.

But one of the main concerns for day traders is commission, or how much is the broker going to take with every trade you make.

Most brokers will earn from your trades whether you win or lose the trade. Therefore, savvy day traders are looking to save on trading costs as much as possible.

However, the trading cost not be your only concern. You should also balance this factor with other features of the broker that can help you become more successful like the tools you can use, research capacity, and trading platform.

So while trading cost is an important factor, it is not the only concern you need to consider.

You must also check with the current rules for day trading in your region. For example, in the United States, day traders should maintain at least $25,000 of equity in their accounts before they can trade as stipulated by the rules of the Financial Industry Regulatory Authority (FINRA).

Market Data and Trading Platform

Time is of the essence in day trading. You can be successful in your trades if you know how to execute your trades in a jiffy. You must be able to move in and out of the trades easily.

It can be a challenge to perform trades fast enough if your broker doesn't use a platform or software with hotkeys.

You need to make fast decisions so you can make extra dollars when the stock suddenly spikes. If the stock rises, you need to be able to place money in your account and make money from it fast. You certainly don't want to be bumbling with your orders. You need fast executions, which is why you really need to use a good broker as well as platform for fast order execution.

Stocks Scanner and Watch List

One of the common concerns among new traders is not knowing the stocks to trade. Every day, thousands of stocks move in the market. However, looking for a setup that is a good fit to your risk tolerance and consistent with your day trading strategy can be difficult.

You need to use a scanner to browse the market and look for good trades.

The most popular stock scanners for day traders are the following:

- StockRover
- ChartMill
- FinViz
- StockFetcher

Community of Traders

Even though day trading can be really exciting, it is also quite difficult and can be emotionally overwhelming.

It is best to join a community of retail traders and ask them questions. Consult them whenever necessary, learn new strategies, and receive some expert insights and alerts about the stock market. But don't forget that you also need to contribute in the community.

You can also talk to each other and share screens and platforms so you can watch each other as you trade. It can be a fun, interactive environment, and you can learn from each other. Through this, you can gain more knowledge and experience in day trading.

You will meet experienced traders in an online community whom you can learn much from, and you can also help other newbie traders in exploring this lucrative business.

If you join an online community, you will see that other day traders lose money often. It can make you feel good to see that losing trades is quite common in this area, and everyone, including seasoned traders still lose money in the process.

Bear in mind that you need to be an independent thinker. Basically, people may change when they join groups. They become more impulsive and unquestioning, nervously looking for a leader whose trades they can mimic. They respond with the crowd rather than using their own minds.

Online community members may be swayed by a few trends, but they could be killed if the trends suddenly reverse. Don't forget that successful traders are usually independent thinkers.

You must develop good judgment so you can decide when to trade, and when not to trade.

Chapter 5 - Introduction to Candlesticks

In order to understand the strategies explored in this book, it is important first to review price action, as well as the basic concepts of candlestick charts. In the 17th century, the Japanese started using technical analysis with the aid of early versions of candlestick charts.

The development of the candlestick analysis is credited to the Japanese rice trader named Homma. While his versions of candlestick charts and technical analysis were quite different from the modern-day version, the fundamental concepts still stand.

Candlestick charts, in their present form, first appeared in the 1850s. It is more likely that the original ideas of Homma were modified and refined over centuries of trading, and gradually developed into a charting system that day traders now use.

In creating a candlestick chart, you should have a data set, which contains the following:

1. Open price
2. Highest price in the selected time frame
3. Lowest price in the same period of number 2
4. Closing price values for each time period that you want to show

The time frame can be one minute, five minutes, one hour, one day, or any time frame that you prefer. The body refers to the hollow (white) or filled (red) portion of the candlestick.

The long thin lines below and above the body signifies the low and high range, and are referred to as wicks (also called tails or shadows). The low is marked by the bottom of the lower wick, while the high is marked by the top of the upper wick.

When the stock closes at a higher price compared to the opening, it results to a hollow candlestick. The bottom of the body represents the opening price. The top signifies the closing price.

When the stock closes lower than the opening rice, a filled candlestick is created with the top of the body signifying the opening price and the lower part of the body signifying the closing price.

In comparison to other methods of charting price action, many day traders consider candlestick charts a lot easier to interpret and more visually appealing.

Each candlestick provides an easy way to interpret price action. A day trader can easily compare the connection between the high and low as well as the open and close.

The connection between the open and close is considered vital information and forms the core of candlesticks.

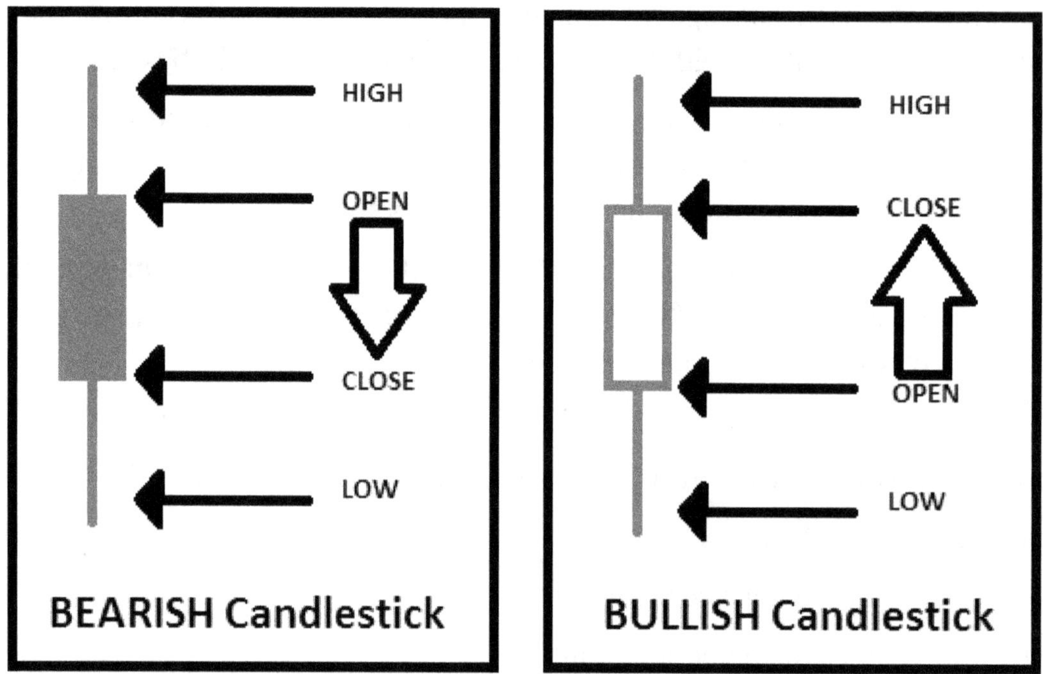

Here is our next rule in day trading:

Rule No. 8 - Filled candlesticks signify selling pressure, hollow candlesticks indicate buying pressure.

Traders are usually categorized into three groups:

1. Buyers
2. Sellers
3. Undecided

Sellers like to charge as much as possible and buyers want to pay as little as possible. The bid-ask spread reflects this permanent conflict. The bid refers to what a buyer offers for the merchandise.

The prices are created by the volume of traders - sellers, buyers, and undecided people. The patterns of volume and prices reflect the general behavior of the stock market.

Take note that as a day trader, your goal is to discover the balance of power between sellers and buyers, and bet on the winning group. You can see this in action if you look at candlestick charts.

Successful day traders are well-versed in social psychology and they are also trained in using computers for charting these prices. The study of mass psychology is crucial in day trading.

The presence of undecided people puts pressure on bearish and bullish trends. Sellers and buyers try to move the prices fast because they know they are surrounded by undecided traders who can easily break the deal.

Sellers know that if they try to hold out for a better price, other traders may step in and sell at lower prices. Buyers are aware that if they don't decide fast, another trader may step in and buy stocks ahead.

The group of undecided traders makes the traders more open to deal with their competitors. Sellers are selling because they are expecting prices to go down. Buyers are buying because they are expecting prices to rise.

The undecided group makes everything happen faster because they create a sense of urgency among traders. Candlesticks can signify a great deal about the general trend of the stock as well as the power of the traders in the market.

Candlesticks are initially neutral. As the time period progresses, the chart can grow to become either bullish or bearish. If a candle is born, traders don't know what it can become. They could be speculative but they don't really know what a candle is until it closes. The battle starts after a candle is born.

The bears and the bulls fight it out and the candle shows who is winning the battle. When buyers are in control, you can see the candle moving up and form a bullish candle. When sellers are in control, the candle can move down and signify a bearish market.

You are probably thinking that this is all quite obvious. However, many traders don't see candles as a battle between sellers and buyers. That little candle is a good reference that can tell you who is presently winning the battle - the sellers (bears) or the buyers (bulls). Candles with large bodies toward the upper part are bullish.

In a bullish candlestick, the buyers are in control of the price action, and there's a high chance that they will keep on pushing the price upwards. The candlestick will not only show you the price. It will also show you that the bulls are winning and that they have more power than the sellers.

Meanwhile, bearish candles signify that the sellers are in control of the price action in the market. It shows you that the sellers are presently in control, so a long position is no longer a good idea.

Candles with the filled body mean that the open was at a high and then the close was low. This indicates a bearish market.

By learning how you can read candlestick charts, you will start generating an opinion on the general behavior of the stock market. This is known as price action. Determining who is in control of the price is a very important skill in day trading. The main goal of a professional day trader is to identify the power between bears and bulls so he can win money.

If bears are stronger, you must sell and sell short. If bulls are stronger, you must buy and hold. Wise day traders stand aside if both camps are in equal power. They just allow the bears and bulls to fight with each other, and enter trades only if they are sure which side is more likely to win.

You never want to be on the wrong side of the trade. Therefore, it is important to learn how to read candlesticks and how to continuously read the price action while you are day trading.

Different Candlestick Patterns

There are numerous chart patterns that you may encounter in other day trading books. These include the following:

- Three White Soldiers
- Three Black Crows
- Stick Sandwich
- Harami
- Falling Three Methods
- Evening Star
- Morning Star
- Dragonfly
- Downside Tasuki Gap
- Dark Cloud Cover
- Abandoned Baby
- Cup and Handle
- Head and Shoulders

However, many of these chart patterns are confusing, and some of them are not useful at all. Wishful thinking is the biggest drawback of these patterns. You may find yourself detecting bearish or bullish patterns, depending on whether or not you are in the mood to trade.

So before this chapter ends, we will discuss two useful day trading patterns. Then in the next chapter, we will explore how you can trade with the aid of these patterns.

Spinning Tops

Spinning tops are candles with similarly-sized low wicks and high wicks that are typically bigger than the body and will usually be a bit more indecisive. In this pattern, the powers of sellers and buyers are almost equal.

Even though no one can control the price, the fight can continue. Normally, the volume is lower in these patterns as traders are just waiting to see who will win the fight between the buyers and the sellers.

Price trends can immediately change after the candles and they, therefore, are crucial to detect in the price action.

Doji

Doji patterns come in varying forms and shapes. However, they are all characterized by having either very small body or no body at all.

Dojis also signify indecision, which is similar to spinning tops. If you see a Doji in your chart, it means there's a strong tension happening between the bulls and the bears. Nobody has won the battle yet.

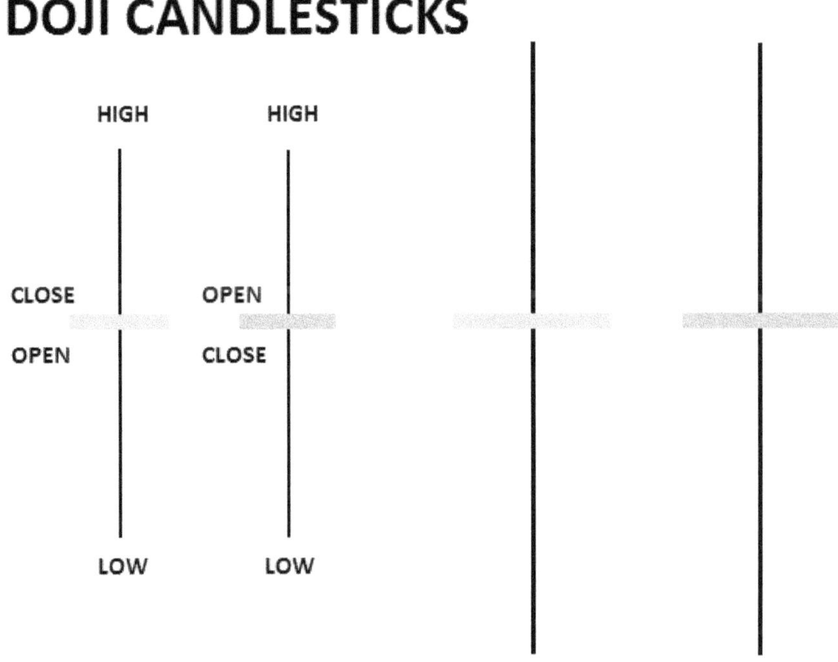

Some types of Doji such as Shooting Star are also indecision charts. However, they may show that the buyers are losing power and that the sellers are taking over.

If the bottom wick is longer like the hammer Dojis, it signifies that the sellers are not successful in trying to push the price lower. This may signify an impending takeover of price action by the bulls.

Remember, all Dojis indicate indecision and potential reversals if they are forming in a trend. When a Doji is forming a bullish trend, it signifies that the bulls have become tired, and the bears are fighting back to take over the price action.

Likewise, when a Doji forms a bearish trend, it signifies that the bears have become tired and the buyers are fighting back to take control of the price action.

After learning about these candlesticks, it is crucial that you don't get too excited, and don't depend on them too much. Always bear in mind that candlesticks are not perfect. If you take a trade each time that you see a Doji forming in a trend, you may end up with considerable losses.

Take note that these candles only signify indecision and not a specific reversal. In order to use these candles effectively, you should look for confirmation candles and use them with other forms of analysis like resistance or support levels, which we will explore in depth in the next chapter.

Chapter 6 - Effective Day Trading Strategies

Finally, we will now discuss the strategies that you can use for day trading. These strategies are based on three important fundamentals:

1. Price Action
2. Technical Indicators
3. Chart Patterns

It is essential that you understand and apply all these three elements in day trading. While some strategies only require technical indicators (like VWAP and Moving Average), it will help you a lot if you understand price action and chart patterns, so you can be a profitable day trader.

This knowledge, especially about price action comes only with regular practice. As a day trader, you must not care about the company and its revenue. You should not be distracted about the mission or vision of the company or how much money they make. Your focus must only be on the chart patterns, technical indicators, and price action.

Successful day traders also don't mix technical analysis with fundamental analysis. Day traders usually focus more on technical analysis.

As we have discussed in Chapter 4, you must look for fundamental catalysts in day stocks. The catalyst is the reason why a particular stock is running. If you have a stock that is running up to 70%, you need to determine the catalyst behind this change, and never stop until you figure that one out.

So, it's a tech company that just got patent approval or a pharmaceutical company that passed through important clinical trials. These are catalysts that can help you understand what is really going on.

Beyond this, don't bother yourself squinting over revenue papers or listening in conference calls. You should not care about these things unless you are a long-term investor.

Day traders trade fast. There are times that you may find yourself trading in time periods as short as 10 to 30 seconds, and can make thousands of dollars. If the market is moving fast, you need to make certain that you are in the right position to take advantage of the profits, and minimize your exposure to risk.

There are millions of day traders out there with different strategies. Each trader requires its own strategy and edge. You must find your spot in the market whenever you feel comfortable.

You must focus on day trading strategies because these really work for day trading. The following strategies have been proven effective in day trading. These strategies are quite basic in theory, but they can be challenging to master and requires a lot of practice.

Take note that these trading strategies give signals relatively infrequently and will allow you to participate in the markets during the ideal times just like how professional day traders do.

Also remember that in the market today, more than 60% of the volume is dominated by algorithmic trading. So you are really competing against computers. There's a big chance that you will lose against an algorithm. You may get lucky a couple of times, but supercomputers will definitely win the game.

Trading stocks against computers means that the majority of the changes in stocks that you see are basically the result of computers moving shares around. On one hand, it also means that there are certain stocks every day that will be traded on such heavy retail volume (as opposed to institutional algorithmic trading).

Every day, you have to focus on trading these specific stocks or the Apex Predators - the stocks that are usually gapping down or up on revenue.

You should hunt for stocks that have considerable interest among day traders and considerable retail volume. These are the stocks that you can buy, and together, the retail traders can still win the game against algorithmic traders.

One principle in day trading that you may find useful is that you must only choose the setups that you want to master. Using basic trading methods that are composed of minimal setups are effective in reducing the stress and confusion, and will allow you to focus more on the psychological effect of trading. This will separate the losers from the winners.

Managing Your Day Trades

Before exploring the day trading strategies in this book, it is important first to know about managing your trade. It is always intriguing when two day traders choose the same stock - the one short and the other long.

More often than not, both traders become profitable, proving that trader management and experience are more important than the stock and the strategy used by the trader.

Remember, your trade size will depend on the price of the stock and on your account and risk management. Beginners in day trading are recommended to limit the size of their shares below 1000.

For example, you can buy 800 shares, then sell half in the first target. You can bring your stop loss to break even. Then you can sell another 200 in the next target. You can keep the last 200 shares until you stop. You can always maintain some shares in case the price will keep on moving in your favor.

IMPORTANT: *Professional day traders never risk their shares all at once.*

They know how to scale into the trade, which means they buy shares at different points. They may start with 200 shares and then add to their position in different steps. For instance, for an 800-share trader, they could enter either 400/400 or 100/200/500 shares. When done properly, this is an excellent way to manage your trades and risks.

But managing the position in the system can be overly difficult. Many newbies who may attempt to do this could end up over trading and may lose their money in slippage, commissions, and averaging down the losing stocks. Rare is the chance that you may scale into a trade. Still, there are times that you can do this, especially in high-volume trades.

However, you should take note that scaling into a trade increases your risk and beginners can use it improperly as a way to average down their losing positions. We have discussed this for the sake of information, and this is not recommended for beginners.

Even though they may appear the same, there's a big difference between averaging down a losing position and scaling into a trade. For newbies, averaging down a losing position can wipe out your account, especially with small accounts that are not strong enough for averaging down.

ABCD Pattern

The ABCD Pattern is the simplest pattern you can trade, and this is an ideal choice for amateur day traders. Even though this is pretty much basic and has been used by day traders for a long time, it still works quite effectively because many day traders are still using it.

This pattern has a self-fulfilling prophecy effect, so you just follow the trend.

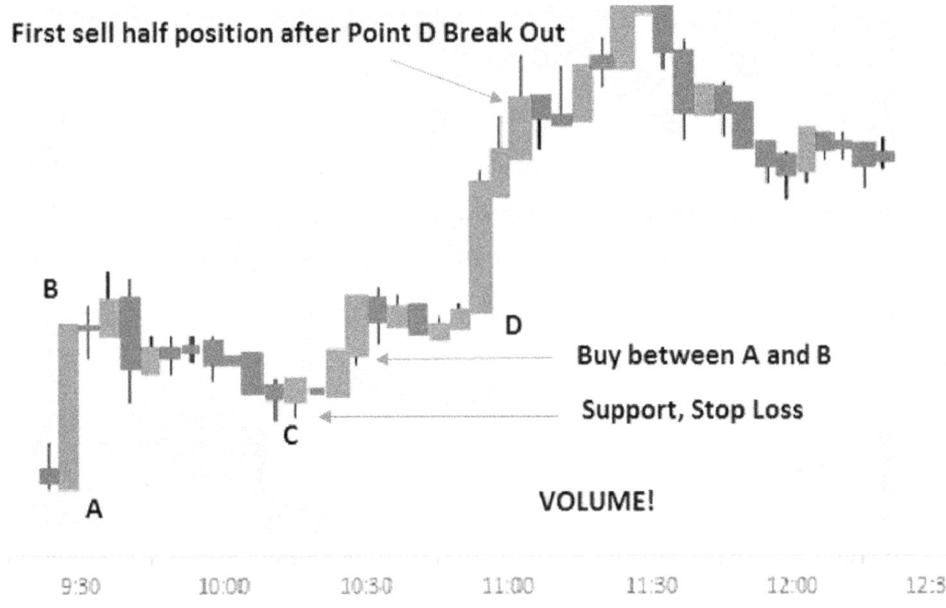

The chart above shows an example of an ABCD pattern in the stock market. This one begins with a strong upwards move.

Buyers are quickly buying stocks as represented by point A, and making new highs in point B. In this trend, you may choose to enter the trade, but you must not be overly obsessed by the trade, because at point B, it can be quite extended and at its highest price.

Moreover, you can't ascertain the stop for this pattern. Take note that you should never enter a trade without identifying your stop. At point B, traders who purchased the stock earlier begin gradually selling it for profit and the prices will also come down.

Still, you must not enter the trade because you are not certain where the bottom of this trend will be. But if you see that the price doesn't come down from a specific level such as point C, it means that the stock has discovered possible support.

Thus, you can plan your trade and set up the, stops and a point to take the profits.

For example, OPTT (Ocean Power Technologies Inc) announced in 2016 that they closed a new $50 million deal. This one is a good example of a fundamental catalyst. OPTT stocks surged from $7.70 (Point A) to $9.40 (B) at around 9 am. Day traders who were not aware of the news waited for point B and then an indication that the stock will not go lower than a specific price (C).

If you saw that C holds support and buyers are fighting back to allow the stock price to go any lower than the price at C, you will know that the price will be higher. Buyers jumped on massively.

Remember, the ABCD Pattern is a basic day trading strategy, and many retail traders are looking for it. Near point D, the volume immediately spiked, which means that the traders are now in the trade. When the stock made a new low, it was a clear exit signal.

Here are the specific steps you can follow to use the ABCD strategy:

1. Whenever you see that a stock is surging up from point A and about to reach a new high for the day (point B), then wait to see if the price makes support higher than A. You can mark this as point C, but don't jump right into it.
2. Monitor the stock during its consolidation phase, then choose your share size and plan your stop and exit.
3. If you see that the price is holding support at point C, then you can participate in the trade closer to the price point C to anticipate the move to point D or even higher.
4. Your stop could be at C. When the price goes lower than C, you can sell. Thus, it is crucial to buy the stock closer to C to reduce the loss. (Some day traders have higher tolerance, so they wait a bit more near D to ensure that the ABCD pattern is complete. However, this is risky as it can reduce your profit).

5. When the price moves higher, you can sell half of your shares near point D, and bring your stop higher to your break-even point.
6. Sell the rest of your shares as soon as you hit your target or you feel that the price is losing momentum, or that the sellers are getting control of the price action.

Bull Flag Momentum

Bull Flag Momentum is a day trading strategy that typically works great for low float stocks, which we have discussed in Chapter 4.

Expert stock analysts consider the Bull Flag Momentum as a scalping strategy because the flags in the pattern don't usually last long. Plus, day traders should scalp the trade in order to get in quickly, make money, and then exit the market.

Below is an example of a Bull Flag pattern with one notable consolidation.

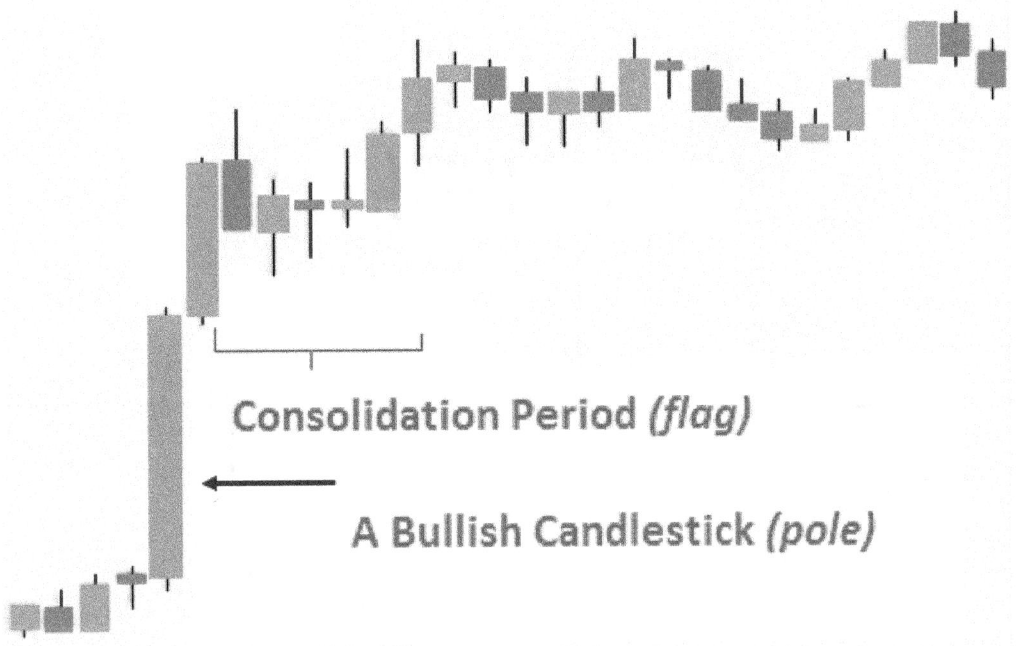

This chart is called Bull Flag because it is like a flag on a pole. In this pattern, you have different large candles rising (pole) and you also have a sequence of small candles that move sideways (flag) or "consolidating" in day trading jargon.

When there is consolidation in the pattern, it signifies that traders who purchased the stocks at a cheaper price are now selling. While this is happening, the price doesn't significantly decrease because buyers are still participating in the trades, and sellers are not yet in control of the price.

Many retail traders will miss buying the stock before the Bull Flag begins. Buying stocks when the price is increasing could be risky. This is known as "chasing the stock". Successful day traders usually aim to participate in the trade during quiet periods and take their profits during wild periods.

This is the complete opposite of how newbies trade. They quickly participate or exit if the stocks start to run, but may eventually lose interest if the prices are slow-paced.

For beginners, chasing the stocks could be an account wiper. You should wait until the stock lands on a high point, then wait for consolidation. As soon as the price breaks up in the consolidation area, you can start buying stocks.

Typically, a Bull Flag will demonstrate several consolidation periods. You may enter the first and second consolidation periods. It can be risky to get into the third and fourth consolidation areas because the price has possibly been quite extended in a way that signifies that the buyers may soon lose control over the price action.

Below is an example of a Bull Flag for Rigel Pharmaceuticals (RIGL).

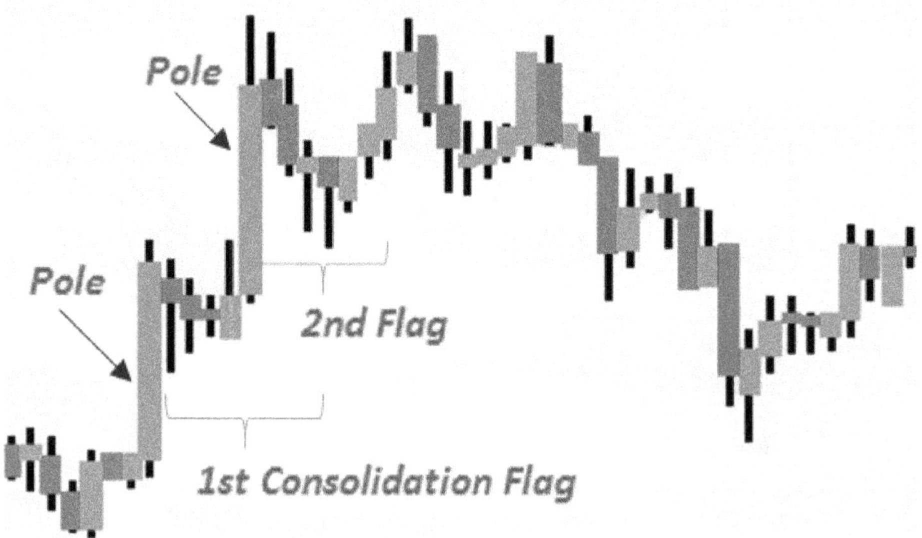

It is usually difficult to detect the first Bull Flag, and without a stock scanner, you might miss it.

As soon as you get an alert for this bull flag, you should immediately check if there's a high relative volume of trading. If yes, it becomes an ideal setup for day trading. Wait for the first consolidation period to be completed, and as soon as the stock begins to move towards its first high price for the day, you should participate in the trade.

The stop loss for the RIGL chart is the breakdown of the consolidation period. The entries and exits are marked in the picture below.

As you can see, if you have to wait for another consolidation period expecting another Bull Flag, you would probably have to be stopped. This is the reason why day traders often enter either the first or second Bull Flag, but they avoid the third one.

Here are the specific steps you can follow to use the Bull Flag Momentum strategy:

1. When you see a stock surging up, you must wait until the consolidation period is complete. Don't quickly participate in the trade or you may lose your account.
2. Watch the stock during the consolidation period. Choose your share size, as well as your stop and exit strategies.
3. Enter the trade as soon as the prices are moving beyond the highest point of the consolidation period. Your stop loss should be at the break below the consolidation period.
4. Sell half of your shares and then take a profit on the surge. Bring your stop loss from the low of the consolidation to your break-even price.
5. Sell the rest of your shares as soon as you hit your target or you think that the price is starting to lose momentum, and the sellers are fighting back to control the price action.

Similar to the ABCD pattern, you should try to buy only around the breakeven point. The Bull Flag pattern is basically an ABCD pattern, which normally happens on low float stocks. This is fast and may vanish a lot faster. Hence, this is more or less a Momentum Scalping Strategy.

Scalpers buy stocks when they are running. They rarely like to buy during consolidation. They often drop faster and brutally, so it is crucial for you to jump only if there's a validation of the breakout.

One way to reduce your risk is to wait for the stocks to break the top of the consolidation area. Rather than buying and holding shares, scalpers usually wait for the breakout and then send their order.

Get in, scalp, and get out fast. This is the principle of momentum scalpers. Participate in the breakout, take your profit, then exit.

The Bull Flag Momentum is located inside an uptrend in a stock. It is also a long-term strategy. It is best not to short a Bull Flag and avoid trading in such momentum. It can be risky, and newbies must be cautious in trading these. If you want to test this out, try one small size at first and only after getting enough practice in simulation. You also need to quickly execute the trade through a platform designed for scalping.

Top and Bottom Reversal

Among the easiest day trading strategies are top and bottom reversals. Retail traders love them because they have specific entry and exit points, as well as a high profit to loss ratio.

In this section, we will learn the following:

- finding reversal setups with the use of stock scanners
- reading Bollinger Bands and finding extremes
- how to use Doji candlesticks to take an entry
- identifying your stops and profit targets
- trailing your winning stocks

Don't forget that what goes up must come down. So, avoid chasing extended trades. The opposite is also true. What goes down will certainly come back. If a stock begins to sell off considerably, there are two possible reasons behind:

1. Hedge funds or venture firms have begun selling their huge positions to the market and so the stock price is affected.
2. Day traders have begun short-selling the stock, but they are covering their shorts a bit sooner. This is where you must wait for an entry.

The stock will follow a reverse trend if short-sellers are trying to cover their shorts. We will illustrate this strategy using several examples so that you can precisely see what to spot on.

In the chart below, you can see the pattern of a stock that has been sold off right after the market opens.

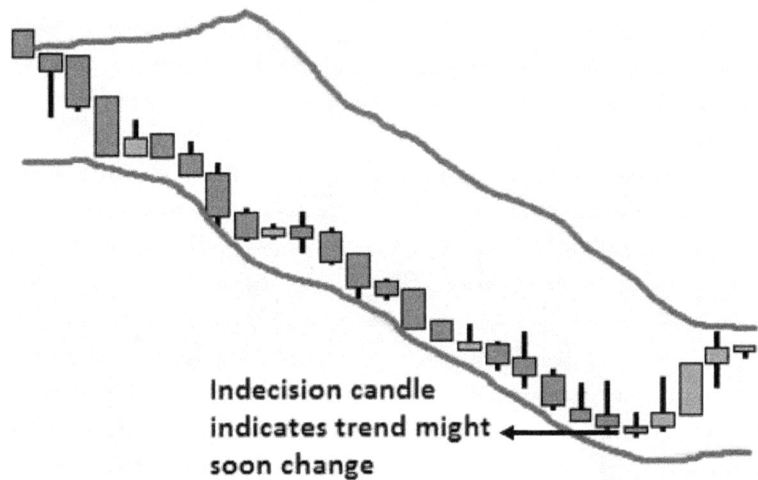

Trends like this are quite difficult to spot for the short side because if you find the spot, it might be too late to participate in the market. But always remember the day trading mantra: What goes up, will come down. Thus, you have the option to wait for a reversal.

There are four important elements in Reversal Strategy:

1. Five candlesticks moving downward or upward
2. The stock is moving outside or near the Bollinger Bands, which indicates volatility. Stocks often stay within these bands.
3. The stock will signal the extreme Relative Strength Index. Try to detect stocks with an RSI below 10 or above 90. More often than not, your day trading platform will have an RSI indicator built into the system.

The first three elements show that a stock is stretched out, and you should monitor the stock on your scanner for all this information. You should also hunt for a specific RSI level, a specific number of consecutive candles, and a specific position inside the Bollinger Bands.

4. You need to be ready if the trend is about to end, normally indicated by indecision candles like Doji or spinning top.

In reverse trading, you need to identify one of the indecision candlesticks - Dojis or spinning tops. These are indicators that the trend will soon turn into a different direction.

Remember, a Doji is a candlestick with a long wick compared to its body. Below is a picture of a bearish Doji.

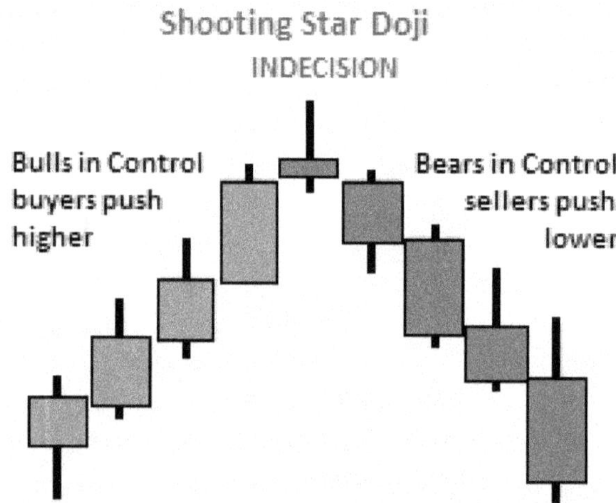

Bearish Doji has a long upper wick that some would call a top and tail, and what others would refer to as a shooting star. This candle signifies four things - the open price, the close price, the high peak of that period and the low peak of that period.

So if you have a candle with a top tail, you know that at some point during the time frame, the price moved up, wasn't able to hold at that level, and was then sold off.

It portrays a bit of a tension taking place between the sellers and the buyers in which the buyers are losing the fight. This is a good indicator that the sellers may soon control the price action and will further push down the price.

This is true with a bullish Doji, which is also depicted in the picture above. It has the longer wick below that some refer to as bottom tail or hammer. If you have a hammer candle with a bottom tail, you should know that at some point during the trading period, the price moved down, wasn't able to hold at the low levels, and was pushed up. This is an indication that there's a battle between the sellers and buyers in which the former is losing the pushdown. This signifies that the buyers are gaining control of the price and are pushing the price up.

For reversal day trading, you should look for either an indecision candlestick or Doji. These are all indications that the trend will soon change. In Reversal Strategies, you need to look for a clear validation that the pattern is starting to reverse.

What you certainly don't want is to be on the wrong side of the reversal trade. Day traders usually call this 'catching a falling blade'. It sounds bad in real life, and it sounds bad in day trading. This means that if a stock is selling off badly (the falling blade) you should not buy on the presumption that it will bounce soon.

If the stocks are on a downward trend, you need to wait for the verification of the reversal. This will normally be:

- The appearance of an indecision candle or a Doji
- The first 5-minute candle to reach a new high point

The second one is usually an entry point. You need to set your stop at the lows. For reversal day trading, the RSI must be located at the extremes (below 10 or above 90), and this final candle must be outside the Bollinger Bands.

After listing your entry requirements, you should then look for an actual entry. For most day traders, the entry is either the first minute or the first 5-minute candle to reach a new high point. The first candle that reaches the new high point is important if you've had a long run of consecutive candles making new lows.

There are instances that you need to analyze the 1-minute chart, but usually, you will need to use the 5-minute chart because this is a much better confirmation. After all, the 5-minute chart is a lot cleaner.

The first 5-minute candle to make a new high is the point at which you can get in the reversal with a stop either at the low of the day or just down around 20 to 30 cents. When a stock goes 30 to 40 cents against you, just admit the loss, acknowledge that you were mistaken about the entry and try again instead of holding.

In some instances, especially on stocks that are more volatile or expensive, you can just use a 20 or 30 cents arbitrary stop when the low of the day is quite far away. Whenever you are in one of these trades, the exit indicators are quite basic. When the stock pops up and then abruptly moves back and down on a bottom bounce, then you stop out for a loss.

When you participate in the stock and it ends up just going sideways, this is an indicator that you are probably going to see a reverse flag. This signifies that the price is probably going to continue to drop. If you get in and you hold for a while and the price stays flat, you need to exit regardless of what happens.

You might make some mistakes, but that's okay. You should not expose your account to the dangers of the unknown. You need to take the right setup, and if the setup is not yet ready, you should head to the exit.

If you make some profits, you can begin adjusting the stop, first to break-even and then to the low of the last 5-minute candle. You can then keep on adjusting your stop as you move up. You should understand that almost all of the big moves will eventually be rectified.

ALWAYS REMEMBER: *What goes up will come down.*

In reversal day trading, one of the primary benefits is the chance to monitor stocks that are moving up, while simultaneously analyzing the potential resistance points and areas that can provide a good opportunity for reversal. This will allow you to resist being impulsive and rushing into the trade.

Instead, you may take your time to monitor the trade and wait for the right moment to start the shift. Day traders usually compare reversal strategies to rubber bands. If the stock becomes really stretched, then they will eventually be due for a correction.

Hence, if a stock is really pushing down, you should understand that at some point, it will bounce and you want to be in the market when that happens. Certainly, you don't want to be in this position if you are still selling. This is a good example of catching a falling blade.

When the stocks are dropping, you need to wait for the validation of the reversal. This is often shown in the first 1-minute or the first 5-minute candlestick to make a new high point. This is your signal to enter the market and set your stop at the lows.

Bottom Reversal

The chart below for the stock history of Emergent BioSolutions (Ticker: EBS) shows a reversal.

The indecision candlestick at the end of the downtrend signifies a possible reversal, and as you will see right after that, there's a big swing back up.

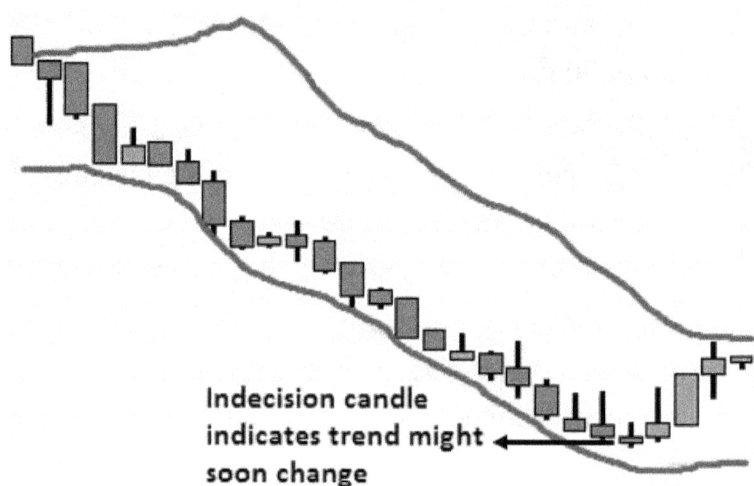

The main advantage of Reversal Trading is that it is less difficult to anticipate when stocks make significant moves. You might miss the time that the stock begins to sell off, and you don't have the time to short the stock for added revenue. However, you can always prepare for the reversal trade.

In analyzing reversals, you need to make certain that you only trade extremes. Take note that a stock that has been slowly selling off all day long usually is not suitable for a reversal.

Whenever you are working with reversals, you need to think of the stocks like rubber bands. You really need to see them stretched out to the downside or for short selling, really stretched out to the upward.

You need to see the big extension, which means you need to see the significant volume. Once you do this, you should look for several key indicators that will suggest that the tide is about to turn, and this is when you need to take the position.

Again, what goes up, will come down. More often than not, these stocks will backtrack in reverse in just a matter of minutes. It is important that you take note of the reversal time.

The key factor to become successful with the top and bottom reversals is trading the extremes. But how can you spot the extremes? Here are the things that you should look for:

1. An RSI of below 10 or above 90

2. A candlestick near or outside the Bollinger Bands

3. Five to 10 candlesticks in a series ending with a Doji or an indecision candle.

The candlesticks at the end usually show that buyers are becoming more powerful and sellers are losing their control. This often signifies the end of a trend.

But please take note that there will be instances when you will see five to 10 candlesticks in a series without much price action. The stocks might be drifting down gradually, but not fast enough for you to sense that this is an ideal reversal. You need to spot on a combination of these indicators all happening at the same time.

The high price should not be a reason to sell short. You must never argue with the decision of the crowd even if the trend doesn't make sense to you. You may choose not to follow the crowd, but never run against it.

Using all of these various factors will help you form a strategy that can be effective because of its remarkable price-loss ratio.

As a refresher, a profit-loss ratio is your average winners versus your average losers. Most newbies end up trading with dismal P/L ratio because they sell their winning stocks early and they hold their losing stocks too long.

This is an extremely common habit among new day traders. However, the Reversal Strategy lends itself to having a bigger P/L ratio.

Let's go back to the rubber band analogy. In following this strategy, you can always purchase stocks if the rubber band is stretched as far as it can. If you keep track of this right, you will be in the market as the rubber band bounces back and you can then ride the momentum right back up.

Here are the specific steps you can follow to use the Bottom Reversal Strategy:

1. Set up a scanner that can show you stocks with four or more consecutive candlesticks that will go down. Once you see a stock hitting your scanner, immediately review the volume and the resistance level or support near the stock to check if it's a good trade.
2. Wait for the confirmation of a Reversal Strategy:
    a. Formation of an indecision candlestick or bearish Doji
    b. Candles that are outside or close the Bollinger Bands
    c. RSI that is lower than 10
3. Buy the stock when you see the stock making a new 5-minute high
4. Your stop loss is the low of the previous red candlestick or the low of the day
5. Set your profit target, which could be the following:
    a. Volume Weighted Average Price (VWAP) - we will discuss this in a bit
    b. The next level of support
    c. The stock follows a new 5-minute high (buyers are once again taking control)

Top Reversal

A Top Reversal is quite similar to the Bottom Reversal. The only difference is that this strategy is ideal for short selling stocks.

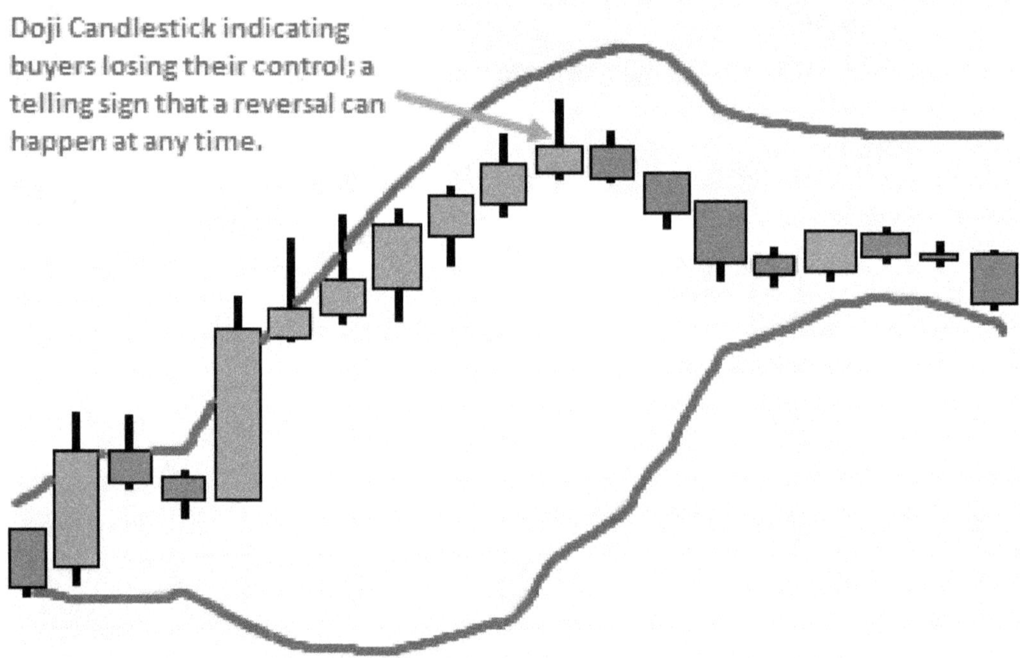

The chart above is the stock movement of Bed Bath & Beyond Inc. Its relative volume is 21.50 and the chart shows six consecutive candles. This particular stock was trading considerably higher than its normal trend, which was caused by day traders looking for unusual trading volume.

Take note that the candles were not located near or outside Bollinger Bands. But the trade was done because it was trading with high volume and formed a good Doji above. The stock was short when the new five-minute candlestick was analyzed with the stop added as the break of the high of the last five-minute candles.

Here are the specific steps you can follow to use the Top Reversal Strategy:

1. Set up a scanner that will show you stocks with 4 or more candlesticks following a rising trend. When you see the stock hitting your scanner, immediately analyze the level of resistance or volume to check if it is a good trade.
2. Wait for the confirmation of a Reversal Strategy:
    a. Formation of an indecision candlestick or bearish Doji
    b. Candles that are outside or close to the Bollinger Bands
    c. RSI that is lower than 10
3. Buy the stock when you see the stock making a new 5-minute low
4. Your stop loss is the high of the previous candlestick or just the high of the day
5. Set your profit target, which could be the following:
    a. Volume Weighted Average Price (VWAP) - we will discuss this in a bit
    b. The next level of support
    c. The stock follows a new 5-minute high (buyers are once again taking control)

Some retail traders focus on reversal trades and base their whole transactions on them. Certainly, reversal trades are the most basic of the various strategies with high-risk reward ratio. Plus, it is always easy to find stocks that are ideal candidates for reversal trades.

Even experienced day traders are now into reversal trades. But take note that reversal trading is not the only effective strategy in day trading. You also need to try Support or Resistance or VWAP.

Moving Average Trend

Some day traders refer to moving averages as possible entry and exit points. Most stocks will begin a downside or upside trend respecting their moving averages in their 5-minute charts.

You can take advantage of this behavior and jump in the trend along moving average. This is below moving average for short selling or above the moving average for going long.

Most newbies usually wonder why moving averages are becoming resistance or support. The main reason is that many traders are looking at these lines and they are making decisions based on these averages. Hence, they have a self-fulfilling prophecy effect. There's no basic reason behind moving averages being resistance or support line.

Many day traders are using 50 and 200 simple moving averages (SMA) and 9 and 20 exponential moving averages (EMA).

The SMA refers to the moving average that is calculated by adding the nearest closing prices, then dividing this number by the time period in the average computation. Short-term moving averages quickly respond to changes in the price of the underlying price. On the other hand, long-term averages require time to react.

EMA is a moving average that highlights the recent price data of the SMA. It responds faster to recent price movements than SMA. The formula for computing the EMA simply includes the SMA and a multiplier.

Most charting software for day trading have built-in moving averages. These are usually ready to use and you don't need to adjust the settings.

Below is an example chart that shows an EMA of nine:

As you should have noticed by now, the stock has formed a Bull Flag and a consolidation period on EMA 9. If you see this signal, it means there's a support holding, so you should enter the market and ride the trend until the price breaks the moving average.

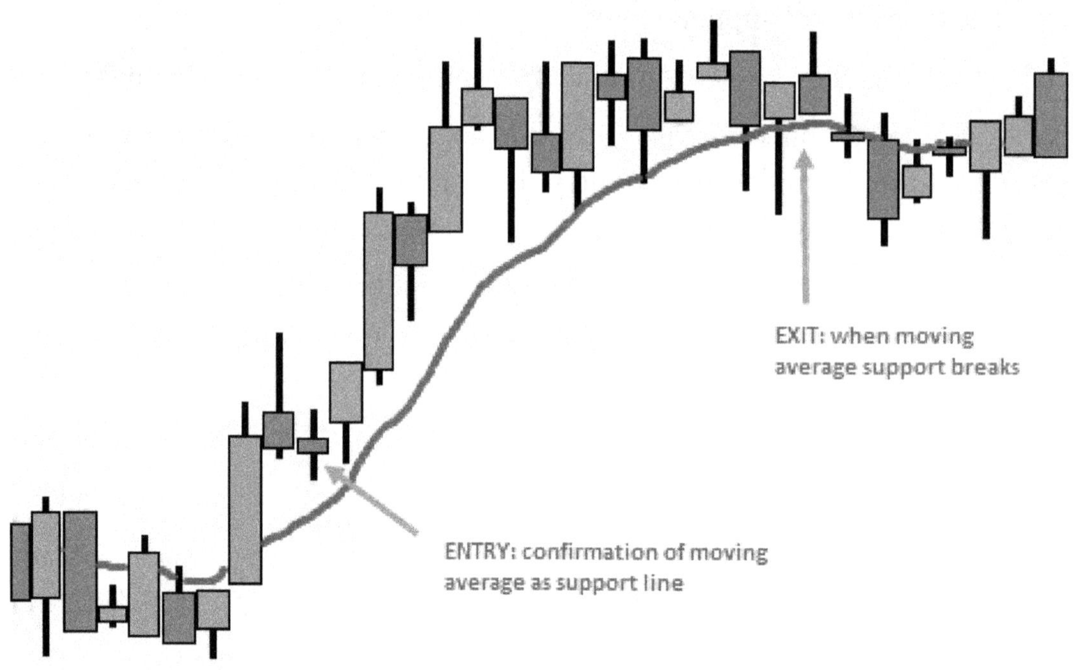

Here are the specific steps you can follow to use the Moving Average Strategy:

1. Keep track of the stock if you notice a trend is forming on its moving averages.
2. Immediately look at the trading data of the previous day to check if the stock is responding to the moving averages in a 5-minute chart. You may follow the 50 and 200 SMA and 9 and 20 EMA used by many day traders.
3. Once you learn which moving average is more suitable to the behavior of the trade, buy the stock after confirming the moving averages as a support. Ideally, you should buy as close as possible to the moving average line. Try to set your stop at 5 cents below the break of the moving average.
4. Ride the trend until the break of the moving average.
5. Avoid using trailing stops, and always monitor the trend with your own eyes. Don't rely on algorithm for this strategy.
6. Take your profit if you see that the stock is moving really high away from the moving average. Don't wait until the break of moving average for your exit.

Some day traders avoid trading moving averages. They see them as potential levels of resistance or support, but they rarely make any trend based on moving averages trend. Take note that in a trend trade strategy, you are often exposed in the market for a significant period.

Some trends may last for as long as three hours, and this could be too exhausting for some day traders. Another drawback with moving average trading is that you are not certain in the stock you want to trade. It can be difficult to know which moving average is accurately acting at a resistance or support level.

As we have discussed, your day trading strategy should depend on your personality, risk tolerance, account size, and trading psychology. This is on top of the brokers and tools that you are using.

Take note that day trading strategies are not something that you can mimic just from attending a class, speaking with a day trader or reading a book. You need to carefully develop your preferred approach, and then stick with it. It makes no sense to stick to moving averages if the ABCD pattern helps you to become profitable.

Volume Weighted Average Price (VWAP)

As you practice day trading, you need to slowly create your own method and stick with it. The best day trading strategy is the one that works for you. There's no good or bad in any of these strategies. It really is a matter of personal preference.

The day trading strategies we have discussed so far were the fundamentals. Over time, numerous strategies have been developed by day traders as they see fit for their choices. One example is the Volume Weighted Ave. Price (VWAP).

A trading benchmark, VWAP is used by retail traders to provide the average price a stock has traded at for the day. This metric is based on the stock price and volume. It is crucial because it will provide you with insight into both the value and the trend of a particular stock.

While other moving averages are computed based only on the stock price in the chart, VWAP also considers the number of the shares that the stock is traded on each price. Most day trading platforms have a built-in VWAP indicator, and you can use this without changing your default settings. This metric will help you quickly identify who is in control of the price action - sellers or buyers.

If the stock is trading above VWAP, it signifies that the buyers are in general control of the price action. If the stock is trading below the VWAP, it is a safe assumption that the sellers are in general control of the price. VWAP trading can be a walk in the park for day trading beginners because so many traders are looking at this metric and are making their decisions in reference to it.

Thus, newbies can easily be on the right side of the trade. If the stock is trying to break the VWAP but not able to, you can instead short the stock because there's a high chance that other traders are also watching the trade, and will also start to short.

A VWAP trading strategy is a simple and easy strategy that you can follow. Many day traders often short stocks if the retail crowd is trying to break the VWAP, but are clearly failing.

Below is an example chart where a VWAP strategy is used:

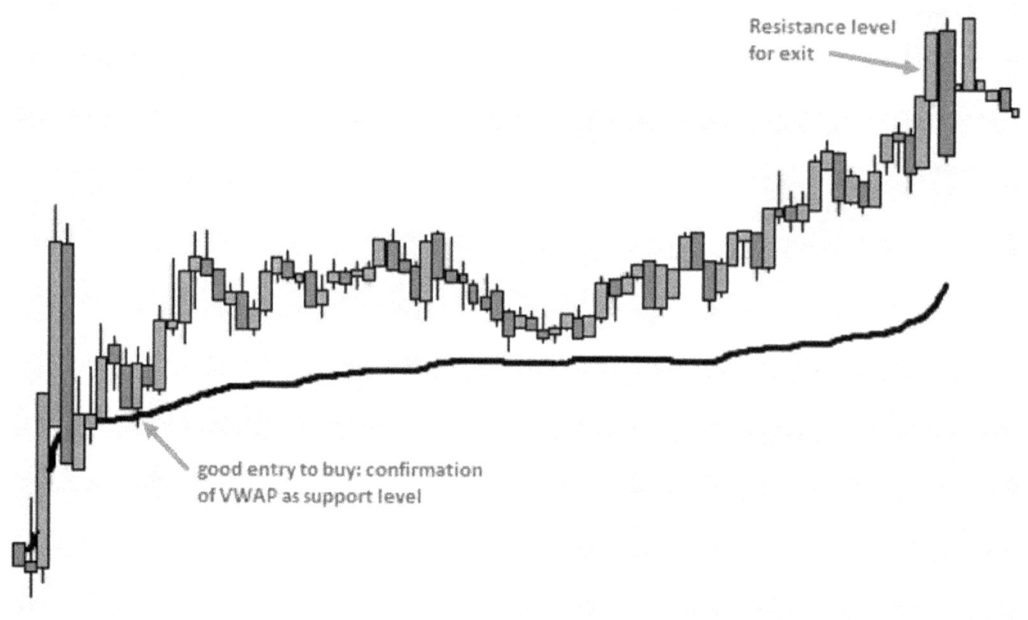

The day trader noticed that this stock rallied support over VWAP, so he bought 1000 shares with the projection that this will move toward an increase. His stop was close under VWAP. He first sold half of his shares and then moved his stop to break-even.

Here are the specific steps you can follow to use the VWAP strategy:

1. Whenever you make your watch list for your day trading, keep track of the price action around VWAP.
2. If a stock is moving towards VWAP, then wait until validation of the VWAP will support or break.
3. You may choose to buy as close as possible to reduce the risk. Your stop will be a break and close the 5-minute chart under VWAP.
4. Keep the trade until you hit your revenue target or until you reach a new resistance or support level.
5. Sell half of your shares near your target profit or resistance or support level
6. Move your stop to your entry point or break-even.

A similar method can also work if you want to short a stock.

Resistance or Support Trading

Horizontal resistance or support trading is another popular approach in day trading. Remember this: the stock market doesn't know diagonal trends. It only recognizes price levels.

This is why horizontal resistance or support lines are ideal benchmarks. On the other hand, diagonal trend lines can be subjective and can often lead to false assumptions.

As a matter of fact, trend lines are among the most deceptive of all day trading tools. You can easily draw a trend line across zones or prices in a manner that can affect its slope and its meaning. For example, if you are predetermined to buy, you may have the tendency to draw a steeper trend line.

Support is a price level where buyers are powerful enough to disrupt or reverse a downtrend. Once a downtrend hits support, it may bounce like a diver who hits the bottom of the sea, and then quickly pushes away. Horizontal lines represent support on a chart as you will see in the figure below.

On the other hand, resistance is a price level where sellers are powerful enough to disrupt or reverse an uptrend. If an uptrend hits resistance, it behaves like a person who hits a branch while climbing a mountain. It will stop and might even fall. Horizontal lines that connect two or more stops represent resistance on the charts.

Minor resistance or support may cause the trends to pause. Meanwhile, major resistance or support may cause the trends to reverse.

Traders sell at resistance and buy at support, which makes their effect a self-fulfilling prophecy. Using this approach, you can shortlist the stocks that you are interested to trade based on the criteria we have established in Chapter 4.

As a reminder, you need to choose stocks with significant catalysts such as news, high revenue report, or new approval from regulatory authorities. These stocks are the ones that day traders are monitoring and planning to trade.

Before the market opens, you can return to your daily charts and find price levels that were recorded in the past to be critical. Looking for price resistance or support levels can be tricky and requires a lot of experience in day trading.

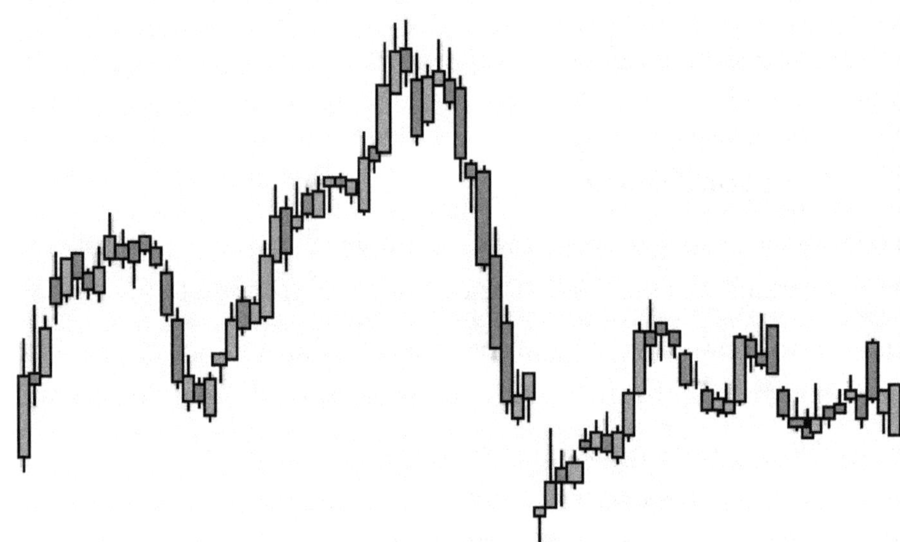

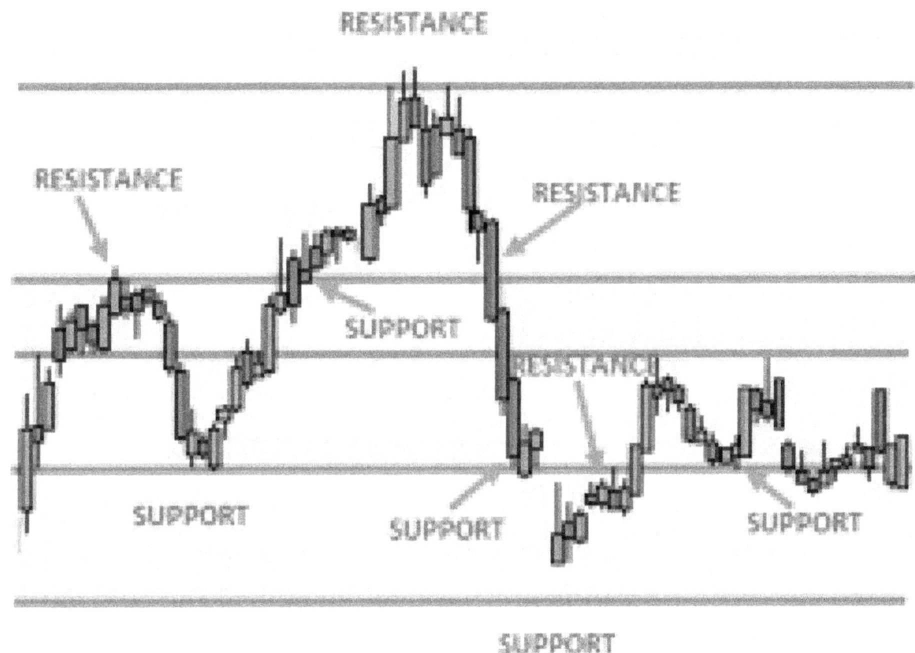

The chart on the left shows the daily chart of SCTY stock without the resistance or support lines. The image on the right includes these lines.

Resistance or support lines in daily charts are not always easy to find. In some instances, you will not be able to draw anything clear. If you can't see anything clear, then you don't have to draw anything.

There's a good chance that other traders will also not see these lines clearly and so there's no point in forcing yourself to draw resistance or support lines. In this case, you can plan your trades based on Moving Averages or VWAP that we have discussed earlier.

Tips in Drawing Resistance or Support Lines

1. You may see Doji or indecision candlesticks in the area of resistance or support because this is where traders are closely battling each other.
2. Whole dollars and half-dollars often act at resistance or support level. If you can't find a resistance or support line around these figures on a daily chart, take note that on daily charts, these figures may behave like an invisible resistance or support line.
3. You must always look at the previous data before you draw the lines.
4. Lines that are touching the price lines have more value. Emphasize these lines.

5. Only the resistance or support lines in the present price range are essential. If the stock price is presently at $40, it makes no sense to find resistance or support lines in the area when it was $80. There's a low chance that the stock will move and reach this region. Look only at the resistance or support area that is close to your day trading range.
6. Resistance or support lines are regions, and not exact figures. For instance, if you find an area around $38.16 as a support line, you should expect the price action movement around this figure, but not precisely $38.16. Depending on the stock price, an area of 10 to 20 cents is a safe assumption. The actual support line might be anything from $38.36 to $38.45
7. The price should have a clear bounce form its level. If you are not sure if the price has bounced in its level, then it is possibly not a resistance or support level.
8. In day trading, it is recommended to draw resistance or support lines across the extreme prices instead of areas where the bulk of the bars has stopped. This is the total opposite of swing trading. In swing trading, you have to draw resistance or support lines across the edges of the congestion areas where the bulk of the bars halted instead of the extreme prices.

Drawing resistance or support lines, while tricky, can be really simple once you have done it a lot of times.

Here are the specific steps you can follow to use the VWAP strategy:

1. When you create your watch list for the day, immediately look at the daily charts for the watch list and look at the area of resistance or support.
2. Keep track of the price action around these areas on a 5-minute chart. If an indecision candle forms around this region, this is a confirmation of that level, and you can enter the trade.
3. Minimize your risk by buying in as close as possible. Stop at the break and close the 5-minute chart below the resistance or support level.
4. Take your profit near the next resistance or support level.
5. Keep the trade open until you hit your target profit or you reach a new resistance or support level.
6. Sell half of your shares near the profit target or resistance/support level, and move your stop near your entry point or for break-even.
7. Consider closing your trade if there are no clear resistance or support levels.

You can also use the same approach if you short a stock.

Other Day Trading Strategies

Day traders usually choose their strategies according to specific factors like size of the account, amount of time that you can commit to trading, risk tolerance, personality, and trading experience.

Ideally, you should develop your own trading strategy and personalize it to your own preferences. Your psychology and risk tolerance are most likely different from other day traders, and from those other traders.

You are probably not comfortable with a $1000 loss, but traders who have big accounts can easily tolerate the loss and eventually make a profit out of the trade.

You can't just mimic other day traders. You should develop your own risk management plan and strategy. Some retail traders largely focus on technical indicators such as moving average crossover, moving average convergence divergence (MACD), or RSI.

There is a lot of technical indicators out there. Some day traders believe they hold the secret and it could be a mix of moving average crossover or RSI. But these are not always effective in the long run.

Basically, you can't participate in a trade using a systemic method and then allow indicators to guide your entry and exit points. This is the core of our next rule:

Rule No. 9 - Technical indicators will only guide you.

They should not dictate you.

Algorithmic programs are trading all the time. If you set up a system for trading that has no input or requires no human insight, then you are in the realm of algorithmic trading. This is not ideal for day traders as you will eventually lose against investment firms that have well-funded algorithms and sizeable trading capital.

Certainly, we can use the RSI in your scanner to guide your day trading strategy, especially for reversal trading. There are also scanners that depend on high or low RSI, but these are more conditioned to look for stocks. By any means, these are not buy/sell indicators.

Develop Your Own Day Trading Strategy

While you should understand these day trading strategies, you should try to find your own place in the market. You could be a 5-minute trader or a 1-hour trader. Some are even swing traders who are more comfortable working with daily or weekly charts.

The stock market is huge, and you can find your own place. You need to consider the lessons in this book as puzzle pieces that together make up the bigger picture of day trading. You can pick up some of the pieces in this book, and you can also choose some of the pieces from your own research. Eventually, you can have all the pieces you need to create your own unique trading strategy that really works for you.

Don't expect that everything you have learned here is applicable to you. You can follow some of the strategies here or completely ditch other strategies you find not useful. The important thing that you need to do for now is to create your own strategy based on your risk tolerance, account size, and personality.

There is a lot of day trading strategies that you have learned here and there will be a lot more, which you will encounter as you practice this trade. As a newbie, you should try to master one strategy. Once you have tested the water with one strategy, you can become a professional trader who has made some profit in the trade. The more you practice, the more you will learn.

This is a career where you must survive until you can make it. You can begin casting out a bit, but first, you have to master just one strategy. You may choose Reversal Strategy, a Bull Flag Momentum Strategy, VWAP trade, or you can develop your own. Limit your options, create your area of strength into a doable approach, and then use this strategy to survive until you are more knowledgeable and experienced enough to create other unique strategies. Never trade without a plan.

Always plan your trade and trade according to your plan. You can't just change your plan once you jump in the trade and you are in an open position.

The reality in day trading is that the profits are not guaranteed. You will lose money. The majority of day traders today are not aware of the insights that you have learned from this book. Many of them are using day trading strategies that are not even proven effective. Some of them don't even have a strategy in place. They follow a bit of advice from someone, or they mimic someone they know.

That method is dangerous. You can quickly lose your trade, and then you may wonder what happened. You may choose to practice for weeks in a day trading simulator, and then trade a bit with real cash for one week, then return to the simulator to improve your weak areas or practice new strategies for another two weeks. This approach is fine.

Even seasoned day traders are still using simulators when they want to test out a strategy that they are working on. While learning the insights in this book and practicing in simulators, your focus should be to develop a strategy to guide your live trades.

There's no mad rush in this career. Day trading is a marathon, and not a sprint. This is not about making $20,00 in one day (even though it is not impossible to do that in day trading). This is about honing a set of skills that you can use to become successful in this career.

Chapter 7 - Day Trading Process

One underlying principle in day trading that you can follow as a beginner is mastering only a few setups that are solid yet profitable. As a matter of fact, following simple trading strategies composed of several minimal setups can help in minimizing stress and confusion. It will also allow you to focus more on the psychological elements of day trading.

After learning the fundamentals of day trading strategies, let's go over the actual process for planning and making a trade. At this point, you should have a basic understanding of the setup that you want to trade. However, as a newbie, you may find it difficult to plan and initiate your trade beforehand.

Setting up your trade can be easy. The challenge starts in figuring out when to enter or exit a trade. This is where you can really make money or break your account.

The key to prevent losses in day trading is to develop a process. Remember, you must plan your trade and trade your plan. Seasoned day traders usually follow a systematic approach to day trading.

Successful day traders know what to do every day. They have a morning routine, they know what to do in developing their watch list, they organize their trade plan, they initiate their trade based on their plan, they execute the trade based on their plan, and at the end of the day, they assess what happened.

You should bear in mind that what makes a trade lucrative is the proper execution of all the steps in the process described above. Write down your reasons for exiting and entering each trade. Anyone can buy a book on day trading and read every page. However, only a small percentage has the discipline for proper execution.

Even if you have a good setup, you can still lose money if you choose the wrong stocks to trade. These include stocks that are manipulated by institutional traders or computers. Or even if you find proper stocks to trade, you could have jumped in at the wrong time. A wrong timing could mess up your trade plan and you will eventually lose money. You can look for good stocks to trade, then enter the trade properly. But if you don't get out at the right time, you may transform a winning trade into a losing one.

All the steps in the day trading process are crucial. Consider something significant that you always do in your life, and then think about how you can do it efficiently. Now, think about how you do it at the present. This is a remarkable thought process for day traders. If you take a trade, you need to make certain that you are focused on the right things either before you enter the trade and during the trade.

Developing a thought process can take away most of the emotional hang-ups that day traders experience when they are looking to jump in a trade, and also managing the trade when they are inside the market.

This brings us to the tenth and final rule in day trading:

Rule No. 10 - Don't allow your emotions to cloud your judgment.

It can be difficult for you to make money in day trading if you are too emotional. If you allow your emotions to rule your decisions, you will lose a lot of money.

Knowledge and regular practice can provide you with a perspective of what really matters in day trading, your approach in day trading, and how you can improve your skills.

Once you have a perspective on what is important, you can easily identify the particular processes that you should concentrate on. The key here is to precisely know your approach.

Beginners usually learn their lessons the hard way - they lose money. But you will realize that trading, following your plan, and the discipline that is inherent in your trading approach can be a reflection of your daily habits, which can contribute a lot to becoming a successful day trader.

For example, Ben is a day trader who has been in the equities and forex market for nearly eight years. Whenever he starts his trading process, he follows the same routine when he gets up in the morning.

He always works out in the morning before the trading session begins. He wakes up at 6 am every day, then he hits the gym from 6:00 am to 7 am. He comes home, takes a shower, and then at 7:30 am he begins writing his trading plan for the day.

Ben discovered that when his body has not been active before trading, he makes poor decisions. There are actually clinical studies correlating exercise to decision making. Individuals who regularly exercise have outstanding scores on performance tests and neuropsychological exams. They also have higher scores on tests that measure memory, cognitive flexibility, and information processing.

Your brain is your number one tool in day trading, so make sure that you take care of it. In financial markets, just being better than average is not enough. You should be excellent in order to win every day.

Sadly, day trading usually attracts people with strong impulses such as gamblers and other people who feel that they are entitled to win. Avoid these mindsets. Stop behaving like an irresponsible teenager.

You must begin developing the discipline of a master. Masters think, feel, and act differently than average people. Try to look within yourself and eliminate your illusions. Change your old methods of acting, thinking, and being.

It can be extremely difficult to change, but if you really want to be a profitable day trader, you need to work on changing and improving yourself. In order to succeed, you need the right form of motivation, know-how, and discipline.

Day trading is a serious business. If you treat this as a hobby, you will not go far.

Successful day traders follow specific morning routines. They wake up early in the morning, they are engaged in exercise, they eat healthy meals, and they are disciplined. As a result, they are awake, alert, and motivated to win the trade.

Following a morning routine can significantly help you prepare your mind for day trading. So regardless of what you do, starting your day in the same routine can lead to sizeable profits.

Rolling out of your bed and then haphazardly opening your computer will not prepare you for the stock market. Sitting on your couch in your pajamas is not the right position to win the game.

Ben's watch list comes from a particular scan that he uses every day. He doesn't need to look from other sources because he is confident that the stocks appearing on his scanner are set up for the trade he wants. He analyzes every stock, in the same manner, using his checklist where he can figure out if it is actually a good trade. His watch list is completed by 8:00 am, and he will not add anything to this list because there is no time to analyze new stocks and plan another trade.

When the market opens at 9:30 am, Ben has his plans in place written on his notebook. He has a good memory but he still writes his plan.

What will I do if the stocks set up to the long side?

What will I do if the stocks set up to the short side?

What kind of setups do I wish to see?

What is my profit target for the day?

Where should I place my stops?

Is the profit area big enough for the trade to be good?

By asking these questions, Ben has a clear advantage over other day traders because he has a battle plan, and all he needs to do is to stick with it. If he has his plan written down on a piece of paper, he can easily review it. This eliminates the anxiety that he used to feel whenever the market opens.

When the market opens, Ben will start looking for his signals and triggers to jump in the trade. There are instances when Ben second guesses himself, but those are rare instances. He has his targets written out, including the technical indicators that he uses for placing his stops. After entering the market, he just needs to focus on hitting his targets and cashing in his profits.

Some day traders believe that knowing the time to get out is the most difficult part of day trading. It can be really hard not to get out of the trade too early, especially if you don't have a plan.

When you have a trading plan and you follow it, you are in a better position to win the trade and cut your losses fast rather than the other way around. This can also help you in keeping your emotions in check during the trade.

It can also help you a lot if you know how to filter out the noise. This will allow you to focus on the trade instead of overanalyzing the situation. After you are done trading, you can start reflecting on how well your plan worked, and how much profit you earned by following your plan. You can start reflecting your trades at night when you review and recap your trades of the day.

Reflection is an important part of the day trading process. Just because you have made money during the day doesn't mean you are a successful day trader. Assessing how you play both sides of the trade is extremely important.

You can start your own trading journal if you want or watch the recap in your trading platform. You can save these insights later for your reference. Some lessons are harder than others because they include losses. However, you should be confident that in due time, you will improve your skills.

Following a process in day trading is crucial because it will help you prepare for trading and provide you the focus for proper execution. It can also help you filter out the emotional and crowd noise. It will provide you with a higher chance of success and offer you a tool to review and assess your trades.

If you know how to focus on the right processes, in the right manner, then you can develop your own approach to successful day trading.

Chapter 8 - Forex Day Trading

At this point, you should have sufficient information about day trading. We also have given you examples, but they are all about equities.

Day trading is not only limited to the equities or stock market. You can also use day trading strategies for other instruments such as foreign exchange, options, and futures markets.

Forex Day Trading

The foreign exchange market (simply known as forex) refers to the actual market where market participants can trade or speculate currencies. It plays an important role in the global economy because the currencies must be converted first before anyone can facilitate business.

For example, if you are located in Japan and you like to buy 300 sacks of curry powder from India, you need to pay your supplier in Rupees (INR). But before you can do that, you need to exchange the corresponding value of Japanese Yen (JPY) into INR.

Forex is also vital in tourism. A Chinese tourist cannot pay in Yuan when in Paris because Yuan is not the accepted currency in the country. Hence, he must exchange Yuan to Francs at the current price.

The need to exchange currencies for either business or personal transactions affect the high liquidity and volatility in the forex market. In fact, the forex market is a lot bigger than the equities market. It is estimated that around $5 Trillion are traded in the forex market every day.

An important feature of this global trading platform is that there's no particular organization or group that manages the trade. You may trade in the forex market via digital channels through over the counter (OTC) transactions.

Instead of a central platform, forex transactions can happen online in several regions around the globe. Unlike in the equities market where you need to wait for the market to open, you can trade in the forex market 24 hours a day and 5 days a week, because the currencies are traded in different financial spots such as Paris, Hong Kong, Zurich, New York, Sydney, Singapore, Frankfurt, Tokyo, London, and New York. This passes through various time zones, so if the trade is closing in Singapore, the platform is just starting in London.

There are three general options in forex market trading:

1. Spot Market

2. Futures Market
3. Forwards Market

Spot market trading is considered as the busiest financial market today because it serves as the main platform for the futures and forwards market. In the past, the futures market has the highest level of activity as it used to cater to private investors, as well as day traders.

However, with the emergence of online forex trading, the spot market has experienced a considerable flow of investment and is now competing with the futures market as one of the busiest trading platforms for speculators and day traders.

Day traders are often trading in the spot market. The forwards market and the futures market are often reserved for organizations that need to hedge their risks to a particular date in the future.

Forex Spot Market

The forex spot market is the platform where day traders can buy and sell currencies based on the prevailing rates. The price can be affected by the current demand and supply and is also affected by different factors such as political situations, economic performances, current interest rates, and currency pair performance perception.

In the spot market, the spot deal refers to the final deal. This is a two-channel transaction wherein one party will provide an agreed currency rate. The transaction is completed if the position is closed.

While the spot market is known as the platform where day traders can trade in present commodities, the trades can be settled also in a matter of days or weeks. In that case, it is known as swing trading and not day trading.

Forex Futures and Forwards Markets

While the spot market is known as the platform where day traders can trade in present commodities, the trades can be settled also in a matter of days or weeks. In that case, it is known as swing trading and not day trading.

On the other hand, there's no actual trading of currencies in the futures and forwards markets. Rather, market participants deal with contracts, which signify a claim to a particular form of currency and a particular unit price. The trade is only settled at a future date.

In the futures market, the trades are settled based on a standard size and the settlement date for public financial markets such as Chicago's Mercantile Exchange. The futures market in the US is administered by the National Futures Association. The contracts in the futures market have specific details including the units for trading, settlement date, and the increase in price.

In the forwards market, the contracts are exchanged over the counter between two traders who will agree on specific terms. Global companies are primarily trading agreements in the forwards market to hedge against the fluctuations in the exchange market. Therefore, this platform is usually not ideal for day traders.

Bear in mind that an important differentiating factor between the forex markets is how we quote currencies. Within the forwards or futures markets, the currencies are always quoted against the US dollar.

Therefore, the pricing is conducted in terms of how many USD you need to purchase a single unit of a certain currency. Take note that in the forex spot market, some currencies are quoted against the US dollars, while there are also quotes where USD is quoted against them. Hence, the quotes from the futures / forwards market and the spot market will not usually become aligned with each other.

As an example, in the forex spot market, the Euro is quoted with the US dollars as EUR/USD. This is also the manner used for quoting currencies in the futures and forwards market. Hence, if the Euro becomes stronger than the US dollar in the spot market, there is also a high tendency for the currency to rise in the futures and forwards markets.

Meanwhile, in the case of the USD / JPY currency pair, USD is quoted against JPY. The current quote in the spot market for this fx pair is 110.27, which means that $1 will buy 110.27 Japanese yen. But in the futures fx market, the quote will be .0090 or (1/110.27), which means that 1 Japanese yen will buy .0090 US dollars.

Therefore, a slight increase in the USD/JPY in the spot market will result in a fall in the yen futures rate since USD will be stronger against the yen, and so one unit of yen will buy fewer dollars.

Forex Swing Trading

This medium-term forex trading strategy is typically used over a period of days to weeks. Swing traders will usually look to set up trades on swings to lows and highs over a certain period of time.

Its purpose is to filter out the erratic movements in the price, which is common in intraday trading. This is also used to prevent setting narrowly placed stop losses, which can force the traders to stop a trade for a short-term market flow.

It is true that the forex market is filled with ratios, charts, and numbers. However, this game is more of an art than science. Similar to artistic endeavors, talent is a strong foundation, but it will only get you so far with your effort and improvement.

Successful traders develop their skills through discipline and practice. They perform self-evaluation to see what is driving their trades, and learn how they can keep greed and fear out of the equation. In this section, we will discuss the tips and tricks that a beginner can use to become successful in forex trading.

Establish your goals and select a trading style that is compatible with your personality

Before beginning a single trade in the forex market, it is crucial that you have some concept of where you want to go and how you can work every day to achieve this destination.

Also, it is crucial that your goals in mind are clear as to what you want to achieve. You should also be certain that the trading strategy you choose will help you achieve your goals.

Take note that every type of trading strategy requires a specific approach and every style is suitable to different risk profiles. For instance, day trading can be ideal for you if you are not comfortable with an open position in the market.

Meanwhile, if you have capital that you believe will take advantage of the appreciation of a trade over a period of several months, then position trading might be ideal for you. Just make certain that your personality is suitable for the trading style you do.

Select a trading methodology and be consistent

Before you start any trade, you should have enough knowledge about the forex market so you can execute your trades with confidence. You should know the specific information you need so you can make the best decision about whether to exit or enter a trade.

Some traders are using technical analysis, while others prefer to look at the underlying fundamentals of the economy of the company, and then use charts to find out the best time to enter the trade. Take note that market fundamentals can drive the long-term trend.

Chart patterns, on the other hand, may provide you with short-term trading opportunities. Just be consistent regardless of the methodology you prefer, and make certain to be flexible as well. The methodology must catch up with the changing forex market platform.

Carefully select your entry and exit frames

Most beginners in forex trading experience confusion because of the opposing data that they may encounter in evaluating charts in various time frames.

For example, the information that can be extracted from an intraday chart could indicate a sell signal, which may show up as a buying signal when viewed in a weekly chart. Hence, if you depend on an intraday chart and use a weekly chart to look for the best time entry, make certain that the two charts are in sync. When the weekly chart indicates a buying signal, you should also wait until the daily chart also shows a buying signal.

Work on the trade expectancy

It is crucial to make sure that whichever system you use, it should be reliable. You can do this by calculating the expectancy.

Using a specific formula, you can revisit past trends and gauge all the trades that you won against the trades that you lost. Then, you can figure out the profitability of the winning trades against how much you have lost on losing trades.

Check your previous 10 trades, then figure out if you have made a profit or loss. Write the trades down and get the total of all the trades you won then divide the answer by the no of trades you won. Below is the formula. W refers to the average winning trade, L refers to the average losing trade, while P refers to the percentage of winning ratio.

$$E= [1+ (W/L)] \times P - 1$$

For example, in your previous 10 trades, you won seven trades, and three losses, 70 percent is your win ratio. If the seven trades gained $3,000, then the average win is $3000/7 = $428.57.

If your total loss was $ 1,000, then your average loss is $1,000/3 = $ 333.33. In using the formula above, you will get: E=[1+ (428.57/333.33)] x 0.7 -1 = 0.60 or 60%, which means 60 percent reliability of the system that can provide you 60 cents on a dollar in the long run.

Create positive feedback loops

You can create a positive feedback loop if your trades are implemented according to your strategic plan. A positive feedback pattern can be created if you execute a trade based on your plan.

Success can breed success, which could in turn provide the confidence you need, especially if the trade is profitable. The habit of sticking to your plan, despite some losses that you may encounter in the process can still result in a positive feedback loop.

Concentrate on your trading strategy and don't be afraid of small losses

In playing the forex market, you should take note that there is a risk of losing all your money. Hence, you should only use your excess money and not gamble your money for necessities such as college fund. Successful traders consider their trading fund as a game fund.

When the game is over, the money is all spent. This attitude can help you to be more positive while trading in forex. Psychologically, you can be well-prepared to accept even small losses.

This is crucial in how you can handle risks successfully. You can become a successful forex trader if you concentrate on your trades and you learn from your minor losses.

Setting Up Your Forex Day Trading Account

Forex day trading is quite similar to stock market day trading because you have first to open your own trading account. Similar to the stock market, every forex account, as well as the services you can take advantage of can be different. Hence, it is crucial that you look for the most suitable platform for you.

In this section, we will discuss the important factors that you should consider when choosing a foreign exchange account.

Trading Leverage

When we speak of leverage, we refer to the opportunity to take control of bigger amounts of cash with minimal capital from your own pocket. The leverage level is directly proportional to the risk level.

Take note that the leverage amount on a platform could vary, according to the features of the account on its own. However, the most popular one is 50:1 leverage. Some accounts could offer a maximum leverage of 250:1.

For example, the maximum leverage of 100:1 signifies that for each dollar that you hold in the brokerage account, you can use up to $100. For instance, if you have an account balance of $100, the brokerage can allow you to trade as much as $10,000 in the fx market.

This leverage could also define the total amount that you can hold in your account or your margin for trading a specific amount. In the stock market, the margin is often at 50%, and the leverage could be 50:1, which can be at least 2%.

In general, leverage is regarded as a primary advantage of trading in the foreign exchange market, because this will allow you to create substantial gains with minimal capital. But leverage could also have extreme downsides when a trade is moving in the opposite direction because the losses could also be big.

With this leverage type, there is always the actual probability that your losses are higher than what you have invested, even though most accounts have safeguard stops to prevent the account from hitting negative. As such, it is crucial that you take note of this when you open a brokerage account, and once you identify your preferred leverage, you can understand the involved risks more.

Fees and Commissions

Another major advantage of forex platforms is that investing through them could be done through commissions, which is unlike stock market accounts where you need to pay a broker a certain fee for every trade.

You are now directly dealing with market players, and you don't have to pass through another layer such as brokers.

Every time you enter a trade, it is the market makers, which can seize the spread. Hence, when the ask/bid for a forex market is 1.5300/50, the market maker can capture the difference between the points.

In setting up your own forex account, be sure to take note that every firm has various spreads on currency pairs that you trade. Even though they are usually different by only several pips, this could be substantial when you are planning to do a lot of trading.

Hence, in setting up an account, be certain that you are aware of the pip and spread of specific currency pairs that you are interested in trading.

You must take note that there are several differences between every forex platform and the programs or software that they are offering. Hence, it is crucial to review every firm before you make a commitment. Every forex trading company may offer various levels of programs and services including the fees beyond and above the actual costs of trading.

Moreover, because of the less strict conditions in the foreign exchange market, you should find a reliable firm. When you are also not completely confident to trade with real cash, you can also try trading in practice accounts or demos.

How to Start Day Trading in the Forex Market

After understanding the most crucial factors in opening your own forex account, it is time to look into what specifically you could trade within the platform. The two primary methods in trading in the forex market include the actual trading (selling and buying) of forex pairs, in which you short currency and long another.

Another method is via buying the derivatives that monitor the fluctuations of a particular currency pair. These strategies are quite similar to the common techniques used in the stock market.

Basically, buying and selling the currency pair is the most popular method, much in a similar manner that many traders are buying and selling currency units.

In this setting, a trader may hope that the currency pair's value will change in a profitable way. If you choose to short a pair, it signifies that you are betting on the possibility that the pair's value will fall.

For instance, let's assume that you want a short position for the USD/JPY pair. You can make profits when the value of the fx pair goes down, and you will lose your investment if it rises. This pair will rise if the USD increases its price against the JPY. Therefore, it is actually a trust on the JPY.

Another alternative is to use futures and options, which are derivative products, so you can make money from the currency value changes. If you purchase a currency pair option, you can gain the privilege to buy a pair on a specific rate. Meanwhile, a futures forex contract could build the agreement to purchase the currency pair at a specific point.

These trading strategies are often employed by more experienced traders, but as a beginner, you should be at least aware of them.

Order Types

In looking for a new trading position, you may have to use a market order or a limit order, which are actually similar when you are placing a new position in the stock market.

A market order can provide you with the capacity to acquire the currency at a specific exchange rate that it is presently trading in the foreign exchange market. On the other hand, the limit order will allow you to identify a specific entry price.

If you are holding an open position in the market, you may have to consider employing a take profit order, so you could lock in your gains.

For instance, let us assume that you are sure that the USD/GBP will react at 1.8700, but you are not completely certain that the price will rise any higher. You can use a take-profit order that will immediately close your position if the price hits 1.8700, which will lock in your profits.

The stop loss order is also a tool that you can use when you want to hold the open positions. This will allow you to figure out if the price could decline prior to the closing of the position and more losses could be accumulated.

Hence, if the USD/GBP rate starts to drop, the investor may put a stop-loss, which could halt the position to avoid any further loss.

When you are also day trading in the stock market, you will realize that the order types that you could enter in the forex trading accounts are quite similar. It is crucial to be familiar with these orders before you actually place your very first trade in the foreign exchange market.

Chapter 9 - Day Trading ETFs and Options

Exchange-Traded Funds are financial securities that involve a collection of securities like equities or even currencies that usually monitor an underlying index.

ETFs also involve different sectors or industries and also use different strategies. In many ways, ETFs are like mutual funds. But they are listed on exchanges and the shares can also be traded by retail traders.

A popular ETF is the SPDR S&P 500 or simply known as SPY that monitors the S&P 500 Index. It contains different types of investments including bonds, commodities, and equities. Because ETFs are marketable securities, it has an associated price, which allows it to be traded.

ETFs also bring together in one instrument some of the paramount features offered by equities and mutual funds. Many ETFs seek to monitor a benchmark index, then trade shares on exchanges such as stock. They are also available for each major asset class such as stocks or equities, bonds or fixed income, cash, and commodities.

ETFs offer a more affordable alternative to obtain exposure to a group that otherwise would have been quite hard to trade.

For example, if you want to put your money in gold, you have different options. You may buy actual gold bars or coins, or you can try trading contracts for gold futures. But these are usually tedious and difficult methods.

The most affordable option here is to get gold ETF shares that follow gold's market price. You can do this with less effort and at a lot lower price. If you project that the whole stock market will rise, you can purchase a stock index such as Dow Jones. You may either purchase DJIA futures contracts or buy all the 30 companies that comprise the Dow Index.

If you like to do this for a cheaper alternative, you can easily purchase EFT shares that follow Dow Jones such as the DIA ETF.

Day traders generally love ETFs because of their high volatility. In this chapter, we will learn how you can trade ETF.

Retail trading is one of the most preferred ETF trading strategies due to its high market volatility. Therefore, day traders can buy & sell ETFs anytime throughout the day. There are different ETF platforms available, but the best ETF today are the following:

- iSHares MSCI Emerging Markets ETF
- ProShares UltraVIX ShortTerm Futures ETF (UVXY)
- Gold Miners ETF (GDX)

- ProShares VIX ShortTerm Futures ETF (UVXY)
- SPDR S&P 500 (SPY)

These are also part of the busiest ETF exchanges in the US. Day traders can take advantage of highly profitable short-term EFT opportunities. But the chances of making a profit by betting on day trading can be limited. This is the reason you have to carefully assess the rules in ETF trading.

Here are the specific steps in trading ETFs:

1. Select the Right Exchange Traded Funds for Day Trading

In the US, the first and the most popular ETF is the SPDR S&P500 ETF or SPY ETF. Day traders are attracted to trade in SPY because it has the biggest AUM and trading volume. The SPY ETF monitors how the world's most famous stock index, the S&P 500, performs.

The top ETFs in the US ranked by Forbes Magazine according to Assets (in billion dollars) are the following

- SPDR S&P 500 (SPY) - $254
- iShares Core S&P500 (IVV) - $146.7
- Vanguard Total Stock Market (VTI) - $94.6
- Vanguard S&P500 (VOO) - $88.2
- iShares MSCI EAFE (EFA) - $78.3
- Vanguard FTSE Developed Markets (VEA) $72.1
- Vanguard FTSE Emerging Markets (VWO) $65.9
- Invesco QQQ (QQQ) $62.1

It is fairly reasonable that most day traders choose SPY ETF as the prime exchange for their day trading. But you should not assume that all ETFs are the same since they are obviously not. If you are not certain which one you should trade, just opt for the most popular and most trusted exchange, which is SPY.

2. Use the 50-period MA (15-Minute Trend)

Among the most commonly used stock trading indicators is the 50-period moving average. This is actually a psychological indicator that many day traders use to analyze the sentiment in the ETF market.

The 50-period moving average is more relevant to the price movement because many traders use it. This is the main reason the 50 MA is used alongside the trading range opening.

The chart below shows the 50 MA in SPDR S&P 500

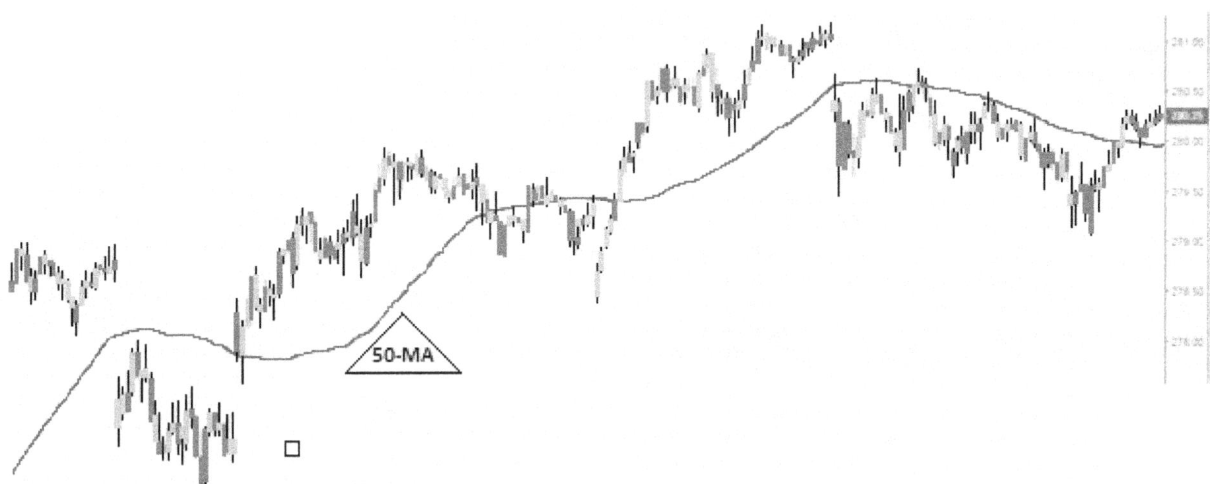

3. Jump into Trade after 10 AM Eastern Time

In day trading ETFs, it is ideal to concentrate on the starting trading range. The trading session in the morning is when smart money typically comes in, and also when the biggest volume happens.

So if you focus only on the AM session, you can avoid being stuck to the chart the entire day, and you can only trade alongside organizational investors.

SPDR S&P500 regularly starts trading at 9:30 AM Eastern Time. However, you should allocate the first half hour after the market opens to observe the trading patterns.

Day trading ETFs is mostly about trading the opportunities during the time of day that is most volatile.

4. Wait for the Price to Hold Over 50-Period MA and Open the Upper Portion of the past 5-day Trade

After analyzing how the market performs during the first half hour of the market session, you should find the price to keep over the key 50-period moving average.

Moreover, the SPDR S&P500 ETF also requires opening the upper half of the past five-day trading range. Just mark the past trading days as well as the peak price of the particular range.

Hold above the 50-period MA if you noticed that on the 6th day you open somewhere near the peak price.

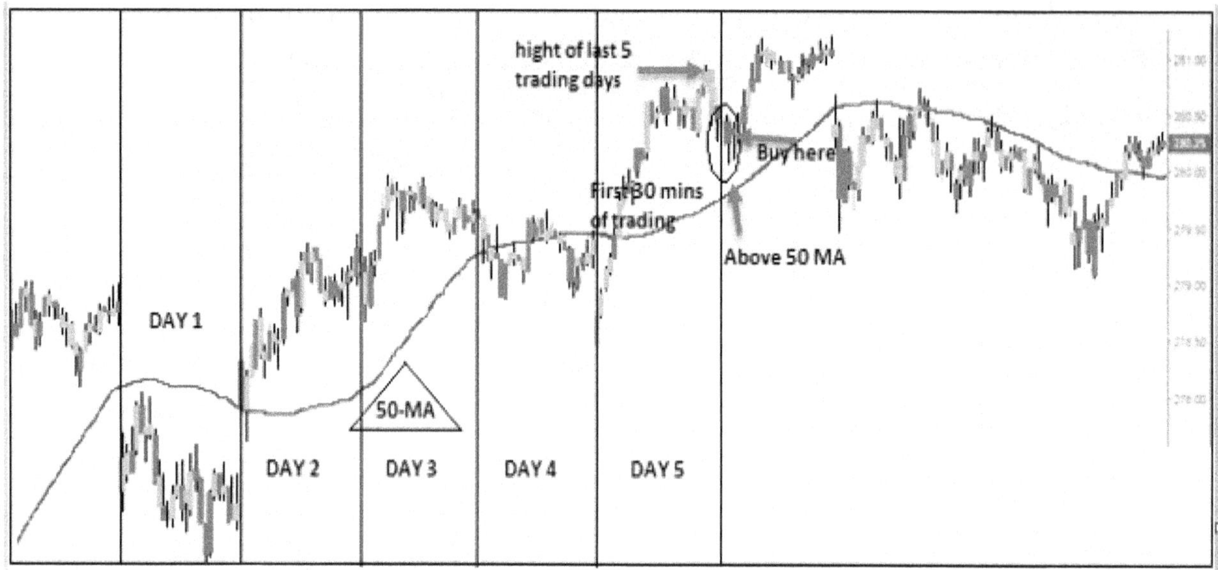

5. Place Stop Loss (25 cents) under the 50-period MA

With this day trading strategy, you need to place your stop loss at 25 cents just under the 50-period MA.

If after the session, the market is breaking under the 50 MA, it means that the bears are getting stronger. Remember this indicator as it is key in making money in ETF day trading.

6. Get Your Profit if the SPY Advances a Dollar

This particular ETF day trading setup depends on the assumption that if each of the conditions above are met, then there's a high chance the SPY ETF will advance at least a dollar. Manually close the trade if you are not able to reach your target profit.

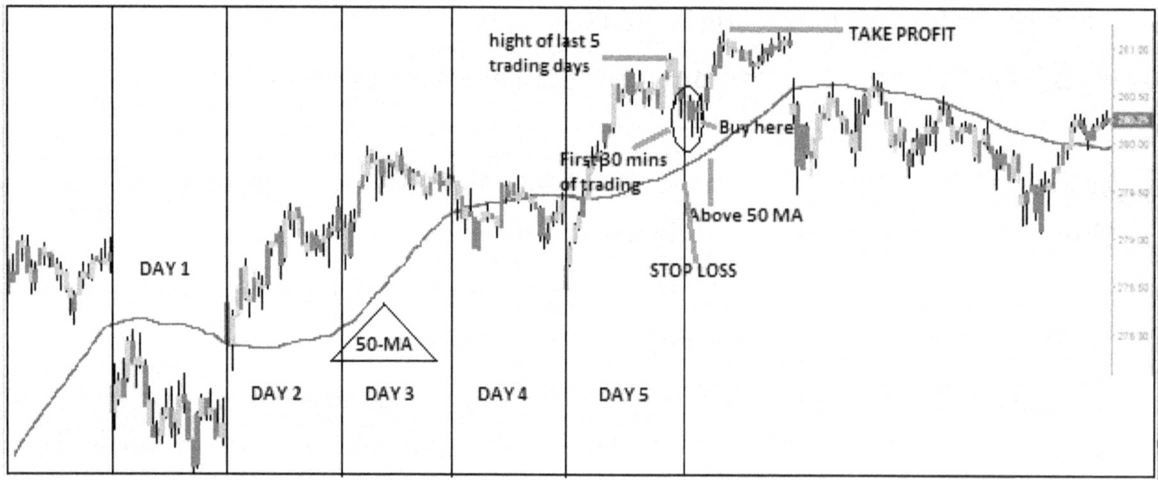

The chart above shows a good example of a buying trade. You can still follow similar rules for a selling trade, only in reverse order.

Day trading ETFs offers basic investment opportunities without investing too much on operating costs compared to equities and forex market. However, you can really make a lot of money as a day trader if you know how to leverage ETF's intraday high volatility.

Options Day Trading

Aside from stocks, forex, and futures, and ETFs. you can also day trade options, which are direct financial derivatives. Options are basically legal contracts that allow you to buy or sell an instrument during or within a pre-established date or exercise date.

If you are selling options, you need to fulfill the terms of the transactions. These could either be buy or sell if the buyer opts to exercise the option before the expiry date.

Day trading options can span across different markets. You may obtain equities options, forex options, ETF options, futures options, and more. These conventional options are also called 'vanilla options'.

Options Contract

If you own an options contract, you will be provided with a number of rights. The options contract includes the following details:

- Types of options (put or call)
- Underlying instrument (equities, bonds, etc.)
- Trade units (the number of shares)
- Strike price (the price at which you can exercise the option)
- Expiry date (the last day you can exercise the option)

Types of Options

Options are usually categorized as risky and complicated investments, and this places off different aspiring traders. There are two types of options:

- Call - These are buying options that will allow you to buy a stock at a certain price.
- Put - These are selling options that will allow you to sell a stock at a certain price.

Aside from the two primary classes, there's a long list of various markets and options available. While not all options are available for day trading, the list includes:

- Equities options
- Mini options

- Index options
- Crude oil options
- Futures options
- SPY Options
- E-Mini options
- QQQ options
- OEX options
- ETF options
- IRA options
- ES weekly options

More often than not, you will find that most options are based on stocks of publicly listed companies such as Amazon or Google. But there is also an increasing number of options based on alternative underlying instruments such as real estate investment trusts (REITs), commodities, currencies, and stock indexes.

If you are interested in day trading stock options, you need to understand that the contracts for these instruments are based on 100 shares of the stock. This rule is not applicable, however, if the adjustments occur as a result of mergers or stock splits.

Most ETF stock options are in the US, and can be exercised at any point between the buying date and expiry date. On the other hand, European options can only be redeemed on the expiry date.

As you learn different financial instruments, you may realize several similarities between options and day trading. These are often based on the same underlying instrument. The composition of the actual contracts also share several similarities.

The main difference is how you trade options and futures. In options, you will get a wider range of available vehicles. You will also find that the trading rules are different. You can trade options singularly or you can buy them alongside futures contracts or stocks to serve like trade insurance.

The Benefits of Day Trading Options

There are several reasons you can make huge profits in day trading options. But aside from financial rewards, day trading options usually has its own appeal to traders.

Low Cost Strategy

Day trading options will provide you with the opportunity to participate and get out in the market faster and with minimum risk compared to other financial instruments such as mutual funds or equities. It is also considerably more affordable to buy an option than to buy the underlying instruments such as shares. Therefore, you can control the same number of shares with minimum capital.

Diversity

Because options are a lot more affordable than purchasing the actual stock, you can take advantage of several opportunities for investments. Therefore, your capital can go further, which increases your potential for profit.

More Benefits for Day Traders

Once the security moves, the day trader can take advantage even more with an option. For example, if a stock moves from $30 to $60, this will bring you a 100% gain in shares. But a call option that moves from $2 per contract to $10 per contract will provide you with a 5x gain. Hence, you can earn more and faster with options.

Advantage over Other Securities

Options have the power to succeed where other financial securities often fail. While some securities fail, options can easily make you money. This is partly due to the fact that you don't need to exercise your option in order to make money. Moreover, high volatility is always attractive for making profits.

Mutually Beneficial for Buyers and Sellers

While options are usually built on stocks, they can give you better benefits if combined. This is due to the fact that you have the option to sell your options so you can create an income on the stocks that you are holding.

But like other financial instruments, day trading options has its own drawbacks. These include the following:

Price Movement Reductions

Price movement is often limited to the time value element of the premium options. In spite of the fact that the value may increase with the price of the underlying financial instrument, it can still be undermined by the loss of time value. But it is interesting to note that the time value for day trading options is relatively limited.

Wider Bid-Ask Spreads

If you compare it to stocks, the bid-ask spread is often wider in options day trading. This is often due to the lower liquidity often found in the options market. This may fluctuate as much as 50% that can further reduce your profit.

These downsides should not discourage you from trying day trading options. As long as you know how to trade and you have your own day trading plan, you can take advantage of income opportunity from options day trading.

Chapter 10 - Biggest Mistakes Beginners Make in Day Trading and How to Avoid Them

While you can make substantial gains from day trading in a single day, there is also the risk of losing all of your money in a single trade. This is especially true if you don't know how to use leverage for your advantage or commit specific ill-adviced practices that can end up draining your account.

There are common day trading mistakes that retail traders usually make in the hope of gaining high returns, but end up losing a lot of money. With knowledge, discipline, and alternative methodologies, you can avoid these trading mistakes.

Chasing Trades

A common mistake in day trading is chasing trades. Instead of focusing on stable and steady profits, some newbies are tempted to chase after fast-moving stocks. They borrow money from the brokerage more than they can afford.

This could wipe out your account. A lot of people who have chased trades and experienced substantial losses are the ones who usually give day trading a bad review. Chasing trades if day trading instruments shoot up could lead to losses. Avoid chasing stocks that you have missed. You will only hurt yourself if you try to chase a train that has started running.

Averaging Down

Beginners in day trading usually experience difficulty when it comes to averaging down. Most of these traders commit this mistake unintentionally. The primary concern with averaging down is not only can it cost you money. It can also cost time, which could otherwise be allocated for other trades that can provide you better returns.

Meanwhile, a higher return is required on the remaining fund in order to initiate replenishment. If you lose half of your capital, it will require 100% return in order to gain back your capital to its original level. Losing huge chunks of capital on a single day or on a single trade can easily cripple the growth of your capital in time.

While averaging down may work on special circumstances, this strategy will eventually result in a margin call or substantial loss because a trend can only sustain itself depending on your liquidity.

News Prepositioning

While you may be aware of certain news events that can influence the market, the direction is still uncertain. You might even be confident about the possible news such as political activities that can affect a sector or an industry, but there is no way to accurately project how the market will behave after the news. There are also added indicators behind the news announcements, which could make the movement highly illogical yet possible.

All sorts of orders can also hit the market and stops could be triggered on different sides of the trade. This usually leads to a back and forth action prior to the emergence of a trend. Taking a position prior to a news announcement can substantially damage your chances of winning the trade.

Quick Trading after News Announcement

A news announcement hits the market and the market players start to react. At first, it seems like a no-brainer to ride the bandwagon so you can take advantage of the market sentiment. If you do this without a plan and without a formidable trading strategy, you may end up losing the trade.

News releases usually result in fluctuation in the market mainly because of hair-pin turns and lack of liquidity in the market assessment of the report. There are even trades that are in the money but would end up quickly turning and bringing large losses as significant swings happen.

Liquidity is crucial for these times, which could mean that losses can probably be much more than expected. Successful traders usually wait for some time for the volatility to subside, so there will be a definitive trend after the hype.

Trading More than 2% of Your Capital in a Single Trade

Take note that higher risk doesn't always mean higher returns. Most traders who risk huge amounts of money on a single trade will typically lose in the long term.

A common rule of the thumb is that you should only risk a maximum of 2 per cent of your capital on one trade. If you have accumulated enough experience and skills in forex trading, you can increase your limit to 3 per cent.

You must also establish a daily maximum risk, which for beginners, can be 2 % of the capital or equal to the average daily profit in a month. For instance, if you have $50,000 in your account (without the leverage), you should not lose $1,000 in a single day.

With this strategy, you can make certain that no single day of trading or single trade could affect the account substantially.

Not Understanding Financial Markets

Regardless of the financial instrument that you choose to day trade - stocks, currencies, or ETFs, you need to really understand the market.

For example, there's always a toss-up between a limit and market order. While the limit order allows establishment of maximum or minimum price for trading securities, the market order is an order to buy or sell instruments at prevailing market rates.

While market orders could be filled quickly, the market has no ability to control the order. Likewise, limit orders can allow the parameters to be regulated. Whether market orders or limit orders make sense to you, you have to understand that you can't miss a fast-paced stock to save a few dollars.

High-quality instruments that are naturally liquid allow the use of either limit order or market order.

Unrealistic Projections

Regardless of your dreams or goals in day trading, the market is insensitive to what you expect. Before you even start trading, you should accept the fact that the financial markets could be illogical and volatile.

In order to avoid disappointments from unrealistic expectations, you should have a trading plan and stick to this strategy when you are doing the actual trade. If the results are steady, still stick to your trade plan. In the forex market, even a minor gain could become substantial in the long run.

As your fund grows over time, the position size could be increased so you can bring in higher returns. Also, if you want to test a new strategy, you should only do so with minimal capital. You can allocate more capital into a strategy if you see positive results.

The financial markets are also quite volatile near the open. You can use certain strategies in the opening, which are not ideal near the closing. The market may become more stable as the day progresses, and there may be a pickup in action towards the close that may require another form of strategy. The key in this fluctuating market is to accept what is provided by the market and don't expect too much from the system.

Relying Too Much on Day Trading Insights Found Online

Learning the fundamentals of day trading is crucial. Exploring proven day trading strategies is also essential. However, as you practice in this career, you need to develop your own strategy.

Nowadays, there is a lot of 'day trading tips' that you can read online. But there's no guarantee that all of them can help you become a successful day trader. It is best to cut through the noise, and learn how to find your own voice. Just remember the day trading process that we have discussed in Chapter 7.

Chapter 11 - The Importance of Continuous Education in Day Trading

Success in day trading is largely based on three essential skills:

1. **Critical Analysis** - you have to assess the tension between sellers and buyers and place your money in the winning group
2. **Financial Management** - You need to practice excellent money management or else you will lose your money in no time
3. **Self-Discipline** - You need to be highly disciplined and stick to your trading plan. You have to avoid getting overly depressed or excited in the financial markets and the temptation to make decisions based on your emotions.

Now after reading this book, you must be in a better position to decide whether or not day trading is really the right career for you. Remember, day trading requires a specific mindset, discipline, and a set of skills that you need to improve in the long run.

It is interesting to take note that many successful day traders are also avid players of poker. They say that they enjoy the stimulation and speculation that comes from this game.

But you need to remember that poker is a type of gambling. Day trading is not because it dwells on the realm of science. It requires skill, discipline, and other skills that have nothing to do with luck like gambling.

Selling and buying financial instruments is a serious business. You must be able to make quick decisions, with no hesitation or emotion. Doing otherwise could lead to a substantial loss of money and also depression in some individuals who don't yet have a formidable mind.

Once you have made up your mind and you have finally decided that you like to begin day trading, the next step is to be properly educated. You must never begin your career in day trading using actual cash. Look for brokers that will allow you to play with simulated accounts but are using real market data.

There are some day trading brokers who will offer access to an account that uses delayed market data. This is not the best simulator to use. You have to work with real-time data so you can make actual decisions.

The majority of simulated data software are premium tools, so you have to save money for this software. Avoid free trials as many of them are cheap platforms. Remember, if you pay peanuts, you get monkeys. Invest in your education, and education in day trading requires an upfront cost.

For instance, let's say that you want to get your master's degree. This goal will easily cost you around $40,000 or even more. Similarly, many diploma or post-graduation programs will cost a lot more compared to the education needed for your day trading career.

When you have a simulated account, you need to develop your own strategy. Try the day trading strategies we have explored in this book. Ideally, you should become a master of one strategy. Reversal Strategies, Resistance or Support, and VWAP are the easiest day trading strategies.

You only have to master a few day trading strategies so you become profitable in this career. Keep it simple. Once you have mastered a strong strategy, make certain that you detach your emotions when you do the trade.

Continue practicing with the level of money that you will trade in an actual account. It can be easy to purchase a position worth $50,000 in a simulated platform and watch 50% of it vanish in a matter of minutes. However, do you have the tolerance to lose this amount of money in real life?

If your answer is no, then you will probably become too emotional while you are trading, and make quick decisions that will ultimately result in substantial loss. Therefore, always trade with the position and size that you will also use in an actual account. Otherwise, it makes no sense to trade in a simulator.

You can move to a real account after training with a simulator and then begin with small real cash. Limit the number of your trades if you are still learning or you feel that you are not emotionally prepared. Continue your self-education, and be sure to reflect on your trading strategy.

Do not stop learning about day trading and the market you want to participate in - equities, forex, ETFs, or futures. These financial markets are quite dynamic. Day trading is quite different than it was a decade ago, and it will be different in another decade.

So continue reading and discussing your performance and progress with other day traders. Learn how to think ahead and keep a progressive attitude. Read as much as you can, but still keep a level of skepticism about everything you encounter, including this book, of course.

Ask important questions, and don't accept 'expert insights' at face value. Ideally, you should join a group or community of day traders. It can be extremely difficult to trade alone.

It can also be emotionally overwhelming. It will help you a lot if you are part of a community of day traders so you can ask questions, discuss options, learn new strategies, and receive alerts and hints about the financial markets. But don't forget that you also need to contribute.

It is essential to take note, however, that if you are part of a community of day traders, you must not always follow the pack. Try to become an independent thinker.

In general, people do change once they become part of a crowd. They become more impulsive, unquestioning, and always looking for a 'guru' whose trades they can follow. They respond with the crowd rather than using their own minds.

Day trading groups may receive some trends together but could lose if the trends reverse. Don't forget that profitable day traders know how to think on their own. Learn how to use your judgment when to pursue the trade, and when to get out.

Conclusion

Thanks again for taking the time to read this book!

By now, you should have a good understanding of day trading and the different financial markets that you can trade. Hopefully, the lessons you have learned in this beginner's guide will help you to decide if this is really a good career for you.

As a recap, I would like you to remember the following day trading rules that we have discussed in this book:

Rule No. 1 - *Day trading is not a get-rich-quick scheme.*

Rule No. 2 - *Day trading is hard.*

Rule No. 3 - *Do not hold stocks overnight.*

Rule No. 4 - *Always ask: is this stock moving because the general market is moving, or there's a unique catalyst behind this movement?*

Rule No. 5 - *Risk management is important for successful day trading.*

Rule No. 6 - *Your broker will trade the stocks for you.*

Rule No. 7 - *Day traders only trade apex predators.*

Rule No. 8 - *Filled candlesticks signify selling pressure, hollow candlesticks indicate buying pressure.*

Rule No. 9 - *Technical indicators will only guide you. They should not dictate you.*

Rule No. 10 - *Don't allow your emotions to cloud your judgment.*

You can print these rules and pin it near where you perform your trade. This will allow you to make a quick reference.

Although this book is only a small slice of all you can learn about day trading, I hope that you have gained enough insights into this topic to have the confidence to get started in your trading journey.

I also encourage you to learn more about the intricacies and the complexities of each financial instrument that you are interested to trade. You should also continue exploring the best strategies so you can find this career worthy of your time and talent.

Book #2

Forex Trading for Beginners

Proven Strategies to Succeed and Create Passive Income with Forex

Introduction to Forex Swing Trading, Day Trading, Options, Futures & ETFs

Introduction

In the past, the forex market was only reserved and exclusive to financial firms, big companies, billionaires, central banks, and hedge funds.

But through the emergence of digital banking and the rise of smartphones, anyone can now participate in this volatile, highly liquid, and exciting financial market.

Successful forex traders are now making big bucks every day, thanks to the availability of forex platforms.

But in my years of experience in the forex world, I also encountered people who have lost a lot of money within minutes.

Certainly, the forex market can make you rich, but not overnight. It still takes knowledge, skills, and discipline in following the most suitable strategies before you can become profitable in the forex market.

Written as a beginner's guide for people who are enticed to join the forex market, this book can help you learn the following:

- The fundamental theories and mechanisms behind the forex market
- The essential skills you need to learn to become successful in forex trading
- The top fundamental and technical strategies that seasoned forex traders are using
- The common mistakes that you must avoid so you will not lose money

The forex world can become a fertile ground for day traders. But this can only be possible if you really understand the basic concepts that influence the biggest financial market in the world.

The objective in writing this beginner's guide is to help you develop a good understanding of the forex market before you even start trading.

Let's get started.

Chapter 1. Brief History of the Forex Market

"Risk comes from not knowing what you're doing." - Warren Buffett

With the worldwide scale of the forex market, you need first to understand important historical events, which are related to the currency system we use today, as well as how the forex market has evolved over time before you try trading or investing in this highly volatile market.

The Gold Standard

The Gold Standard model was established in 1875 as a global currency model. This became one of the early milestones of the forex market. Prior to this standard, countries in the 19th century usually used precious metals like gold or silver for international payments.

The main disadvantage of this system is the volatility of gold and silver prices as they are influenced by the supply and demand. For example, depletion of primary gold reserves in a specific country can have lasting effects on the prices of gold.

In the gold standard, governments or companies have to agree to convert their currencies into specific equivalent of gold and vice versa. Hence, the currency should be backed by actual gold in reserve. And so, the governments during the 19th century had to secure sufficient gold reserves to catch up with the demand for exchanging foreign currencies.

Leading world economies of that time such as Great Britain and China had already established the value of currency. Eventually, the distinction in the price of gold between two currencies was regarded as the rate of exchange between the two currencies. This became the early standard for trading currencies.

At the onset of World War I, the gold standard eventually became obsolete. Because of imminent danger from the Axis Power, many European countries had to finance massive military projects. Gold reserves were not enough as they needed to complete the project within a limited timeframe.

After the war, some countries re-established the gold standard, but most economies discarded the system when war again erupted in the 1940s. However, gold continued to be valued as the preferred channel for international payments.

The USD Standard

Before the end of World War II, the Allied Forces deemed it crucial to establish a currency system to solve the downsides of the gold standard. So in 1944, a meeting was convened at

Bretton Woods, NH to deliberate on a new currency management system. The resulting system was later on called the Bretton Woods System.

The Allied Forces agree to adhere to the following:

- Use a fixed rate system for trading currencies
- Use the United States Dollar as the primary reserve currency to replace gold
- Form three worldwide agencies to manage economic activities: the International Monetary Fund (IMF), the World Bank, and the General Agreement on Tariff and Trade (GATT).

Bretton Woods became the birthplace of the US Dollar as a global reserve currency. Furthermore, USD was also established to be the only currency to have an actual equivalent of gold reserves.

As such, the US had to execute a series of balancing the deficit payments to make sure that the currency is the most stable in the world. However, in the 1970s, the US gold reserves were not sufficient to sustain the economic activities of the world.

In 1971, US Pres. Richard Nixon ended the Bretton Woods System by officially declaring the termination of the gold reserve system for the USD. In spite of the fact that the Bretton Woods system was a short-lived system, it still made an important contribution for the present-day world economy.

When the Bretton Woods disintegrated, world governments gradually embraced the floating rates for foreign exchange. But in 1976, the Jamaica Agreement led to the permanent elimination of the gold reserve standard. However, this didn't mean that government totally adopted the floating rate system. Many governments were still using floating rates, pegged rates, or dollar rates.

Floating Rates Mechanism

This exchange mechanism is established if the exchange rate of a currency is permitted to freely change in value according to the market forces of demand and supply. However, the central bank or the state could still interfere to ensure the stability of the currency if the exchange rates experience high fluctuation.

For instance, if the currency of a country is falling too much, the government may choose to increase short-term interest rates. This will in turn cause the currency to slightly appreciate. But take note that this is a macro perspective as central banks usually employ several tools for currency management.

Pegging refers to the practice of a country establishing a fixed exchange rate for another currency so that it becomes more stable compared to regular floating rates.

In particular, pegging will allow the currency of a country to have a fixed rate for the exchange with one or a specified group of foreign currencies. In addition, the currency may only fluctuate if there's a significant change in the pegged currencies.

In 1997 and 2005, the Chinese government pegged its currency to the US dollar at USD 1 to CNY 8.28. The disadvantage of pegging is that the value of the currency is now on the discretion of the economy of the country. For instance, when USD significantly increases its value against other denominations, the value of the Chinese yuan will also increase.

Dollarization

Dollarization happens if a country decides not to use its own currency and adopts the United States Dollars as its currency. Even though dollarization normally bestows a country with higher stability, the disadvantage is that the central bank of the country cannot make any form of monetary policy or print its own money.

Countries that adopted the US dollar include Zimbabwe, British Virgin Islands, Palau, Marshall Islands, El Salvador, East Timor, and Ecuador.

Chapter 2 - Forex Trading As A Business

"The expectation that you bring with you in trading is often the greatest obstacle you will encounter." – Yvan Byeajee

The forex market has boomed and it is now considered as one of the hottest financial markets today. It has been around for decades now, but the recent rise of trading technologies has made it accessible to private traders on a scale that is unprecedented.

At its core, forex trading is all about speculating the value of one currency against another. The key words in the preceding sentence are "currency" and "speculating". It is important to look at forex trading in these two dimensions.

First, forex trading is speculative similar to trading stocks or other financial instruments with the hope that it will increase its value and you as a trader will make a profit.

Second, the financial securities that you are speculating with are the currencies of different countries.

If we view these two dimensions separately, forex trading is both about the market speculation dynamics, as well as the factors that affect the value of currencies. If we combine these together, we get the biggest, most exciting financial market in the world.

In this book, we will see forex trading using these two perspectives, viewing them separately and integrating them to provide you the insights you need in order to trade successfully in the forex market.

Speculating as a Business

In general, speculating is all about taking risks in the hope of making money. However, it is neither investing nor gambling.

Investing is about reducing risk and maximizing returns, typically over an extended period of time.

Gambling is about playing with money even if you are not certain that you will win.

Speculating (also known as active trading) is about taking calculated risks to try making profits, normally over a very short time horizon.

In order to be a successful trader in any market (not just forex market) you need the following:

- Knowledge
- Decisiveness

- Perseverance
- Financial Resources
- Technological Resources
- Emotional Discipline
- Financial Discipline
- Dedication (Energy and Time)

But even if you possess all the traits listed above, there's no substitute for crafting a comprehensive trading plan. It can be foolish to open a business without first developing a plan. Therefore, you must not expect a resounding success in forex trading if you can't develop a realistic trading plan and follow it.

Consider forex trading as a business, and approach it as you would a real enterprise. Take it seriously. Moreover, you should not try to take the outcome of your trading too personally. Financial markets are susceptible to irrational movements, and the market doesn't care or know who you are and what you do. It will move even without you.

Currencies as Financial Instruments

You are probably aware that the forex market is the largest financial market in the world in terms of daily trading volumes. The forex market is also unique in many respects. The liquidity is ever-present because of the huge volume in this market.

The forex market also operates 24 hours a day, six days a week, which can provide day traders with access to any market at any time. Furthermore, there are severe restrictions - no requirements in selling a currency pair short, no limits on the sizes of positions, and no daily trading limits.

When you are selling a pair in a short position, you are expecting for its price to fall. Because of the way currency pairs are quoted and because of the fluctuations in the forex market, short positions are quite as common as long positions in the market.

The majority of the action takes place in primary currency pairs that pit USD against Eurozone (countries in Europe that have adopted the euro as their currency), Switzerland, Great Britain, and Japan.

Plus, there's also a lot of trading opportunities in the minor currency pairs that see the USD traded against Australian Dollars (AUD), Canadian Dollars (CAD), and New Zealand Dollars (NZD). Then there's also the cross-currency trading that directly pits two non-USD currencies like Japanese Yen against Swiss Francs.

Depending on which forex brokerage you are dealing with, there are around 15 to 20 different major currency pairs. Many individual traders are now trading currencies online (on a PC, tablet, or even mobile phone) but still through a brokerage firm.

Online forex trading is usually performed on a marginal basis that permits individual traders to trade huge amounts by leveraging the amount of margin on deposit. Trading with leverage is one of the key features of the forex market.

Also known as margin trading ratios, the leverage can be quite high, sometimes as high as 200:1 or even higher. In this leverage, a margin deposit of $1000 will allow you to control a position size of $200,000.

Trading with leverage is the backdrop against which all the trading will occur. It has its advantages, but it has its own requirements and rules as well. But you must remember that trading with leverage is like dealing with a two-edged sword. It can amplify your losses and gains that makes risk management the key to any lucrative trading strategy.

Before you begin trading in the forex market, you need to really understand your risk capital or the money you are willing to lose. Managing risk is the key to any successful trading plan.

Without a risk management-centric strategy, margin trading could be short-lived. With a proper risk plan in place, you stand a better chance of surviving losses in your trade and make money in the process.

The forex market is not affected by economic downturns as they do in other financial markets such as equities. Selling a currency pair is normal in this market, which is quite different in other financial markets. For instance, in the stock market, day traders don't usually sell stocks because of the financial risks involved.

Due to the fact that selling is quite common in currency market, it is virtually immune to financial downturns. Traders are always trading currency pairs, so something is always going up even in times of economic crisis.

Currency rates are primarily affected by information. Every financial market is driven by information, but the forex market has its own unique roster of information dynamics.

At any given moment, numerous cross-currencies are at play in the forex market. After all, the forex market is setting the value of one currency in relation to another currency.

Therefore, you are at least looking at information that is affecting two major economies of the world. Factor in other national economies, and you have a considerable information flowing through the market.

Market Fundamentals Driving the Forex Market

Fundamentals refer to the general grouping of information that reflects the political and macroeconomic conditions of the countries whose currencies are being traded.

More often than not, if you hear someone talking about currency fundamentals, he or she or referring to the economic fundamentals.

The basis of economic fundamentals are the following:

- Interest rate levels
- International trade flows
- Economic data reports
- Monetary policy
- International investment flows

Confidence or faith that the market is placing in the currency is an essential element of any currency's value. If political events like a political scandal, war, or a divisive election are perceived to undermine confidence in the leadership of a nation, the currency value could be affected negatively.

Gathering and making sense of this information will be part of your routine as a forex day trader.

Technical Drivers in the Forex Market

If you hear the word technicals in any financial markets, it usually means technical analysis, which is a method of analyzing a market that involves trend-line analysis, chart analysis, and mathematical studies of price behavior like moving averages or momentum trading.

Technical analysis is also crucial in forex trading so don't ignore the technicals. If you are also engaged in other financial markets, there's a big chance that you already worked with technical analysis. If you want to actively trade in the forex market, then you need to familiarize yourself with the basics.

Don't be intimidated by the name. Technical analysis is just like a tool that you can use to complete a job similar to a cellphone. You don't have to understand the whole mechanism of a cellphone before you learn how to use it. However, you need to know how to use it properly so you can use it to call someone, send a text message, or use mobile applications.

Technical analysis is crucial in currency trading because of the amount of fundamental data hitting the market at any point in time. Forex market traders regularly apply different forms of technical analysis in order to define and refine their trading strategies with a lot of traders trading currency pairs based on technical indicators.

Take note that forex trading is just one type of market speculation, and speculative trading involves inherent dynamics in the market.

The forex market is composed of hundreds of thousands of various traders with different perspectives of the market and each expressing his view by either selling or buying various currencies at different times and price points.

So on top of understanding the specific fundamentals of a currency and getting to know technical indicators, you also need to really appreciate market dynamics (also known as market psychology or sentiment). This is where trading with a plan comes in.

The Importance of a Trading Plan

It is important first to settle your trading style before you start developing your forex trading plan. Various trading styles basically call for variations on trading plans, even though there are a lot of overarching rules in trading that are applicable to all styles.

Trading style all boils down to how you approach currency trading in terms of the following:

Time Frame

You need to determine how long you would hold your position. Some forex traders look at short-term trade opportunities. This is known as day trading. Meanwhile, some traders are trying to capture more significant movements in forex prices over days, weeks or even months.

Currency Pair

Are you looking to trade in different currency pairs or are you more interested to focus your energy into few pairs?

Risk Appetite

How much money are you willing to risk and what is your level of expectations for your trading profits?

Rationale

Are you technically or fundamentally inclined? Are you looking to develop a systematic trading model? What strategies are you looking to follow? Are you comfortable in following forex trends? Or are you more inclined to become a breakout forex trader?

Don't worry if you still don't have answers to these questions. Hopefully as you read this book, you can choose the forex trading approach you are interested to pursue.

You can try different strategies and styles by using demo accounts. But don't forget that your goal is to zero in your trading style that you feel comfortable with and that you can pursue regularly.

In addition, you also need to consider other factors such as your individual circumstances such as personal discipline, temperament, finances, free time, family, and work obligations. These are essential variables and you are the only one who knows how they impact your forex trading.

Regardless of the trading style you choose to pursue, achieving success can be challenging if you don't set your trade plan then follow it. Remember, trade plans will help you avoid losing a lot of money from bad trades and can also help you win big in the market.

Moreover, your trading plan serves as your guide, which helps you explore the trades after the emotions and adrenaline begin pumping regardless of what the market presents to you. But this doesn't mean that forex trading is any easier compared to other financial markets.

However, it is proven that trading with a plan will significantly improve the probability of your success in the forex market over time. Also, you need to understand that trading without a plan is a guaranteed way to lose money in the forex market.

Sure, you may make money from a few trades, but a day of reckoning will eventually come to any trader who is only guided by his guts. This is always the trend in any financial markets.

The starting line of any trading plan is to determine an opportunity for trading. Do not wait for any writing on the wall that will tell you what and when to trade. You must devote your effort and energy in looking for lucrative opportunities for trading. In this book, you will learn some expert insights on forex market behavior in different settings.

Trading Plan Execution

Forex trading begins once you step into the market and you open a position. The way you approach this initial step is as important as the trade opportunity itself. Remember, if you have never enter the position, you will not be able to exploit any trade opportunity.

And possibly, nothing is more disappointing as a trader than identifying a trade opportunity, having it to go the way you are expecting, but you can't reap the results because you have never opened a position in the first place.

The money and energy you invest in studying, tracking, and assessing the forex market comes to a solid outcome only if you open a trade. This process is a lot easier by developing your own trading system with setups and trigger points that can help you in entering the trade.

Placing the trade is just the start. The mere fact of owning a trading plan doesn't mean that the market will keep on rolling. You must actively engage in managing your position in order to maximize it if the position is a winner then reduce the damage if the market is going against your expectations.

In order to retain most of your earnings, you should have an active trade management plan in place. With the right strategy and discipline, it can be easy to earn money in currency trading. The real challenge comes in maintaining your profits.

It is crucial that you learn how to keep yourself on the ground. The forex market will always move, usually a lot quicker than usual. Moreover, new information will be coming into the market. Later in this book, we will look at various ways that you can keep track of your active trades and also how and when you must adjust your trade strategy depending on time and events.

Trade exits serve as the finale of the whole process, where you can either make money or lose money unless of course you exit at the entry price. This is just the way the market works.

Even though your trade is still active, you should take note that you are still in control and you may choose to exit the trade at any time. We'll take a look at important tactical considerations that you need to bear in mind when it is time to close the trade.

Your trade is still not complete even after you have exited the position. If you really want to treat forex trading as a serious business, you must reassess your immediate past trades so you can obtain a more general perspective about recent trends and method of execution.

One way to focus on your trades is to document your trading history. Carefully study your previous trading style so you can gain insights on strategies that are effective.

Chapter 3 – The Forex Market

"The goal of a successful trader is to make the best trades. Money is secondary." - Alexander Elder

The foreign exchange market (commonly known simply as the forex market, or just FX market) is the biggest and most liquid of all financial markets around the world.

This financial market is the crossroads for global capital, the intersection via which worldwide investment and commercial flows are dynamic.

Global trade flows such as if a South Korean company buys French-made furniture, were the original basis for the development of these markets. But today, global financial flows dominate trade as the main non-speculative source for market volume.

Whether it's a Canadian pension fund investing in Australian Treasury bonds or a Swiss insurer allocating assets to the stock markets in Hong Kong, or a Japanese conglomerate buying a Brazilian manufacturing plant, each international transaction has to pass through the forex market at some stage. As such, the forex market is considered as the ultimate market for traders.

The forex market is open 24 hours a day and six days a week. This enables traders to quickly act on events and news as they happen. This is the trading platform where $500 million trades can easily be completed in a few seconds and may not even affect the whole market. This is one unique trait in the forex market. Try selling or buying units in other markets and it will be chaotic.

Organizations like IG Group, CMC Markets, Oanda, Saxo Bank, and Forex.com have made the FX market accessible to retail traders. This allows you to trade the same forex units with hedge funds and big financial conglomerates.

Trillion Dollar Market Volume

The average daily forex trading volumes in the forex market exceeds $5 trillion daily. Now, that's a lot of money. To provide you some idea on this volume, this is around 10 times the everyday trading volume of the stock markets around the world combined.

And remember, that volume is daily!

But take note that this high daily trading volume that you might have seen in newspapers or in other books on forex trading, actually overstates the size of what the foreign exchange market is really about - spot forex trading.

Spot Forex Trading

"Spot" pertains to the rate where you can trade currencies at the moment. Bear in mind that in the equities market, the rates that you can trade is basically a spot rate. This term is basically used to identify the difference between a spot or cash trading from futures trading, in which the delivery date of the units are settled on a future date.

The spot forex market is settled in two trading days. Unless explicitly written in a contract, the spot rate is more likely what you trade with your forex broker.

Forex Market Speculation

Even though financial and commercial transactions in the forex markets represent significant nominal sums, they still fade in comparison to the amounts based on speculation.

At this point, the huge majority of forex trading volume is based on speculation - traders buy and sell for short-term gains based on hourly and daily fluctuations.

Forex trading experts estimate that upwards of 90% of daily trading volume is derived from speculation, which means commercial or investment-based forex trades account for less than 10% of daily global volume.

The breadth and depth of the speculative market means that the liquidity of the general forex market is unparalleled among worldwide financial markets.

The majority of spot forex trading, around 75% by volume, happens with primary currencies that represent the largest economies of the world. Trading primary currencies is significantly free from government regulation and happens outside the authority of any national or international organization.

Moreover, the movement in the forex market regularly functions on a regional bloc basis where the majority of trading happens between the EUR bloc, JPY bloc, and USD bloc signifying the biggest global economic blocs of the world.

Trading in currencies used by developing nations like the Philippines or Argentina, is usually referred to as exotic forex trading or emerging market. While trading in emerging markets has significantly grown in recent years, in terms of volume, it still remains the same way behind major currencies.

Because of some internal catalysts (like local restrictions on forex transactions) and some external catalysts (like geopolitical crises and the crash of financial markets making the emerging market challenging to trade) the emerging market is significantly less liquid that can turn off small investors.

Always Be Mindful of Liquidity

Liquidity pertains to the market interest and trading volume available at any point in time for a particular financial instrument. The higher the liquidity or the deeper the market, the faster and easier it is to buy or sell an instrument.

As a forex trader, you need to always be mindful of liquidity because this will allow you to figure out how fast the currency prices will move between your trades. Remember, the forex market has high liquidity so you will usually experience huge trading volumes but with minor price changes.

The market is called a thin market or illiquid if its price moves a lot faster on relatively lower trading volumes. In comparison, a stock market has medium-level of liquidity because it only trades during specific hours.

Take note that in this guide, we will always refer to liquidity because this is one of the most important factors that can affect price action and movement. Even though the forex market has high liquidity, the volume may vary throughout the trading day and across different currencies.

For forex day traders, variations in liquidity yearns more on strategy rather than tactics.

If a hedge fund company requires millions of a particular company, its analysts will first look on the tactical side of liquidity such as how much the trade will cause price fluctuations depending on the performance of the trade and its time.

But for day traders who generally trade in smaller units, the trade size is not a major concern. The strategic liquidity level is an important factor in timing of when and how prices are most likely to behave.

Throughout this book, we will take a closer look on fluctuations on liquidty and market interest with a special lens relevant to trading in particular forex pairs.

Trading Day Around the World

The foreign exchange market is active 24 hours daily from the beginning of business hours on Monday morning in Asia straight through end of business hours in New York. At any point in time, depending on the time zone, leading financial centers such as London, Tokyo, or Sydney, are active and open.

Aside from leading financial centers around the world, numerous financial organizations also operate 24 hours a day. This provides an ever-present source of market interest. Forex trading centers are even active during holidays when other markets such as futures or stocks are closed.

While it's a holiday in Sydney, for example, Hong Kong, or Singapore may still be active. It might be National Founding Day in Japan, but if it's a business day, Toronto, London, and New York and other financial centers are still trading currencies. New Year's Day is probably the only holiday common around the world, and even that depends on the day it falls on.

Opening of Trades

There's no official starting time for forex trading, but the market is active when Wellington, New Zealand starts on Monday morning. This is around Sunday afternoon in North America, Monday morning in Asia, or Sunday night in Europe. (Note: This still depends if Daylight Savings Time or DST is active in your time zone.)

Take for example the Sunday open, which signifies the beginning where forex markets trade again after trade closes in North America on Friday. This is 5 in the afternoon Eastern Time. This is the first opportunity for the forex market to react to news and events that could have happened over the weekend.

Prices may have closed Tokyo trading at one level, but depending on current events, they may begin trading at various levels at the opening on Sunday. Weekend gap risk or Sunday open gap risk refers to the risk that the forex rates open at different levels on Sunday versus Friday close.

The gap refers to the price level movements where prices are unable to trade in between. As a retail trader, you should understand the Sunday gap risk and know what events are expected to happen over the weekend.

There's no guaranteed set of political events and there's no way to rule out what could transpire such as a natural disaster, a geopolitical conflict or a terror attack. You just need to be conscious about the existence of risks and consider it into your forex trading strategy.

Of the usual pre-determined events over the weekend, the most typical are the national referenda or elections or the quarterly G20 meetings. Make certain that you are aware of any major events that are scheduled. For example, during the height of the debt crisis in Europe, numerous last-minute bailout decisions were decided over the weekend. These developments have major implications for the financial markets when they opened.

On a typical Sunday opens, prices basically pick up where they left off on Friday afternoon. The price spreads in the opening of the interbank market will be much wider than the usual because only New Zealand and 24-hour trading desks are active in this period.

The opening price spreads of 10-30 points in the primary currency pairs are not uncommon during the early trading hours. Once banks in Australia and Asia centers enter the forex market over the next few hours, market liquidity starts to improve and the price spreads start to narrow to more regular levels.

Because of the wider price spreads during the early hours of Sunday open, many online trading platforms don't start trading until 5 pm Eastern Time on Sundays. During this period, the liquidity enables the platforms to offer their regular price quotes.

With these things in mind, it is crucial that you are aware of the trading policies of your brokers in connection with the Sunday open, particularly in terms of trading executions.

Asia-Pacific Trading Session

According to the survey results released by BIS in 2014, the trading volumes of the forex markets in Asia Pacific accounts for around 21 per cent of the average global volume. The largest financial trading centers in this region are Wellington (New Zealand), Tokyo (Japan), Hong Kong, Sydney (Australia), and Singapore.

News announcements from Japan, Australia and New Zealand shall hit the forex world in the first session.

Australia and New Zealand reports are regularly issued in the early morning local time, which is roughly mid-morning in the US Eastern Time.

News announcements from Japan are usually issued before the 9 am session in Tokyo, which is roughly around 7 pm in the US Eastern Time.

In some trading days, important Japanese reports are issued in the afternoon, which is roughly around 4 am US Eastern time. The whole trading movement for the NZD, AUD, and JPY can be set for the whole trading session, depending on the the substance of the news reports and what they mean for the market.

Moreover, news reports from China mainly about Asian economy, interest rate changes, comments from political leaders, and policy changes can also affect the market.

In some days, American sources of information such as the Federal Reserve can also affect the other regions such as when an official issue a controversial comment on the US economy or if the interest rates in the US suddenly changes.

Because of the sheer size of the Japanese market as well as the significance of the Japanese current events, majority of the action in this trading region revolves around currency pairs that involve JPY such as EUR/JPY, AUD/JPY and of course USD/JPY.

Japanese companies and financial firms are also active in their own time zone so you should watch out from these sources if you have interest in JPY currency pairs.

For forex day traders, the general liquidity in major forex pairs is enough to predict the price movements. In less liquid, non-regional currencies like GBP/USD or USD/CAD, the price movements may be erratic or even non-existent depending on the market environment.

With few reports from Canada issued for the next half-day session, there could be limited interest or reason for this pair to move. But if an important market player has the need to start a transaction in this pair, the price movement can be bigger than normal.

European Trading Session

European trading centers begin to open around the middle of the Asian session. At this time, the market is in full swing. These financial organizations, especially London (United Kingdom) contributes more than half of the global total trading volume. UK alone comprises about 30% of the global average volume (BIS survey, 2014).

The European trading session overlaps with half of the trading day in Asia and also 50% of the North American trading session. Thus, the market interest as well as the liquidity is at its highest peak in this specific time window.

News announcements from Europe (as well as countries like UK, Germany, France, and Switzerland) are typically issued in the early morning hours of Eurozone trading.

Hence, some of the most important price movements and trading fluctuations occur in currencies from this region such as GBP, CHF and EUR. This includes cross-currency pairs in Europe such as EUR/CHF and EUR/GBP.

The Asian trading session begins to dwindle down roughly around mid-day in Europe and North American financial centers open several hours later around 7 am US Eastern Time.

North American Trading Session

Due to the overlap of the trading sessions in North America and Europe, you should always be mindful of the trading volumes in these specific time zones. Some of the biggest and most important price movements happen during the crossover between the trading sessions of these two regions.

The trading volume in North America accounts for around the same percentage of Asia Pacific that is roughly 25% of the daily trading volume.

The trading session in North America starts when important economic information in the US are released. Remember, key decisions in the forex market mainly involve the USD.

Most data reports coming from this region are released at 8:30 US Eastern Time with other financial centers issued later in the day not later than 10 am. Some financial reports in the US are released at various times at mid-day or not later than 2 pm. This activated the New York forex market in the afternoon. European centers begin to wind down the daily trading sessions around noontime.

There is also volatility when the European trading closes down. A significant trend that occurred before early afternoon in Europe or in New York can still be reversed if sufficient volume of trades happen to cover shorts or take profit.

An overwhelming trend can also further extend as more traders are trying to jump on board prior to the closing of the trading session. Take note that there's no fixed formula that the European trading follows in the closing session. But it is almost predictable that considerably volatility in the market occurs around this time.

On regular trading sessions, liquidity dwindles down in the afternoon session in New York. This can be a bit of a challenge for day traders. On more "peaceful" days, the usually lower liquidity often results to sustained price action.

On more active days when prices usually move around, the lower liquidity could add more price movements because few traders are pursuing better liquidity and better currency prices.

Like the European close there's no fixed method in which the North American session will play out the movements. Therefore, you must be aware that lower liquidity conditions have a high tendency to prevail and adapt accordingly.

Higher volatility and a chance for lower liquidity is more apparent in the low-liquid major pairs especially GBP/USD and USD/CHF.

Trading volume and interest in the North American region basically continue to dwindle down as the trading day moves toward later afternoon session in New York. This is also the time, which sudden changes usually occur. But the new trading session begins as Wellington and Sydney opens in the afternoon in North America.

London is considered as the center of the forex market world. But there's a lot of opportunities if you take advantage of the salient moments in the North American and Asian sessions.

As a forex trader, you must remember that if you are trading in Asia, and there's no significant news announcement, the trend caused by the North American session prior to today's trading usually prevails.

Important Daily Times and Events

Aside from the market interest and liquidity movement during worldwide forex trading day, you also need to be aware of key daily events that tend to happen around the same time every day.

Options Expiry

Currency options are usually set to expire either at the New York expiry (10 a.m. Eastern Time) or the Tokyo expiry (3 p.m. Tokyo time). The option expiry in New York is the more important expiry option since it has the tendency to capture both North American and European option market interest. Once an option expires, the underlying option stops to exist.

Remember, any spot market hedging done based on the option being suddenly alive should be carefully monitored. This triggers important price changes in the hours leading up to and just after the expiry time of the option.

The variety and the amount of currency option interest is just too big to suggest any one method to spot the prices. However, if you are getting some volatility around 10 am Eastern Time, this could be caused by the expiry of some currency options.

Establishing the Rate at Currency Fixtures

Currency fixing refers to a set time every day when the prices of currencies for business transactions are fixed or set.

There are scheduled currency fixtures in different financial centers around the world. However, the two most important are the London Time (4 p.m.) and the Tokyo Time (8:55 a.m.).

From a trading perspective, these fixtures may see a surge in a specific currency pair (usually 15 to 30 minutes) to the fixing time that suddenly ends precisely.

A sharp movement in a particular currency pair on fixing-related buying, for instance, may suddenly come to an end at the fixing time and see the price immediately drop back to where it was before.

Traditionally, the London Forex Fix is benchmarked to WM/ Reuters fixing rates.

Squaring Up on the Forex Futures Markets

One of the biggest futures markets in the world, the Chicago Mercantile Exchange (CME), offers forex futures through the International Monetary Market (IMM) subsidiary exchange. A forex futures contract specifies at which a specific currency can be purchased or sold in the future.

The trading of currency futures closes every day on the IMM at 2 p.m. central time (CT) or around 3 pm in the East Coast. Numerous traders in the futures market usually square up or close any open positions at the end of every trading session for margin requirements or to limit their exposure overnight. The last hour leading to the closing of the IMM usually creates a surge that spills over into the spot market.

Market liquidity is usually at the lowest in the afternoon in New York. This results in sharp movements in the futures market that can trigger volatility in the spot market around this period.

There's no easy way to tell if or how the IMM close will cause a movement in the spot market in New York, so you have to be aware of this.

The USD Index

The USD index is a futures contract that is listed in the New York Board of Trade (NYBOT) and Financial Instruments Exchange (FINEX) futures exchanges that is based in Dublin.

The dollar index refers to the average USD value against a basket of six other primary currencies. However, this is heavily weighted towards currencies in Europe.

Here are the specific weights of other currencies in the USD index:

- Swiss Franc (3.6%)
- Swedish Krona (4.2%)
- Canadian Dollar (9.1%)
- British Pound (11.9%)
- Japanese Yen (13.6%)
- Euro (57.6%)

Take note that the European currency share of the basket (Switzerland, Sweden, United Kingdom, and Eurozone) accounts for 77.3%.

USD is the most powerful currency today with the majority of forex trading normally involving the dollar on one side of the pair. Global commodities are valued in USD and numerous global currency reserves maintained by central banks are in USD.

It is not surprising that the USD is considered as the most liquid currency in the world.

As a day trader, you need to know if the USD is strong or weak. The USD index allows you to do this because it provides you a wider perspective of how the dollar is performing in the G10 forex space. As a forex trader, you should follow the USD index especially its technical developments.

Forex and Other Financial Instruments

While forex market is the largest financial market in the world in terms of daily trading volume, it is not the only financial instrument that you can trade. Aside from currencies, you can also trade gold, oil, and of course company equities or stocks.

You have probably heard about the supposed interconnectivity of forex to these financial instruments. Unfortunately, much of the information out there are not true at all and you should learn how to determine which one is true and which one is just pure hype.

Seasoned forex traders usually look for a link between two different financial instruments depending on individual circumstances. You must be careful in getting caught up in these "connections".

Even if there's an apparent connection between two instruments (moving in harmony or inversely against each other) it usually happens over the long term - months or even years. This connection usually provides minimal information on how the markets will connect in the short term, which is an important factor to consider if you are a forex day trader.

And even if two instruments are connected with each other in the short-term, there's no certainty if the correlation will persist in the long-term.

For example, depending on where you look at the performance of gold and USD (inverse connection) you may still find a correlation co-efficient (not less than -0.2 and not more than -0.8). Remember, if you see a zero correlation in the charts, it means that the two instruments are not correlated at all.

Different financial instruments are traded in their own markets, so they behave in their own internal dynamics based on the market interest, trader positions, and significance of news.

There's a possibility that the financial markets might overlap and will demonstrate various degrees of correlation. And as a trader, it will help you if you are also aware of what is happening in other financial markets.

But you should look at each market in its own right and to have your own strategy and trading plan for each instrument.

For now, we can briefly discuss other important financial instruments and see their correlation with currencies.

Stocks

Stocks refer to the units of shares in the equities market. The movement in the stock market follow individual prospects for each company, sector or industry that you hold shares.

On the other hand, currencies are much larger securities that usually fluctuate in response to various economic and political developments.

Hence, there's minimal logic that the stock market is correlated to the forex market. Long-term correlation studies bear this out with the co-efficient of 0 between the main USD pairs and the stock markets.

There are some instances that the currencies and stocks cross each other, even though this is rare and for short-term only.

For example, when the equity market volatility peaks on (such as when S&P 500 loses higher than 2 per cent in a single trading day) the USD can also experience more tension than the usual. However, there's no way to predict this through correlation studies.

NASDAQ may dwindle down during an unexpected rise in interest rates, while the USD may even increase on the sudden surge.

Meanwhile, the Japanese stock market can be affected by JPY value mainly because of the significance of the export sector in the Japanese economy.

A sudden rise in the value of JPY may cause a negative response in the equities market because this would make exports more expensive and thus could affect the value of import sales.

Fixed Income Markets

Fixed income markets mainly trade bonds, wherein you are guaranteed an income within a specific time. The bond market has a more intuitive correlation to currencies compared to equities because the bonds and currencies are both significantly affected by interest rate movements.

However, the short-term market dynamics of supply and demand usually affects the efforts to establish a possible correlation between the two instruments for short-term.

In some instances, the forex market could respond first based on the changes in interest rate movements. There are times that the bond market could reflect the changes in the expectations on the interest rate with the currencies trying to follow.

If you want to become a forex day trader, you should look at the current yields of government bonds on major currencies so you can monitor the possible changes in interest rates.

Gold

In Chapter 1, we have learned that gold was used by governments to back up the value of their currencies. While this is no longer the case today, gold is still used by investors and traders as a hedge against inflation and it is also a much more valuable alternative to the USD.

For long term, the correlation between gold and USD is typically inverse. If the dollar is weaker, then gold is stronger. If the dollar is stronger, then gold is weaker.

But for short term, the two markets have their own interest level and liquidity that makes the correlation between them too tedious.

Basically, the gold market is a lot smaller compared to the currencies. Thus, if you are also interested in trading gold, you should also monitor the movement of USD.

Robust movements in the price of gold can attract the attention of forex traders and typically affect the dollar inversely.

Oil

Some financial experts say that there's a correlation between oil and currencies especially JPY and USD. This is basically based on the premise that because some countries are oil-producing countries, their currencies are influenced by the oil price.

The assumption is, if a country is importing oil, then its currency is affected by the oil price fluctuations.

However, correlation studies show no clear link to back this up, especially in the short-term. If there's a correlation in the long-term, this is usually against the USD as much as more than any currency regardless if the country is importing or exporting oil.

Take note that oil is seen as an input to calculate inflation and also considered as a factor that can limit the general growth of a country's economy.

Higher oil price may lead to higher inflation rate and the other way around. Because of the fact that the US is significantly reliant on energy, and also heavily driven by capitalism, it favors lower oil prices.

If you also want to speculate in the oil market while trading currencies, you need to consider the fluctuation in the oil prices when you look at growth projections and inflation of a certain country.

But remember, there are other factors that affect the overall financial markets, not only oil price.

Chapter 4 – How Forex Trading Works

"You don't need to be a rocket scientist. Investing is not a game where the guy with the 160 IQ beats the guy with 130 IQ." - Warren Buffett

Just like any other financial market, the forex market also has its own trading norms and jargon.

If you are new to forex trading, you may need some time to learn the terminology and mechanics of the market. But basically, you will see that most forex norms are quite straightforward and easy to understand.

One of the largest mental obstacles facing newbies to forex trading is really understanding the concept that every trade in the forex is composed of buying and selling.

For example in the equities market, if you purchase 200 shares of Amazon, it is clear that you now own 200 shares and you hope that the share price will increase. If you like to exit this position, all you have to do is to sell all your shares or a percentage of it.

But in the case of forex trading, we need to understand the concept of exchange. If you are looking for USD to go up, you need another currency for the benchmark.

If USD is stronger against another currency, it also means that the other currency will go down against USD. Viewing this in the language of equities market, you are actually selling money. Remember, if you are selling shares, you are buying money.

Currency Pairs

To put it simply, the currency market refers to trading two different currencies. Currency pairs have abbreviations or nicknames that refer to the pair but does not necessarily involve the individual currencies.

The USD is the main currency against which other currencies are traded in the forex market. According to the Bank of International Settlements (BIS), USD is involved in 87% of all reported transactions in the forex market. Its position as the dominant currency has remained virtually unopposed for more than five decades.

The central role of USD in the forex market is rooted from several fundamental factors:

- USA is the largest economy in the world
- USA has the biggest and most liquid financial markets in the world
- USA is a global military superpower with stable political climate

As a result, USD is now the main international reserve currency and it is also used for numerous international transactions. For instance, oil is priced in USD. So even if you are a

Countries	ISO Currency Pair	Conventional Name	Market Nickname
United States and Japan	USD/JPY	Dollar-Yen	None
Eurozone and United States	EUR/USD	Euro-Dollar	None
New Zealand and United States	NZD/USD	New Zealand-Dollar	Kiwi
Australia and United States	AUD/USD	Australian-Dollar	Oz or Aussie
United States and Canada	USD/CAD	Dollar-Canada	Loonie
United States and Switzerland	USD/CHF	Dollar-Swiss	Swissy
United Kingdom and United States	GBP/USD	Pound-Dollar	Cable or Sterling

Chinese oil importer buying crude from Saudi Arabia, you need USD to settle the transaction.

Major Currency Pairs

USD is involved in all major currency pairs with designations expressed using the codes established by the International Standardization Organization (ISO) for every currency.

The table below shows the commonly used currency pairs with their traditional names and market nicknames.

Note: Eurozone is composed of all member countries of the European Union that have adopted the Euro as their currency. This includes Austria, Spain, Belgium, Slovenia, Cyprus, Portugal,

Estonia, the Netherlands, Finland, Malta, France, Luxembourg, France, Italy, Germany, Ireland, and Greece.

Some newbies are confused over currency names and nicknames when they read market commentaries or following the market in general. To avoid confusion, you need to understand if the forex analyst or writer is referring to the currency pair or the individual currency.

For example, if an analyst is discussing a study suggesting that Australian Dollars is expected to be weaker the next few months, the discussion refers to the currency itself (AUD in this case) expecting that USD/AUD will go upwards (USD is strong and AUD is weak).

But when the analysis suggests that Aussie is expected to be weaker in the immediate future, it now refers to the currency pair, which indicates a forecast that USD/AUD will go downwards (USD weak / AUD strong).

Primary Cross Currency Pairs

While the bulk of forex trading happens with USD, cross currency pairs provide an alternative way to trade forex.

Basically, cross-currency pair (simply crosses or cross) refers to any pair, which doesn't involve the USD.

The rates for crosses originate from their corresponding USD pairs but independently quoted and normally with a lower spread compared to what you can obtain from directly trading USD.

Take note that the "spread" pertains to the difference between the offer and the bid or the rate at which you could trade. You will encounter the spread in almost all finance markets.

Cross currencies allow traders to directly move target trades to particular individual currencies to take advantage of important events or news.

For instance, forecast suggests that CAD has the lowest prospects of all major currencies to go forward, based on economic outlook or interest rates. You may take advantage of this by selling CAD. But to what pair?

You may consider the USD, possibly buying USD/CAD (buying USD and selling CAD). However, you think that the prospects of USD are not much better than CAD. After taking a closer look, you identified a currency that has a much better outlook (such as strengthening economy or rising interest rates), say the New Zealand Dollar (NZD).

In this case, we are looking to buy CAD/NZD cross (buying CAD and selling NZD) to take advantage of your projection that the NZD has the best potential among major currencies and CAD the worst.

Cross trading can be particularly effective if major cross-border mergers and acquisitions (M&A) are released. If a Japanese conglomerate is buying an Australian software company, the Japanese company needs to sell JPY and buy AUD to fund the acquisition.

For M&As, you need to watch out for the cash portion of the transaction. If the transaction involves stocks, then there is no need to exchange currencies to raise the needed cash.

The three major non-USD currencies (GBP, JPY, and EUR) are presently the most actively traded cross currencies. These are known as the sterling crosses, yen crosses, and euro crosses. The rest of the currencies (NZD, CAD, AUD, and CHF) are also traded in cross pairs.

Base Currencies and Counter Currencies

If you study the currency pairs, you may realize that the currencies are combined in a seemingly peculiar order. For example if Aussie-yen (AUD/JPY) is a yen cross, then why is this not called a "yen-Aussie" and written JPY/AUD?

The quoting norms evolved over the years to follow conventionally strong currencies as opposed to traditionally weak currencies, with the strong currency coming first. It also reflects the norm in market quotations where the first currency in the pair is called the base currency.

The base currency refers to what you are buying or selling when you are trading the pair. This is also called notional or face amount of the trade. Therefore, if you buy 50,000 GBP/AUD, you have just purchased 50,000 pounds and sold the equal amount in Australian Dollars. If you sell 50,000 CAD/GBP, you just sold 50,000 Canadian Dollars and purchased the equivalent amount of British Pounds.

The counter currency refers to the second currency in the pair. As such, it is also known as the secondary currency. It also refers to the denomination of the price fluctuations and ultimately what you earn and lose will be denominated in the counter currency. If you buy CHF/AUD, it goes up and you take a profit, your gains are not in francs but in Aussie.

Long, Short and Flat

Like other financial markets, the forex market also uses the same names in discussing market positioning. But due to the fact that forex trading involves trading currencies at the same time, you need to be really accurate on the contextual definition of these terms, especially if you are a newbie.

Long Position

Long position refers to a trade position wherein you are buying a unit of security. In the forex market, this refers to buying a currency pair. If you are long, it means you are searching for rates to move higher, so you may sell it at a better price compared to when you purchased the security.

If you want to close a long position, you are interested to sell what you have purchased. If you are purchasing at different price levels, you are sustaining longs so your position is “getting longer”.

Short Position

Short position refers to selling units that you never owned in the first place. In equities, shorting a stock refers to borrowing the stock so you can resell the units (less the broker fees).

In the forex market, this refers to the actual trading of two currencies, which means you are selling the “base” and buying the “counter”. Therefore, the exchange is still present, but just in reverse order and in reference to the quoting terms for currency pairs.

Once you have sold a currency pair, it is now called getting short, which means you are now searching for lower rates so you can buy it back and then make profits from the difference.

When you are selling at different price levels, you are going for shorts and so your position is getting “shorter”. In other financial markets, short selling are bounded by certain restrictions and usually considered too risky for many day traders. But in forex trading, getting short is quite common as getting long.

“Sell high and buy low” is a common mantra in financial markets. But take note that the forex pair prices are not absolute because they only indicate the relative values between the two currencies.

Due to the fact that currencies may rise or fall relevant to each other in long-term and medium trends, and short-term market activities, currency pair rates can easily go down or up.

In order to leverage this activity, forex traders usually go short to take advantage of declining currency rates. Players from other financial markets may find it risky to short sell. However, this is just something that you need to embrace.

Flat Position

When you are in a flat position, it means you have no position in the market. It also called a square position. If you are currently in short, you need to buy currencies so you can “square up”. When you are long, then you need to sell currencies so you can go “flat”. A square position generally carries no financial risk or exposure.

NOTE: The only time that you don't have financial risk or exposure is when you are square.

Profit and Loss

Seasoned traders in any financial market are trained in analyzing Profit and Loss (P&L) reports to ascertain if they are winning or losing the trade. Bear in mind that these financial markets are not theoretical or academic. You can earn or lose a lot of money within minutes. If you want to actively trade currencies, you have to really master P&L.

Understanding the mechanism behind P&L is crucial, especially if you are interested in online marketing trading. In this case, your P&L will directly affect the margin level you need to recover.

The slight movements in your margin account will help you figure out how much you can buy and sell and also the duration of the trade if the rates are not looking good for your current position.

Liquidations and Margin Balances

One of the key advantages of forex trading is that you can use the leverage that will enable you to obtain a bigger exposure to a market while only using a small percentage of your capital.

Margin refers to the initial capital that you have to post in your trading account in order to start trading. This margin will now become your starting balance. This now becomes the basis on which all your trades will be used as collateral. This is similar to a collateral that a bank will ask you before approving a loan.

Not similar to margin-based stock trading or futures market, online forex brokers don't usually issue requests for more leverage so you can sustain more open positions. As an alternative, they establish margin ratios to open positions, which should be sustained regularly.

If the margin balance of your account falls below the needed ratio even for just a few moments, your broker may close out your positions without any prior notice.

This usually happens if your account is currently in a losing position. When your broker liquidates your positions, you are most likely tied in and the size of your margin balance can be reduced.

Make certain that you are totally aware of your broker's requirements for leverage and policies for liquidation. The requirements may vary depending on the size of your account.

Some brokers may liquidate your trading account when you go under the margin limits. Other brokers, on the other hand, may just close out your largest losing trades until you can fulfill the recommended ratio again. Please go over the terms and conditions relevant to leverage and liquidation before you sign up.

Market-to-Market Computations

Many online brokers will provide you actual market-to-market computations, which will show your account's margin balance. This computation will show your profit and loss (unrealized) according to the exact moment that you can close your positions in the trade.

Depending on the trading platform used by your broker, if you are long, the computation will use the exact moment that you can sell as the basis. If your position is short, the rate will be based on the exact moment you can buy.

On the other hand, margin balance refers to the total amount you have deposited initially, as well as your P&L (both realized and unrealized).

Once you go flat (close all open positions at full), all of your earnings will be diverted to your margin balance. If you partially close some of your positions, only the corresponding percentage of your P&L shall be realized and will be diverted to your margins.

The unrealized P&L shall continue to fluctuate based on the remaining open positions and so will your total margin balance. If you have a winning position open, you'll have a positive unrealized P&L and your broker may increase your margin balance.

When the market is moving against the positions the unrealized P&L will be negative and your broker may reduce the size of your margin balance. Take note that the prices in the forex market are always changing, so your total margin balance and market-to-market unrealized P&L will also change.

Using Pips to Calculate Profit and Loss

The computations for P&L are quite mathematically direct. Forex analysts only use the pips you have lost or gained and the size of your position as bases.

Pip refers to the basic increase of price changes on the prevailing rates of a currency. Pips are also referred to as points, so you may find these terms used interchangeably.

It's not certain where the word pip came from. Some say this is an abbreviation for percentage in point, but it may also refer to the FX response to the bips or bond traders that refer to the bps or basis points.

Even the conventionally strong pip is now being updated as electronic trading continues to develop. It is true that a pip is the smallest increment of fluctuations in the currency price rates.

However, you should take note that online forex trading is rapidly progressing to use decimals in pips, wherein you can trade 1/10 pips. Furthermore, half-pip prices have been the norm in specific currency pairs in the interbank market for several years. But as a newbie, it is ideal that you stick with pips for now.

Now, let's take a look at several currency pairs so you can get an idea of what a pip is. Many currency pairs are quoted in five digits. The position of the decimal points depends on whether it's a yen currency pair - if it is, there are two digits after the decimal point.

For the rest of the currency pairs, there are 4 digits after the decimal point. In all cases, the pip is reflected in the last digit. Below are some of the major currency pairs and crosses. Take note that the underlined digits are the pips.

- USD/JPY: 101.4**3**
- USD/CHF: 0.907**4**
- EUR/USD: 1.353**5**
- EUR/JPY: 138.0**1**
- GBP/USD: 1.614**2**

Take a look at GBP/USD. In this case, if the rate increases from 1.6142 to 1.16162, it has increased by 20 units. When the rate moves from 1.6142 to 1.6122, it just went down by 20 pips. Pips offer an easy way to compute the P&L. To turn the movement of the pip into a P&L computation, all you have to do is to determine the size of the position.

For a 100,000 position (GBP/USD) the 20-pip move is equal to $200. Whether the amounts are negative or positive depend on whether you are short or long for every move.

You may take time to really study the P&L pip calculation, but this is not usually a concern since most online trading platforms will compute the P&L for you instantly, both realized when the trade is closed or unrealized if the trade is open.

However, calculating the P&L is crucial so you can effectively manage the risk and structure the trade. This will help you to understand the P&L implications of a trade strategy that you are considering so you can maintain your margin balance and gain control of your trade.

Really understanding your P&L can help you avoid costly mistakes such as placing a trade that is too high or placing stop loss orders beyond your price where your account falls under the needed margin. You need to at least compute the price point at which your position will be liquidated once your margin balance declines under the recommended ratio.

Interest Rates and Rollovers

One market norm that is peculiar to forex is rollover, which refers to a transaction where an open position from the settlement date is rolled over into the next value date.

The rollovers signify the intersection of interstate markets and forex. After all, currencies represent monetary value.

The rollover rates are based on the difference in interest rates of the two currency pairs that you are trading. This is because what you are actually trading is cash.

Yes, the currency is cash. When you go for long, it's similar to depositing cash into a bank. When you go for short, it's like you are borrowing money from a bank. Just as you would expect to earn interest from your bank deposits or pay interest for a loan, you should also expect an increase in holding a currency position over the changes in value.

The caveat in forex trading is that if you carry over an open position from value date to the next, the transaction involves two banks. One account has a positive balance (long) and the other account has a negative balance (short).

But because your accounts are in two different currencies, the two interest rates of the country using the currency will apply. ***Interest rate differential*** refers to the difference between the interest rates in the two countries. The bigger the interest-rate differential, the bigger the effect from rollovers. The lower the interest rate differential, the lesser the effect from rollovers. It is ideal to look for the benchmark or base lending rates for each country.

Leading financial market websites can provide you the relevant interest-rate levels. This includes www.fxstreet.com or www.marketwatch.com.

Bear in mind that rollover rates have a more significant impact on you, depending on the size of your position. They have a larger impact on someone trading in the millions compared to someone who is only trading in thousands.

But regardless of the size, it is still ideal to understand how a rollover can affect your trade. So it is important that you know how interest rates can affect the currency rates. After all, the interest rates are expressed in percentages and currency rates are in decimals.

Take note that the deposit rates can yield actual cash returns that are netted, and produce a net cash return. This net cash return is then dividend by the size position that provides the currency pips or the rollover rate.

Valuation Date and Trade Settlements

In discussing forex trading, we are implicitly referring to trading in the spot market, in which the securities are delivered immediately. In the real world, immediate means several business days. This allows banks and financial organizations to have time to settle a trade.

In forex trading, spot refers to the settlement of the trade in two business days, which is also known as the value date. The time is needed to allow for the processing of the trade across different time zones and for the currency payments to be completed around the globe.

Remember, the forex market operates on a 24-hour trade basis starting at 5 p.m. Eastern Time and ending the next day at 5 pm. So if today is Tuesday, spot currencies are trading for value on Thursday assuming there are no holidays in between.

On Tuesday 5 pm ET, the trade date becomes Wednesday and the value date is changed to Friday. If you have an open position on Tuesday at 5 pm ET closing, your position will be shifted to the next value date, in this case from Thursday to Friday or a rollover of one day.

If you completed the position the next day (Wednesday) and completed the trade date square, there are no rollovers because you don't have a position. The same is true if you can't carry a position through the daily closing at 5 pm ET. On Thursday trade dates, the spot currencies are usually trading for a Monday value date. On Wednesday 5 pm ET, the value date changes from Monday to Tuesday or known as a Weekend Rollover.

In this rollover computation, it will be a five-day rollover (Thursday, Friday, Saturday, Sunday, and Monday). Therefore, the cost of the rollover will be five times the usual daily cost. The only exception to the two-day spot convention in forex trading is USD/CAD because the primary financial centers in Canada and United States are sharing the same time zone. Therefore, wire transfers and communications can be easily processed.

It will only take one business day to settle USD/CAD trades. The weekend rollover for USD/CAD happens on Thursday after the 5 pm ET closing when the value date moves from Friday to Monday. This is only applicable to USD/CAD and not to other pairs that involve CAD such as EUR/CAD or CAD/JPY.

Value Dates and Market Holidays

Take note that value dates are based on individual currency pairs to consider banking holidays of countries involved. The rollovers can be longer when there's a banking holiday in one of the countries whose currency is part of the trade.

For instance, if it's Wednesday and you are trading CHF/USD, the typical value date would be Friday. However, if there's a banking holiday in Switzerland, Swiss banks are not open to settle the trade.

Therefore, the value date is adjusted to the next banking holiday that is common to Switzerland and the United States, usually the following Monday. In this case, the weekend rollover will take place at the closing of the trade on Tuesday at 5 pm ET when the value date would be shifted from Thursday to Monday (skipping over the holiday on Friday). This is a 4-day rollover.

What will happen at the change in value date at 5 pm ET (Wednesday)? There will be no rollover. Since the value date for trades made on Wednesday is already Monday, no rollover is required because the trades settled on Thursday are also for settlement on Monday. This is referred to as a double value date, which means two trade dates (Wednesday and Thursday) and are settling the same value date (Monday).

Several times every year (typically around Christmas, New Year, or Spring Break in Japan) when multiple banking holidays in different countries cross over several days, the rollover period could be as long as 7 or 8 days. Therefore, you may earn or pay seven or eight times the rollover fee in a single day, but you may not face any rollover fees for the remaining of the holiday period.

Rollover Transactions

Rollovers are typically performed by forex brokers if you hold an open position that has already passed the valuation date. Rollovers are applied to the open position by two offsetting trades, which result in the same open position. Some online forex brokers apply the rollover rates by changing the necessary rate for the open position.

Meanwhile, other forex brokers apply for the rollover credit or debit directly to the margin balance. Here are the important pointers you need to remember about rollovers:

- Forex brokers will apply rollovers to positions that are open after 5 pm ET
- Your broker will not apply rollovers if you are not carrying a position over the change in value date. Therefore, if you are square at the close of every trading session, then you don't need to worry about rollovers.
- Rollovers represent the cost of holding an open position or the interest rate return
- Rollovers represent the difference in interest rates between currency pairs in an open position. However, they are applied in currency-rate terms
- Rollovers are composed of net interest you have paid or you have earned, depending on the movement of your position
- You can earn money through rollovers if you get short a currency with the lower interest rate and go long a currency with a higher interest rate
- You will lose money if you long a currency with the lower interest rates and short a currency with the higher interest rate
- Some forex brokers apply spreads to rollovers that can deduct any interest earned by your position
- Rollover credits/costs are based on the size of your position - the bigger the position, the bigger the gain or cost to you

- You should consider rollovers as a business expense and should not be considered as a catalyst in your trading decisions

If you will trade a relatively big account with an online forex broker (around $25,000) it is possible to negotiate a tighter rollover spread. This will allow you to capture more of the profits if you are in the right position or you can reduce the cost.

Currency Prices 101

We will now begin exploring how actual forex trading works. But before that, it is first important to get a glimpse of the mechanism behind currency prices. If you want to become a forex day trader, you should always be mindful of currency prices.

When you are trading in the forex market, you are trading a currency pair. And when you buy something, you should be always mindful of the price. So in this section, we'll take a look at how online forex brokers show currency prices so you can properly execute a trade.

Different brokers use different formats to present currency prices in their platforms. A comprehensive picture of what the currency prices mean will allow you to navigate the various platforms used by forex brokers and also help you identify important features that can help you in the trade.

Bids and Offers

Whenever you use a forex trading terminal, you will typically see two prices for each currency pair.

The number on the left is referred to as the bid and the number on the right is referred to as the offer or the ask. Some brokers present the numbers on top (offer) and bottom (bid). An easy way to tell the difference between the numbers is that the bid price is always lower compared to the offer.

Currency price quotes have two parts - the deal price and the big price. The latter refers to the first 3 numbers of the entire currency rate and is usually show in a faded font or smaller font.

On the other hand, the deal price refers to the last two digits of the currency pair and is usually shown in a brighter font or a larger font.

Spread

This refers to the difference between the bid and offer prices. Many online forex brokers are using spread as the basis of their platforms, especially for retail forex traders.

Basically, the spread serves as the charges or the commission that your brokers will charge you for facilitating the trade. While some brokers promote their service as "zero commission" chances are they are still earning from the spread.

The spread is also regarded as the remuneration that forex brokers receive from being an important player in the market. It varies from one broker to another and will also depend on the currency pair that you are trading.

The spread is generally lower if the currency pair is more liquid. Bigger spreads could result in less liquid currency pair. This is especially true for cross currencies.

Trade Execution

In the Final Chapter, we will explore the steps in signing up for your own forex account. Ideally, you should first register with a demo account so you can get a feel for executing deals before you spend your own money for forex trading.

There are two main ways to execute a forex trade - live trading and orders through a broker.

In live trading, you can access the market platforms to trade currency pairs at current prices. Remember, you should have a solid trading plan before you execute a trade because once you make a live deal, it is already settled.

What about if you suddenly changed your mind during a live trade? You have to execute another trade so you can correct the mistake. This is usually expensive as changing minds in the market will cost you money.

There are different ways to enter the forex market, and this will all depend on the setup of your preferred broker. Most brokers have live-streaming functions that will allow you to quickly see the prices and enter into the deal with only several clicks.

Many online brokers now also have their own mobile apps that you can easily use for quick forex trading. Only a few years ago, day traders had to use devices that must be plugged into a desktop computer or a specialized terminal.

With the introduction of forex trading apps, retail traders can now participate in the market using their phones anytime and anywhere. Today, you can trade while watching your kid play basketball or waiting for your order to arrive in a restaurant.

But mobile phone trading also has its disadvantages. For instance, if your smartphone has unreliable internet connection or your battery is low, then there's the risk of going offline when you are executing a trade.

Below are helpful tips when you are trading on your mobile phone:

- Before you execute a trade, make sure that your battery is enough to sustain online trading.

- Avoid trading if you are currently in a place with bad mobile reception. You may lose money if you can't monitor your trade.
- Maximize your internet connection by closing other apps while you are trading.

Orders

Orders are generally used by forex day traders to take advantage of profitable market movements even if they are not able to execute a trade personally. Remember, the forex market never closes so a considerable movement may happen while you are sleeping.

Many forex traders have their other occupations that also require focus. In order to respond to the market without being there, you can use orders. Day traders use orders in order to:

- Protect profits and minimize losses
- Capture sharp price fluctuations
- Minimize risk in highly volatile windows
- Automatically execute a trade from entry to exit
- Safeguard trading capital from significant losses

The forex market can be extremely volatile and usually difficult to predict. With orders, you can capitalize on short-term market movements and also place a limit on any adverse effect of price movements.

Effective use of orders can also help you in quantifying the risk that you are taking. A sound forex trading strategy should always include a solid strategy for using orders.

Types of Orders

Bear in mind that not all types of orders are available for day traders. So you should always ask your broker about the orders you can use before you sign up with any account.

Stop Loss Orders

Forex traders use this type of order to limit the possible losses when the market is moving against your current position. Without a stop loss order in place, you are exposing your trade to a high risk.

If you are in a short position, then the order for stop loss is to buy at a higher price compared to the prevailing rate in the market.

If you are in a long position, then the order for stop loss is to sell at a lower price compared to the prevailing rate in the market.

Trailing Stop Loss Orders

Seasoned forex day traders know how to quickly stop losing positions and allow their winning trades to take profit as much as they can.

You can mimic this strategy through a trailing stop loss order. When you have a winning trade, you can wait for the next market to follow a reversal and take you out instead of choosing the right exit. A trailing stop loss order will allow you to work on a fixed number of pips from your entry rate.

NOTE: Not all brokers can provide you with a trailing stop loss order. If the platform you have chosen doesn't have this feature, you can copy the trailing stop but you have to do it manually by changing the rate on your usual stop loss order. But this is still dragging especially if you are not a full time day trader.

Take Profit Orders

This type of order is used by forex traders to automatically close a trade if the position reaches a specific predetermined level.

For example, if you buy a currency pair CAD/USD at 1.1780 and you add a take profit order at 1.800, the trade will be closed and the profit will be protected if the currency pair reaches the 1.800 level.

This order is automatic so you don't need to constantly keep track of the market for the best time to exit.

If you set a take profit order, you also need to set up an order for stop loss. This move is quite similar to a take profit order but this one is designed to minimize your possible losses when the market doesn't follow a lucrative trend.

Take profit order is an important tool for retail traders because it safeguards your profits when there's a sharp reversal in the market. Remember, the forex market is highly volatile and the trades can easily change from making money to losing money in a matter of minutes.

This order is usually used by traders who use fundamental metrics such as the average true range that can help in determining the best way to enter or exit points.

Also take note that take profit orders are commonly established based on your trading plan. This order can be opened short or long depending on your position.

Ideally, you should set this order at a higher level if your trading plan is based on a significant movement in the market. On the other hand, you should place a closer take profit if your fundamental strategy is to protect your profit before any market turn.

It is usually a false assumption that taking profit in the short-term will allow you to sustain a positive capital and beat the market. This rarely happens. Some traders take profit levels too close to the opening price, which usually leads to losses.

As a newbie trader, it is essential for you to understand the basic principles of financial management to make certain that you will actually win the game.

In figuring out where to place your take profit order, resistance and support levels are also crucial. When to take profit and market direction can help you determine market lows and highs. A fundamental viewpoint in this case is to take profit before high-impact price movements.

Remember to focus on major price levels and just ignore the horizontal lines in a forex chart.

Limit Orders

Some newbie forex traders are confused over take profit and limit orders. This is not surprising because a take profit order is actually a form of a limit order.

The primary difference is that take-profit orders will minimize or close open positions. Meanwhile, limit orders open new positions or add to prevailing positions in the same line of movement.

Take note that limit order pertains to any order that activates a favorable trade compared to the prevailing market price. At this point, you should always remember the classic mantra in trading - buy low and sell high.

If you place a limit order to buy, then the trade execution is entered at a price under the current market price. If you place a limit order to sell, then the trade execution is entered into a price that is better than the current market price.

OCO Order

OCO is abbreviation for One-Cancels-The-Other Order. This is a special type of a stop loss order, which is usually added with a take profit order. It serves as a stand-by protection order for open positions.

In this order, your forex position shall stay open until one of your existing order levels is triggered by the market. The effect is closing the position. If your position reaches an order level and triggered, the other order will be quickly cancelled.

Contingent Orders

You may also choose to combine several forms of orders in building a solid strategy for your trade. You may use contingent orders to place on your trade even if you can't go online. This usually provides peace of mind to traders knowing that your contingent order has all the bases covered and you are clear in your defined risks.

Contingent orders are also known as if-then orders because it requires the IF order to be fulfilled first before the second part to be triggered.

Chapter 5 – Making Sense of Forex Market News

"Don't blindly follow someone, follow market and try to hear what it is telling you." - Jaymin Shah

At any given moment, any number of real-world forces are at work in the forex market. This includes geopolitical events, interest rate decisions, and economic data.

These forces are filtered through the collective consciousness of the market and translated into price actions. As a forex trader, you need to focus on trying to make profits based on the price movements. But bear in mind that you are not the only trader in the market.

Hundreds of thousands are also active in the forex market, and they are all assessing the same information and data, but more likely they are working on different assumptions.

To provide another perspective, the trades are based on different conclusions that is what ultimately moves currency prices. This will bring you back to the observation - if it's not one thing it's another. This all boils down on how the forex markets process information and there are a lot of information out there.

Even seasoned traders who think they have seen it all can still be mesmerized by new and unexpected outcomes in the market. Hence, you are not alone when it comes to making sense of market information just to make immediate trading decisions.

Your objective is to avoid "paralysis by analysis" and to absorb and understand as much as you can about the market drivers. The goal is to make successful forex traders. Hopefully, this book will provide you a better understanding of the types of market information that drives the market so you can effectively interpret and apply this information.

Where to Source Market Information

Before you can analyze tons of information about the market, you first need to know where to source information in the first place. Organizational traders employ teams of strategists, analysts, and economists to provide them with real-time observations and interpretations.

But don't worry as any information that these big traders are getting are also available to retail traders. However, you should exert extra effort to find, read, and make sense of it.

Have you ever boarded a moving car?

The art of boarding a moving car requires you to begin running alongside the running car before you grab a handle and board. If you are just there flat-footed and you try to board, you will lose your arm.

This is an ideal metaphor to describe the forex market.

Any day trader who will try to jump in without first getting up to speed will be up for failure. Getting up to speed in the forex market means learning what present themes are driving the market. In order to do this, you need to know where to find market sources and how to interpret information.

However, getting up to speed will take some time. Therefore, you should not be in a rush to begin trading based on several hours or days of reading. Ideally, you should dedicate a month worth of research on different currency pairs. You should also familiarize yourself with what is going on before you consider yourself ready to board a moving train.

One way to prepare yourself for the forex market is to use a demo account offered by online forex broker. In just a month, you will experience a full cycle of economic data indicators as well as majority of market events such as central bank meetings that will provide you a first-hand experience of how the market moves and shifts to new market information.

An exciting part of forex trading is that there's always something going on. Remember, a busy road is filled with running cars. So don't worry about missing your ride because there's always another one that will come for you.

Market Pulse

With the popularity of online forex trading in recent years, there's been a growth of currency-specific online sources that are catering to the needs of day traders.

To save space, we will not review these sites in this book, but you should check out www.fxstreet.com, which is a site that features different sources of forex market analysis.

Twitter is also another reliable source of information, particularly around important news releases and breaking news events. If you're looking at forex research from different information sources, you need to be mindful of who has provided the analysis.

If you are not aware of the backgrounds or identities of the forex analysts, you might be relying on the work of someone who just have few months of market experience. This is not exactly a sophisticated insight.

If you are in doubt, you should focus on the reports that are developed by market analysts you really trust or major financial organizations. Many online forex trading platforms also provide different types of market research and analysis, so if you're deciding which broker you must open your account with, you should look at the quality of its research.

Sources of News

In the past, people tend to focus on mainstream financial press that provide continuous coverage of the major financial markets including forex.

Their websites offer regular intraday updates that can cover data releases and announcements, typically with some organizational commentary, too. This will allow you to better understand the reasons behind market behavior. The best sources of financial news are Reuters, MarketWatch, and Bloomberg.

Some of the most credible analysts tweet their insights throughout the day, and you can also follow most of the major news outlets to gain a fast perspective of what is happening.

There are also reliable blogs such as Baby Pips and Forex Factory. Be sure to check out several sources and narrow down to the ones that are working for you. Just keep in mind that what you will read from these sources has already happened, and the market has digested the information and so the prices might have been adjusted accordingly.

In interpreting news and information, you should always ask yourself the source of the information as you must always differentiate fact from rumor or opinion.

Moreover, you should also try to figure out how old the information is. You have to gauge the timeliness of the news and the extent to which the market has already responded on it.

Sources for Real-Time Market Information

The forex market moves on information quite fast, and the organizational players basically have different live feeds from the primary accredited news sources such as Reuters, Bloomberg, and Dow Jones.

Nowadays, one of the fastest ways to obtain real-time news, particularly information releases is from Twitter that provides you access to unlimited news sourced and could be an effective way to access real-time market news.

Event Calendars and Economic Data

The forex market revolves around economic events and data, and you need to find a reliable market calendar so you can see what is coming down the road next.

Ideally, you should look for market calendars that contain all the major upcoming economic releases showing the time of the update, the market forecast, and the previous report cited.

Aside from data reports, you should also keep an eye on economic events such as central bank rate-setting meetings, the issuance of the minutes of those meetings, speeches by chief bankers, and significant meetings such as monthly gatherings of finance ministers.

Insights from these events usually move the market in the short term and if you are not watchful of them, you could be blindsided. In a bit, we will discuss how the forex market anticipates events and information, and how this behavior can affect the prices. But at this point, you should understand that you can't anticipate anything that you don't know.

Currency Forecasts

Many of the financial media are keen on organizational predictions of where the forex market is headed, and you will likely encounter a lot of monthly, quarterly, and yearly exchange rate forecasts in your market research.

However, you should treat these as indicators of general market sentiment and outlook rather than solid trading advice. Many forecasts are heavily skewed to present circumstances and are a much better guide to what the market is really thinking at the moment compared to where rates will actually be in the next few months.

Gossip

Despite its professional image, the financial markets are also susceptible to gossip. True or untrue, rumors may still affect the market behavior in the forex world.

One example of gossip that drives the market is called the whisper numbers, which are rumors of economic data prior to its scheduled release. These rumors have the tendency to roil short-term market positions that traders opened in anticipation of an economic report, and they also affect the subsequent reaction of the market to the report.

For instance, a whisper number that suggests a bad picture of a data report from the US, which was originally predicted to be weak in the first place, may see the USD come under extreme pressure before the release date.

If the real number is revealed and it's weak but still in line with the forecasts, but not as low as projected by the whisper number, then the USD could rebound because the worst fears were not true.

On the other hand, large market orders are rumors that usually hold water, but not certain or absolute. These are normally linked with large organizational players or central banks that are trading in the forex market.

The typically mention a price level, so pay attention to the price level as a possible source of resistance or support. When the price level is broken, the order either wasn't real or has already been filled. In both cases, the price level has given way, possibly triggering a further directional move.

Nowadays, gossips spread fast, and day traders usually have to contend with them several times every day, which in due time may reduce the effects on the market.

The problem with gossip is that there's no easy way to figure out if they are true and even if you can, you have no way to be sure of the price reaction that is ultimately the key to deal with gossip.

Surprisingly, gossips have the uncanny habit of spreading after relatively extensive attempts to break through significant technical levels or directions moves.

You should take note that a technical level test or intraday move is underway. A tight strategy for exit is also crucial to protect your trades if that market turns tail. If there's unproven information behind a sudden reversal, you can typically find out only after the fact anyway. However, a tight exit plan could save you from getting left behind in the reversals.

Market Themes

At any given point in the forex market, several themes can dominate the attention of the market. Market themes are at the core of actual forces presently affecting the market. These are what market analysts and commentators are talking about when they are trying to explain what is happening in the market.

But on top of that, themes serve as the filters through which new data and information are digested by the market. They all come in different sizes and shapes and they have different effects on the market over time.

Some are longer themes that can activate the direction of the market for months or even years, such as the persistence of the US trade deficit. Other themes may only hold for weeks, days or even a few hours such as a controversial tweet from a central banker.

Market themes generally come in two primary forms that are co-existing in parallel universes but they also overlap a lot of times. The two main forms of themes that we like to focus on are technical themes and fundamental themes that we will discuss in the later chapters.

Currency Fundamental Drivers

Every currency has its own set of fundamental factors in which it is being assessed by the market.

The basic fundamental environment is all present, but it is also subject to change similar to economic conditions that will change in the course of business cycles.

Fundamental themes will also change in relative importance to one another, with specific themes being pushed to the side for a specific period if events or news focus the attention of the market on other, more important themes.

As you continue, bear in mind that each theme is applicable to each and every currency but in different degrees at any given moment. You will learn some examples of what will probably happen to a currency based on the context of information means for each theme.

Interest Rates Movement

Interest rates are typically the single most important factor that drives the value of a currency. However, it's not just about where the interest rate levels are now, even though this is still undeniably important.

What really matters most is the general direction, their level in the future, and the timing of any changes. Remember, financial markets are always speculating on the direction of interest rates, although the interest rate changes are relatively not frequent.

For instance, as of press time, the Bank of England hasn't changed the interest rates level since 2009. The interest rate changes and speculation over the market direction are the primary drivers of the value of a currency on a daily basis as well as over longer time frames.

The data inputs that drive the interest rate outlook are focused on inflation reports and economic growth data. Take note that the stronger the growth picture, the higher the inflation pressures are. This will result in interest rates to move higher, typically improving the outlook of a currency.

If the inflation readings are lower or the growth outlook is weaker, the interest rates are more likely to move lower or remain steady, usually damaging the currency in the long run.

Bond markets also have a huge impact on the direction of interest rates and are considered the best real-time measurement tool for interest rate markets. The central banks can only affect short-term interest rates that are driven by the target interest rate of the central bank.

However, longer-term bond yields with the 10-year maturity as measurement tools can reflect the long-term view of the market as well as the direction of future interest rate movements.

Lower interest rates in bonds could point to a weaker economic perspective and the possibility of lower interest rates ahead. This can usually damage the currency while higher yields could result in a positive economic outlook and the possibility of higher rates, normally supporting the currency.

The influence of interest rate themes can be felt by the market if the interest rates of the two currencies are seen to diverge - when one interest rate of a currency is expected to move higher and the other is lower or at the same level.

For relative changes that may favor one currency over the other, you should keep track of the three-month yield spreads - the difference between the yields of two government bonds. However, rates don't necessarily have to diverge to affect currencies. The yield of one currency may just move higher faster than another, and the widening spread between the two will be apparent in the long run.

Growth Prospects

Economic growth outlook is the linchpin to several factors that determine the value of a currency. This includes the attractiveness of a nation's investment climate, and the interest rate outlook.

Not surprisingly, the stronger the growth prospect, the better a specific currency is likely to perform relative to currencies of countries with weaker growth prospects.

Stronger growth of the economy can increase the probability of higher interest rates down the road as central banks usually seek to limit rapid growth to head off inflationary strain.

Meanwhile, weaker growth data increases the prospect of potentially lower interest rates as well as damaging the outlook for investment. Numerous data reports for growth reflect only a specific sector of a country's bigger economy such as the real estate market or the manufacturing industry.

Depending on how important that sector is to the bigger national economy, those reports have the tendency to be interpreted as more or less important.

For example, industrial production is more important in Japan compared to the US because of the more significant role manufacturing plays in Japan. Also, there's no fix recipe for how growth data will affect the value of a currency, but if the interest rate outlook is basically neutral, as in no solid conviction on the movement of the rates of the two currencies, the growth theme becomes more significant.

Combating Inflation

As a forex trader, you need to monitor fiscal policy developments. The inflation theme has more nuances compared to the growth theme in terms of its implications to the value of a currency.

Depending on the bigger picture, it may produce starkly different result for a currency. Basically, if there is a good outlook for growth, and inflation is too high, you can say that it is a forex plus.

On the other hand, if the growth is weakening or low, and inflation is too high, you can say that it is forex negative. In both cases, the interest rates could be steady to high. However, a low-slow growth case added with high/higher interest rates increases the risks of an economy falling into a recession that could ultimately lead to interest rate cuts.

In view of this, currencies are a bit fickle in that they are attracted to higher interest rates some of the time, but not always. The same scenario happens if a central bank is holding rates that are too high for too long, normally based on combating inflation, and the market starts to speculate that an economic hardship is imminent.

This market behavior is actually not unusual if you think that the forex market is basically always looking for future interest rates. In considering inflation data into the interest rate theme, you should be aware of how the general growth theme is holding up. If there's good growth, and inflation is high due to economic strength, higher inflation readings will be supportive of the currency.

If there's a slowdown and inflation is still high, the impact on the currency will be less positive and probably downright negative.

Financial Stability

The Eurozone Debt Crisis (2009 to 2013) and the Great Financial Crisis in the US (2008 to 2009) shone light to financial stability as another general theme in the forex market.

During the early days of the crisis, the financial players (banks and insurance companies) was deeply affected and needed massive intervention from the government to avoid a meltdown.

The succeeding economic turmoil later revealed excessive government debt levels as well as budget deficits as a threat to economic growth and sovereign debt.

The journey to recovery among developed countries remain a difficult choice and the levels of government debt and the risk for sovereign default still looms.

Regardless if it is quantitative easing in the United States or high debt levels in Europe, financial stability and perceptions of credit ratings can sway over national currencies, typically for the worse.

One way to measure market fears is to keep track of government bond yields. Higher bond yields could mean investors are selling bonds over fears of a default and not because of growth expectations. Therefore, the currency at risk may suffer alongside government bonds.

Measuring the Strength of Structural Themes

Beyond financial stability, inflation, growth, and interest rates, several other significant themes usually assert themselves, mostly in the structural aspect or the general picture of how the economy is performing.

Bear in mind that structural themes can be fleeting. They may be in full force today but can drop altogether tomorrow. These themes are normally peripheral to those we have discussed in the previous sections, but they can still exert important influence on currency pairs by their own right.

In addition, they can also boost the impact of the main themes similar to throwing kerosene to a fire. Here are the basic recurring structural themes:

- **Deficits** - Both trade and fiscal deficits are normally considered as forex negatives. During times of low to slow growth, the effect of deficits can be magnifies as the credibility of a currency is scrutinized such as the case with euro. In times of stable or high growth, deficits could have less influence but are still a negative hanging over the general prospect.
- **Employment** - Employment is an important factor in the long-term performance of an economy and the main driver of interest rates. As long as employment is increasing, the long-term economic outlook will be supported. However, if the employment growth starts to falter, as reflected in the labor reports, the economic outlook will tend to be marked down. Sharp unemployment increases are among the triggers to interest rate cuts by central banks, which goes back to the main interest rate theme.
- **Geopolitics** - Political tensions were not always all-present as they seem today, from trade war against China, to North Korean nuclear tests, to upheaval in the Middle East. During times of geopolitical tension, safe currencies such as Swiss franc and Japanese yen tend to outperform the riskier currencies such as NZD

or AUD. Considering the size of the American economy and wide military involvement, the USD is also vulnerable. When geopolitical tensions subside, the market is fast to revert to pre-existing conditions.

- **Government changes or uncertainty** - Government changes and uncertainty in the political climate can certainly damage the sentiment of the market towards the concerned currency. But immediately after the issues are resolved, political issues tend to quickly fade.

Technical Themes Assessment

Technical themes are probably a bit harder to understand compared to fundamental themes especially if you are not familiar with technical analysis.

But to put this more simply, there are instances that currency prices move simply because currency prices are moving. The fundamental political or economic themes may not have dramatically changed, but the price levels have, and this is usually enough to bring primary market interest out of the guesswork.

In many cases, breaks of major price or technical levels will be in the direction suggested by the prevailing fundamental themes, but the timing is usually suspect and could leave traders dubious. However, sizeable price movements tend to take a life on their own, forcing market players to take action based on price shifts alone.

Moreover, the prevalence of technical analysis as the fundamentals for numerous trading decisions could add weight to current fundamental-driven activities, generating yet another theme to drive the movement. This is the technical theme.

It could be a trending market movement, which attracts trend-following forex traders who don't care about the underlying fundamentals. These traders will keep on pushing the market in the direction it is going, possibly beyond what the fundamentals would dictate.

If a currency pair has broken through significant technical levels, it can attract breakout traders - speculator who focus on jumping on breaks of key price levels, searching to participate on the move for an easy trade. However, nothing will be easy, and breakout forex traders may take the hit if the breaks are not true and the ranges will survive.

The added interest entering the market in the direction of the market again propels price faster than it may regularly go. Getting a sense of where a currency pair stands from a technical perspective is always crucial even if you don't base the trades on technical analysis. The technical theme also stems from different actual considerations that all relate back to the currency prices.

Options Interest

The forex options market is huge and considered as one of the reasons that the spot market is as massive as it is. Options hedging is one of the largest sources of spot market movement outside short-term spot speculation. If spot prices have been trading in popular regions, option interest has the tendency to accrue caused by any considerable changes in the market.

When the ranges are broken, sizeable option-related interest is often pushed to emerge into the market and leverage the movement of the price breakout. This could sustain new exposures or unwind your financial hedges.

Hedgers

Hedgers are forced to participate in the market when a rapid and unexpected price movement develops. Different firms identify an inner hedging rate for corporate and financial management purposes. As long as they are capable of selling above or buying below the rate, they are looking good. When the market moves sharply, they could be forced to jump in on the direction for fear of not ever seeing the inner hedging rate again.

Consensus Expectations

Take note that data reports and news events don't just happen right away. The forex markets evaluate incoming data reports that are relative to market forecasts, normally referred to as consensus expectations or just consensus.

Consensus expectations refer to the average economic forecasts made by economists from leading financial organizations, academe, or private investments firms. News agencies such as Reuters and Bloomberg ask economists for their projections of upcoming information collate the results.

The outcome average forecast is what appears on market calendars, which indicate what is expected for any given data report. The consensus will then become the baseline against which the incoming data will be assessed by the market.

For economic data, the market will compare the actual result - the economic figure, which is actually reported against the consensus (what was expected). The actual data is usually interpreted by the market in the following ways:

- Worse Than Expected - The data is weaker than the projected consensus. For reports on inflation, a worse-than-projected reading could signify that the inflation was higher than forecast, or more inflationary.

- In Line or As Expected - The actual data report was at or quite close to the consensus prediction.
- Better Than Expected - The report was basically stronger than the consensus prediction. A better-than-projected reading on inflation reports means inflation is lower than expected or more benign.
- As Expected or In Line With Expectations - The actual data report was at or very near the projected consensus.

Moreover, the degree to which a data report is better or worse than predicted is crucial. The deviation to the report will affect the release of the data. In assessing central bank statements and commentary from monetary policy makers, the market is assessing the language used in terms of leaning towards steady to lower interest rates (dovish) or leaning towards increasing interest rates (hawkish).

Chapter 6 – Forex Theories and Models

"The goal of a successful trader is to make the best trades. Money is secondary." - Alexander Elder

There are several theories and models behind the foreign exchange market. While you don't have to master them all, it is still ideal to understand the general ideas behind the research.

The primary economic theories found in the forex market are more about the parity settings. Basically, parity refers to the economic justification of the price at which the currency pairs must be traded according to important factors such as interest rates and inflation. According to these economic theories, if the parity setting cannot sustain, there is an arbitrage opportunity for market players.

But arbitrage opportunities, like in other markets are often immediately discovered and discarded before even providing the individual investor the chance for capitalization. Other forex market theories are based on economic factors such as capital flows, trade, and how the country is running its monetary operations.

Asset Market Model

In the Asset Market Model, you have to look into the flow of money into a country from foreign sources for buying assets such as bonds, stocks, and other financial assets.

If you see that the country is experiencing large surge of foreign investments, the price of its currency will rise as the domestic currency has to be purchased by these foreign investments. This model also considers the capital account of the balance in comparison to the present account.

This model is popular among forex investors as the capital accounts of countries are beginning to significantly surpass the current account as foreign money flow increases.

Balance of Payments Theory

There are two divisions in a country's balance of payments - the capital account and the current account. These two measure the outflows and inflows of goods and capital of a country.

In the balance of payments theory, you have to look at the present account that deals with tangible goods trade so you can get a general direction of the exchange rate.

One indicator that a country's exchange rate is not in balance is if it runs a large current account deficit and surplus. In order to adjust to this condition, the exchange rate should be adjusted gradually.

Look if the country is running more deficit (higher imports vs exports) as the currency is more likely to depreciate. Meanwhile, a surplus (higher export versus import) will lead to the appreciation of the country's currency.

You can determine the balance of payments of a country by using the formula below:

BCA + BKA + BRA =

BCA refers to the present account balance

BKA refers to the capital account balance

BRA refers to the reserves account balance

Economic Data

Economic theories could affect the movement of the currencies in the long-run. When it comes to daily or weekly transactions, forex players focus more on economic data.

Countries are often regarded as the largest companies in the world and that holding currency is basically getting a share of that country. Economic data like the current Gross Domestic Product (GDP) figures are usually regarded to be similar to the latest earnings data of a company.

In a similar manner that current events and financial news could influence the stock price of a company, news involving a country could also have a significant effect on the movement of the currency of that country.

Significant changes in the political condition, GDP, consumer confidence, unemployment rate, inflation, and interest rates could result in substantial losses or gains depending on the nature of the news and the present situation of the country.

The volume of economic news that you might need to monitor every day from around the world could be overwhelming. However, as you go along the forex market, it will become a lot more clear which news could have the largest influence. Below are several economic factors that are basically regarded to have the biggest influence in the foreign exchange market.

Retail Sales

The data on retail sales measures the volume of sales that retailers have gained during the period. This basically reflects spending in the country. The data does not cover all stores, but only monitors a basket of stores of different types to gain an idea on how people are spending.

This data will provide you a general ideal of the country's economic stability. In general, strong spending indicates a strong economy. In the United States, the retail sales data is released by the Department of Commerce once a year.

Employment Data

Another economic indicator that you should take a look when you are into forex is the employment data or the number of people who are currently employed in the country.

In the United States, this data is called non-farm payrolls and published by the Bureau of Labor Statistics every first Friday of the month. In most instances, strong increase in employment shows that a country is experiencing a strong economy, while the opposite means otherwise.

If a particular country is going through significant problems in the economy, strong employment data could affect the currency price, because it is an indicator that the economy is recovering.

Meanwhile, high employment could result to inflation, so this indicator might affect the currency price. To put it simply, the movement of currency and economic data will usually depend on the circumstances that are prevailing if the data is released.

Gross Domestic Product (GDP)

The GDP of a country is used as a measurement of all the completed goods and services that a country has produced during a specific period of time. Calculating the GDP is divided into four divisions: total net exports, business spending, government spending, and private consumption.

Economists regard GDP as the best measurement of the economic health of a country with GDP increases indicating economic growth. As you already know, a healthy economy entices more foreign investments.

This will usually lead to increases in the currency value, as the money moves into the country. In the United States, this information is published by the Bureau of Economic Analysis.

Durable Goods

Durable goods refers to those who can last longer than three years such as automobiles, gadgets, and home appliances. The data for durable goods is used to measure the volume of manufactured goods that are produced and shipped for a particular period of time.

This data will provide you a general idea of the amount of individual expenditure on these goods on top of the information on the health of a specific sector. In the United States, this data is published by the Department of Commerce.

Capital and Trade Flows

Transactions between countries build large cash flows, which could have a significant effect on the currency value. Remember, a country that is importing more than its exports may experience depreciation on its currency because of its need to bid its own money to buy the exporting nation's currency. Moreover, higher investments in a country could lead to significant increases in the currency value.

The data on trade flow takes a closer look at the difference between the exports and imports of a country. There is a trade deficit if the imports are higher than exports.

In the United States, the Department of Commerce publishes the trade flow data every month. This shows the volume of goods and services that the country has imported and exported during the previous month.

Meanwhile, the data on capital flow focuses on the fine distinction in the currency volume that is surging through exports or investments to currency that is being offered for foreign imports or investments.

In general, there will be a surplus of capital flow if a country is enjoying a high volume of foreign investments where foreign investors are buying domestic assets like real estate and stocks.

The combined total of the trade and capital flow of a country is known as balance of payments data. This is divided into three categories: financial account, the capital account, and current account.

The financial account focuses on the cash flow between countries mainly for investments. The capital account focuses on the exchange of cash between countries for the purpose of buying capital assets. The current account focuses on the flow of goods and services between countries.

Macroeconomic and Geopolitical Events

The most extreme fluctuations in the foreign exchange market is often influenced by geopolitical and macroeconomic events such as financial crises, changes in the monetary policy, elections, and wars. These can all change or reshape the economic condition of the country, which includes its market fundamentals.

For instance, an election gridlock in a country could place a large strain on the economy of a country and may affect the volatility in the region and thus affecting the currency value. In forex trading, it is important that you are updated on these geopolitical and macroeconomic events.

Interest Rate Parity (IRP)

IRP is quite similar to PPP, because it suggests that there should be no arbitrage opportunities if the two assets in two countries have the same interest rates and the risks for each country is also virtually the same.

The law of one price is also the basis of IRP, because purchasing one asset in one country must also yield the same return as the same asset in another country. Otherwise, the exchange rates will have to be adjusted to bridge the difference.

Below is the formula for getting the IRP:

$$(i_1 - i_2) = \left(\frac{F - S}{S}\right)(1 - i_2)$$

F - refers to the exchange rate in the forwards market

S - refers to the exchange rate in the spot market

I_1 - refers to the interest rate in country 1

I_2 - refers to the exchange rate in country 2

In terms of interest rates, the most concentration by market participants is placed more on the bank rate changes of the country's central bank. This is used for monetary adjustment and establishment of the monetary policy of the country.

In the United States, the bank rate is determined by the Federal Open Market Committee (FOMC). This rate is used by commercial banks for lending and borrowing to the US Treasury.

The FOMC convenes eight times every year to discuss the current economic factors and decide whether to lower, raise, or not change the bank rate. Forex market participants should take note of the outcome of these meetings to guide you in forex trading.

Monetary Model

This forex model concentrates on the monetary policy of a country to help in figuring out the exchange rate.

The monetary policy of a country primarily deals with the supply of money in the country, which is determined by the amount of money printed by the treasury as well as the interest rate set by the central bank.

Countries that adopt a monetary policy, which quickly grows its supply will likely experience inflationary pressure because of the increased circulation. This may lead to currency devaluation.

Purchasing Power Parity (PPP)

PPP is an economic theory, which states that the price levels between two countries must be equivalent to each other after adjustments in the exchange rate. This theory is founded on the one price law, in which the cost of a similar good must be the same regardless of the location.

According to this theory, if there is one major difference between two countries for the same product after the adjustment in the exchange rate, there is a need to create an arbitrage since the product could be obtained from the country, which can sell it for a cheaper price.

Below is PPP's relative version:

$$e = \frac{\Pi_1 - \Pi_2}{1 + \Pi_2}$$

e - refers to the change rate in the exchange rate

'Π_1 - refers to the rate of inflation in country 1

'Π_2 - refers to the rate of inflation in country 2

For instance, let's say that the inflation rate of country A is 10% and the rate of inflation in country B is 5%, then country A's currency must appreciate at least 4.76% against that of country B.

Real Interest Rate Differentiation Model

This forex theory basically suggests that countries with higher real interest rates will likely experience an increase in their currencies compared to countries with lower interest rates.

The main reason behind this is that investors are more likely to invest their money in countries with higher real estate interest rates so they can earn higher returns. The country with the higher real estate interest rate will likely bid up its currency exchange rate.

Theory and Practice in the Forex Market

Understanding these foreign exchange theories could help you understand the underlying principles of the forex market and how it affects or affected by economy.

But take note that there are theories that are conflict with each other, so there is no certainty that these are not 100% accurate to help you in projecting the fluctuations in the forex market. Their application may likely vary according to the market conditions, but it is still crucial to know the core concepts behind these theories.

At this point, you might be a bit overwhelmed by the large volume of data that is being published and that you should monitor as you try forex trading. In spite of this, it is crucial to know what news announcements could affect the currencies that you are betting your money on.

After understanding the economic factors that are driving the foreign exchange market, we will next take a look at the two primary strategies that you can use in trading in the forex market - fundamental analysis and technical analysis.

Chapter 7 - Fundamental Analysis and Fundamental Strategies in Forex Trading

"I believe in analysis and not forecasting." - Nicolas Darvas

In the stock market, fundamental analysis measures the true value of a company. A fundamentalist (one who mainly use fundamental analysis) base his decision to invest or trade in stocks according to the calculation.

Somehow, this is similar in the foreign exchange market, where fundamentalists are also looking into the true value of the countries and their currencies. They are also watching out for economic announcements in order to gain an idea of the true value of the currency.

In general, geo-political events, economic data, and news reports from a certain country are regarded similarly to announcements about stocks and companies used by investors to gain insight of their true value. The value may change over time because of several factors including financial strength and growth. Fundamentalists are focusing on this data to assess the currency of the countries in the currency pair that he is interested in.

In this Chapter, we will discuss the top forex fundamental strategies that are used by traders and investors today.

Forex Investment Strategy - Forex Carry Trade

The forex carry trade is an investment strategy wherein a trader is offering a currency that has lower interest rates and buys a currency with higher interest rate. To put it simply, you are lending currencies at a higher rate and borrow at a lower rate. In using this strategy, you can make profits through the difference between these two rates.

Remember, when you are leveraging a trade, even a slight movement between the rates could result to great profits or greater losses. Aside from capturing the differences on the rates, the traders also focuses on the increasing value of the currency, because money flows into the currency that is high-yielding that increases its value,

One good example of this is the carry trade of the Japanese yen in 1999, when the country lowered its interest rates to almost 0%. Investors eventually capitalized on these lower interest rates by borrowing substantial amount of Japanese yen, which was converted into USD to purchase US treasury bonds.

These bonds guaranteed as high as 5%. Because the Japanese interest rate was basically zero, the investors are not paying any substantial amount to borrow yen and made a lot of profit from the US treasury bonds. Through proper leverage, you can substantially increase your profits in forex trading.

For instance, a 20 times leverage will yield a return of 30% on a 3% yield. If you have $500 in your account and you have access to 20 times leverage, you can control $10,500. If you try the carry trade strategy from our example, you can earn 3% per annum. By the year-end, your $10,000 investment will be $10300. Take note that you have only invested $1,000 from your pocket, so your actual return is 30%.

But bear in mind that this strategy is only applicable if the value of the currency pair appreciates or not changing. Hence, many forex traders who are using the carry trade strategy focus not only on earning from the interest of the difference between the interest rates, but also for appreciating capital.

For the sake of giving simple examples, we have simplified the transactions given here. It is crucial to take note that there is a minimal difference in interest rate that could lead to huge gains when you apply the leverage. Many forex brokers need a small margin for earning interest rates for implementing the carry trade strategy.

Transactions through carry trade strategy could be complicated through the changes to the exchange rate between the currencies. If the currency is low yielding and it appreciates against a currency that yields higher, the profit you can earn between the two yield might be discarded.

The main reason that this could happen is that for investors, it could be too much to carry the risks of currency that are yielding high. Hence, they usually choose to invest in safer but lower yielding currencies.

Take note that the carry trade strategy is ideal for investors who are looking for long-term profits in the forex trade. Hence, this strategy will make you vulnerable to different changes over time like increasing rates in the currencies with lower yield. This also entices more investors and could result in currency appreciation that could diminish the profits you can make through carry trading.

News Trading

Significant news events around the world could have a large impact on the foreign exchange market, which usually render all analysis meaningless. Take note that the forex market is a 24-hour market, and there is no way to schedule the announcement of news. Changes in the market according to the economy and data could hit any type of trader wherever you are and whichever currency you choose to trade.

If you are in Europe and you want to trade Swiss Francs, you can always read news from Europe. If you prefer Yen or Yuan, then you have to watch for news from Japan, China, and

Asia in General. Same goes for other currencies. You have to check the news every day to be updated on any information that could affect your trading.

In the equities market, significant news are often about the publication of corporate earnings, profits, macroeconomic data, profits per share, etc. In the forex market, significant news that affects the market can be announcements from the Central Banks, political events, economic news, inflation reports, and more.

Among the first lessons for beginners in the forex market is when trading, you must be careful in the market during significant news announcements. Nonetheless, you may still find yourself trading during the news, and usually it is not because of being selfish or greedy. Some traders just like the feeling of excitement or adrenaline rush. Some are addicted to the thrill, but most forex traders are only after the profits. After all, you are mainly trading for profits, and the risk is a natural part of the process.

There are always two currencies involved in forex trading. If you are planning to open a position, the news from the two countries must be taken into consideration alongside other foreign news that may affect the currency pair.

For instance, if your decide to trade CHF/NZD, aside from assessing the possible results of the news from Switzerland and New Zealand, and the effect that it could have on the pair, you should also consider significant news from Europe and Asia or anywhere because the news may cause any movement in the financial markets.

If there was a really good economic data from Australasia, the pair will rally because it means that demand for European products may likely to follow an upward trend. The opposite may happen if the economic conditions in Europe are not that strong. It could affect the worldwide financial market and the traders may likely choose currency alternatives such as USD and Yen.

After establishing the significance of understanding the news and the impact it may have on the price, the next step is to learn how you can use news releases to your advantage. There are two primary methods of using the news trading strategy - the short term and the long term.

Short term news trading is a bit more challenging because of the volatility as well as the tighter stops. More often than not, minutes before and after, there are whipsaws with the rate frantically moving in both directions. Short term news trading is also divided into several strategies.

One method is to sell the currency spike after a bad news. There are instances that even after bad announcements, the price slightly increases for several seconds or even minutes. This is the best time to sell, particularly if it is at some significant resistance or level.

On the other hand, buying after bad news, because of past good data may cause a currency pair to form an uptrend. Even though infrequent, worse than expected news should not be ignored, although this will not affect the general outlook of the situation. Hence, after an initial fall, you should look to buy the immediate response from the market.

In looking for long-term trading opportunities according on economic news, it is crucial to assess both the previous and current data. This is because there are instances that news may take weeks or months to be significantly absorbed by the market. You can use the information to see a larger picture and the impact that it may have on the currency you want to trade. The long term trends are built by fundamental factors that are founded on numerous economic pieces over a specific period of time.

For example, the currency pair GBP/USD has started an uptrend a year ago, and this trend continued ever since. On the other hand, EUR/GBP is following a falling trend for some time now. Take note that these trends have not started out right after.

This has been made possible by the economic data, which came out from Britain during the previous two years or even longer. Majority of the news was about the expected recovery of the economy of Britain long before the trend began to form. Through careful analysis and projection, a trader should have placed his bet on the British Pound and gained from around 2000 pips.

Market Momentum

All forex traders have their own style in trading - some may be bearish, and some may be bullish. Hence, market sentiment is the style of the different traders combined, which produces the general condition of the market.

There are instances that every indicator is pointing in a specific direction but the market is moving in the opposite. There are instances that the fundamental condition of the economy can be considered as bearish for a particular currency, and nevertheless, it keeps on fluctuating upwards in comparison with other currencies.

One example of this is the high movement of the USD/EUR that started in 2012 until early 2017. The European economy in general was not progressing with many member countries still suffering the effects of the recession, inflation falling, and political unrest in some countries. In the US, the economy was recovering in spite of the fair conditions in Europe, the currency pair still rises to an average of 1.40.

It is crucial for forex beginners to be familiar with market sentiment. You will not only be able to read the market sentiment in general, but you can also successfully trade and make profits not only in the foreign exchange market but also in other commodities as well. More often than not, the market sentiment is easy to analyze, because you only need to focus on the primary trend of a particular pair such as the good trend in EUR/USD between 2012 and 2014.

You will surely encounter some tips on forex trading on the importance of the trend as an indicator in forex trading. Somehow, this is true as the trend will allow you to find out the market sentiment. But there are times that trends can be difficult to read. For instance, a day trader who trades every 15 minutes to one hour, may see the trend pointing in single trend. But hours later, the trend may change and so you can lose money.

Trends can really change fast. The larger trends within the daily or four-hour chart could have been trending in the opposing direction, and so the trend that a day trader might be looking at could just be the larger trend's correction. Hence, before you place an order according to a lower chart timeframe, you have to check the larger charts first. Through this, you will be able to sense the market sentiment and find the pairs you can position your bets on.

Why Focus on One Currency Pair?

Focusing on a single currency pair one at a time is a good way to become familiar with the general market sentiment. Through this, you can gradually master reading currency pairs. Many lucrative forex traders are successfully trading according on their price action sense. In this strategy, you must keep track of how quick a specific pair is moving in two directions.

When the uptrend is quicker than the downtrend, it means that the market is more open to buy immediately, which indicates a more bullish general market sentiment. In addition, you can also monitor how a currency pair responds to financial news that is relevant for the currency pair.

For instance, if the economy in the UK is good, the GBP/USD could bounce up according to the recovering economic data. This signifies a more bearish general market sentiment.

The market sentiment can even be more bearish when the recent announcement in the economy has not yet progressed to form an uptrend.

If you are trading in stocks, you could assess traded volume since the stock market is focused on the stock floor. Take note that this is not true when it comes to forex market investing.

In the foreign exchange spot market, the ideal volume indicator is the COT or Commitments of Traders Report, which is released every 7:30 GMT Fridays. This report contains the net long and short trades of non-commercial and commercial trades in the futures forex market. By reading the COT, you could assess how the market players are positioning, which will have an impact on the forex market.

In general, going with the trend is the best form of trading in the forex market. Through this logic, it is clear that you sell when there are more net shorts, and you buy once there are more net longs. However, there are instances that it is ideal to just ignore the trend. If the buying signals are considered in the extremes, you might need to wait for a while or sell if needed.

If every trader has purchased in the market, there are very few traders who could buy, and so a currency will not be able to follow an uptrend if there is not enough buying activities. Hence, a reversal is imminent because the currencies could close the buying positions. It is also ideal to bet on this report or indicator for long term or medium trend trading, since it comes out every week. When you're into short-term trading, this report can help you in evaluating the trends.

Global Events

Monitoring worldwide events are crucial in sensing the mood of the market. Many of these events may happen on one continent and may seem irrelevant to a currency pair that you are trading. Nonetheless, the whole world is now connected thanks to the power of the Internet, and so any news that is considered globally significant has the possibility to have any impact on the market, especially in the foreign exchange market.

For instance, the rise of ISIS in the Middle East has a significant effect on leading currencies around the globe. When you think about it, CHF has in no way related to the crisis in the Middle East. But as a safe and stable currency, it has surged higher because of the fear of another world war.

In summary, market sentiment is a crucial indicator that you can use in trading in the foreign exchange market as well as other financial markets. All these indicators could establish the sentiment for traders to decide on their strategy.

This can be really challenging for a beginner, but if you want to be profitable in the forex market, it is crucial to have an in-depth learning and try these proven fundamental strategies.

At this point, you should have a basic idea on the general economic and fundamental concepts that form the basis of the foreign exchange market and affect the movement of the currencies.

A key concept that you should learn from this Chapter is that the countries and their currencies, like companies, are continuously changing their values according to fundamental indicators such as interest rates and economic progress. As a beginner in the forex market, you should also have an idea how specific economic factors could affect the currency of a country.

In the next chapter, we will discuss technical analysis as well as the related strategies on how to pick trades in the forex market by looking into the technical indicators.

Chapter 8 - Technical Analysis and Technical Strategies in Forex Trading

"What seems too high and risky to the majority generally goes higher and what seems low and cheap generally goes lower." - William O'Neil

Among the fundamental concepts of technical analysis is that the future price movement could be predicted by looking into past movements.

Because the foreign exchange market is a 24-hour market, you get a chance to assess a huge volume of data, which you can use to measure the price activity, which increases the statistical significance of the projection.

Many investors and traders in the forex market are using technical tools like indicators, charts, and trends.

In general, it is crucial to take note that technical analysis interpretation could stay the same regardless of the assets that you are keeping track. In this Chapter, we will discuss the most popular forex strategies based on technical analysis.

Currency Pair Movements

In doing technical analysis in the forex market, you need to determine if a currency pair may follow a trend in a specific spot, or if it has the probability to remain in the range or go against the trend.

A common way to figure out these traits is to place trend lines, which links previous market levels that have derailed the rate from rising up or declining.

These resistance and support levels are popular among "technicals" to find out if the current trend shall continue.

In general, most currency pairs like GBP/USD, USD/CHF, USD/JPY, and EUR/USD have demonstrated the best performances in the past.

On the other hand, the pairs that have shown better likability to follow the ranges are the pairs that don't involve the USD or known as the crosses.

Minimal Rate Inconsistency

There are different players in the foreign exchange market such as large banks and hedge funds. These large players are equipped with complex computer systems to continuously keep track of any inconsistencies between the various currency pairs.

With these programs, it can be rare to see any significant inconsistency to last longer than a matter of seconds. Many traders are using technical analysis because it presumes that all factors that could affect the currency rates such as psychological, social, political, and economic - have already been considered into the present exchange rate by the market.

With many players and with high volume of transactions every day, the trend as well as the capital flow becomes important instead of trying to determine a rate that is mispriced.

Technical Forex Indicators

Forex traders who prefer technical analysis use various indicators alongside resistance and support levels to help them in projecting the movement of the forex rates in the immediate future. Take note that understanding the different technical factors or indicators is crucial and may require further study on your part.

Among the indicators that you should learn well include stochastics, moving averages, Fibonacci retracement, and Bollinger Bands. Take note that these tools are not often used as an independent indicator but rather alongside chart patterns and other indicators.

Fibonacci Indicator

The Fibonacci Indicator is a common indicator used in technical analysis in the forex market. This strategy heavily depend on the pullback and to completely understand how this works, you should revisit your understanding of the forex trend.

In looking at every price action separately, it is quite difficult to look for a pattern. Taking a closer look at the larger picture will allow you to identify the trends.

For hundreds of years, the Fibonacci ratios and numbers have been popular among artists and mathematicians. These figures signify many things in mathematics, in nature, and even in the financial markets.

Although Fibonacci is a classic concept in mathematics, you don't need to be well adept in the subject so you can use these figures in calculating projections in the forex trading platforms. All you have to do is to make a decision according to the lines that appear on the charts.

By taking a closer look on how far the pullback has reached on the Fibonacci scale, we could figure out if the price could pull back again or turn into a bearish or bullish trend. As long as the price will remain above the specific line, you could expect the trends to pull back through a rising trend. When the price crosses the line, you should treat it as a beginning of a bearish trend that will indicate that it is time to close the position.

Horizontal Level Indicator

Horizontal Levels are among the most simple but quite useful concepts trading in the forex market. These are fundamentals in most forex trading strategies and could help you in studying charts. But you can also use them as a separate strategy instead of a mere tool to ride along with other strategies.

In monitoring the most clear-cut price actions and identifying the horizontal levels, you can make profitable trades. In completely becoming familiar with the horizontal levels of advanced charts, you can identify trends that you might have otherwise ignored.

Many forex traders regard horizontal levels as equally essential as price action that is ultimately regarded as the core of forex trading. Evaluating the integration of the change in price as well as the horizontal levels could allow you to be familiar with the trend and project the movement of the market. Even though horizontal levels could be a simple strategy in trading in the forex market, many popular forex traders like George Soros and Warren Buffet have recognized horizontal levels as a pillar for their strategies.

Horizontal levels could help you spot certain parts on a chart where the change on the trend could likely to happen. This could help you to decide where you could put a stop, or if you want to enter a trade, but you are not sure of the best time in doing so.

Take note that timing is critical in most trading strategies in the forex market and you should take extra caution in evaluating horizontal levels to find the proper time and position a good trade. Take note that horizontal levels are used as a basis for many other forex trading strategies, but when used separately, it is often not sufficient and should be used alongside other forex strategies.

The ideal method in using horizontal levels to your advantage is through the analysis of swing points, which refer to the points where there is a change in trends. By marking the horizontal levels on these places, you can find the prices where there could be a likely change in the trend.

Take note that swing points are more likely to recur themselves. Resistance levels could turn into support levels, and the other way around. When you mark the horizontal levels on your graph, you can project the next point of the swing will likely to happen and exit or enter a trade at the right time.

Ranging Market Indicator

Horizontal levels can be used in ranging markets, which refers to the condition in which the price has clear lower and upper boundaries.

By monitoring the price when it is approaching a limit, you can project with precision the points where the price could be more likely to continue the trend.

It can be hard to predict the price, and may even break down the boundary as you are deciding to enter the trade. But in general, this forex technical strategy is safe and very reliable.

In a chart, the horizontal levels will continue to rise and fall between distinct boundaries. You can mark the boundaries as horizontal levels so you could utilize them for your advantage.

Then, the next move is to wait for the moment that the price will go near the boundaries so you can finally place your trade. Remember, the price will unlikely jump over the horizontal level of the boundary, so you could place a trade hoping for a switch in the trend, and so the price could return to the horizontal level.

If the price is approaching an upper boundary, the trend is usually bearish and so the price will likely go down. On the other hand, when the rate is approaching a lower boundary, the trend is often bullish and an uptrend in the price may happen.

The reward and risk levels could also quite easy to select in this market type. The level of risk must be below or above the boundary that you have entered in the trade from, and the reward level must be on the opposing boundary of the ranging market.

Divergence Indicators

Aside from the market fundamentals, traders and market analysts are using several indicators to determine the price movements of a specific instrument.

Understanding these divergence indicators will provide you a basic approach of detecting patterns and projecting the price trends. Using these indicators is what makes signals in the forex market helpful, as you can use them for live analysis of price action.

Divergence is one such indicator, which can help you to significantly increase your profits in the forex market. The probability of entering in the correct direction at the best time could increase if you use this indicator alongside others such as support or resistance levels, stochastics, RSI, and moving averages.

Just by recognizing the name of the indicator, you could simply know that the divergent approach is a form of trading in deviation or disharmony. The indicators and prices normally follow in a similar direction and also at similar rates.

When the price reaches a high-high trend, the indicator must also reach a high-high trend, and if the price also reaches a low-high trend, then the indicator should follow as well. The same goes for higher lows and lower lows.

When the indicators and the price are not in harmony, then it can be true that some type of change will happen. Therefore, divergence is computed between the lows and highs of the prices. The ideal metrics for trading divergence are volumes, MACD, stochastics, and RSI.

Divergence could be easy to spot, as you only need to draw several lines in a chart. However, there are instances that traders are looking too hard at the charts, which makes them see things that are not actually helpful in making the trade.

For instance, when liquidity is low or during consolidation, some minor divergences between indicators and price could form. However, this doesn't mean you should consider them actual divergences.

Chapter 9 - Basic Forex Trading Skills You Need to Learn

"I think investment psychology is by far the more important element, followed by risk control, with the least important consideration being the question of where you buy and sell." – Tom Basso

There are many ways to become a successful forex trader. For example, if you want to be a forex trader under a financial firm, they usually hire people who have a strong background in the hard sciences, engineering, or math.

In starting your career as a forex trader, there are basic skills you need to learn. This includes the following:

1. Analytical skills
2. Research skills
3. Focus and Control
4. Money management
5. Psychology

Basic Trading Skills

Analytical thinking is a basic skill that every forex trader should have. You must be able to analyze the available data within a limited time frame.

Forex trading is a numbers game and the platform is filled with patterns, indicators, and charts that you need to analyze quickly. You also need to develop your analytical skills so you can easily identify trends in the forex market.

Reading Currency Quote

When you are quoting a currency, you are doing it in relation to the currency of another country in a way that the value is defined by the other currency's value. Hence, if you want to know the forex rate between the Swiss Francs (CHF) and Chinese Yuan (CNY), the forex quotation will look like this:

CHF/CNY = 6.95

This is known as the currency pair. In this pair, CHF is the base currency, while CNY is the counter currency. The former always has a value of one unit, and the latter is what that one base unit is equivalent in its denomination. This fx pair means that CHF1 =

6.95 Chinese Yuan. So if you have one Swiss Franc, you can buy 6.95 Chinese Yuan. Take note that the fx quote includes the currency symbol for the currency pairs.

You can quote a currency pair either indirectly or directly. An indirect quote is basically when the local currency is the base currency, while a direct quote is basically a forex pair wherein the domestic currency is the quote currency.

Therefore, if you are looking for the United States Dollar as the domestic currency and the Japanese Yen as the foreign currency, an indirect code will be JPY/USD, while a direct quote will be USD/JPY

In a direct quotation, the quoted currency could vary, while the base currency has a default value of one unit. Meanwhile, in the indirect quote, the domestic currency has a default value of one unit, while the foreign currency has a variable value.

For instance, if Japanese Yen is the domestic unit, a direct quote will be 109.37 USD/JPY, which means that 1 unit of USD can buy JPY 109.37. The indirect for this will be inverse (1/109.37), 0.0091 JPY/USD, which means with 1 JPY, you can buy USD 0.0091.

In the fx spot market, most currencies are traded against the USD, and this is often referred to as currency base. These are all direct quotes and true to the above CHF/CNY that indicates 1 CHF is equal to 6.95 CNY.

You must remember that not all currencies have the USD as the base. The currencies used by the British Commonwealth such as the New Zealand Dollar, Australian Dollar, and the British pound are all identified as the base currency against the USD. This is how we also quote the Euro. For these situations, the USD is positioned as the counter currency, and the fx rate is known as an indirect quote. Hence, EUR to USD is quoted as 1.19, because one unit of Euro can buy 1.19 USD.

The exchange currency rates are quoted up to four digits after the decimal place. One exception to this is the Japanese Yen, because this currency is quoted only up to two decimal places.

If a currency quote is given without the USD as a component, this is known as cross currency. The most popular cross currency pairs are the EUR/CHF, EUR/JPY, and the EUR/GBP. In general, currency pairs expand the trading horizons in the fx market. But you should bear in mind that they are not that much popular compared to the currency pair that uses USD as the base currency.

Buying and Selling Price

Like in stock markets, if you are trading currency pairs, you have to refer to the buying rate (bid) and the selling price (ask). Take note that these are still in relation to the base currency. If your strategy is to long (buying a currency pair) the asking price refers to the rate of quoted currency, which should be paid so you can purchase one unit of the base currency, or how much the market is willing to sell a unit of the base currency in reference to the currency quote.

On the other hand, when you go short (selling) a currency pair the bid rate signifies how much of the quoted currency you can get when you sell a unit of the base currency or how much the market is willing to shell out for the currency (quoted) in reference to the currency base.

Remember, the figure on the left of the slash is the bid rate, while the next two digits to the right of the slash are the asking price. Take note that it is customary to quote only the last two digits of the full price. The bid is also smaller compared to the asking price. Below is an example:

USD/CHF = 1.3000/05

Ask = 1.3005

Bid = 1.3000

Buying this fx pair signifies that you like to purchase the base currency, and so you have to refer to the asking price to know how much in Swiss Francs the market will charge for US dollars. Based on our asking price, you can purchase $ 1.00 with 1.3005 Swiss Francs, which is the currency that you are quoting.

But if you want to sell this fx pair or in other words you want to sell the currency base using the quoted currency, you have to refer to the bid. This signifies that the market will purchase $1 base currency for a price that is equivalent of 1.3000 Swiss Francs, which is the currency that you are quoting.

The base currency (whichever you are quoting first) always refer to the one in which we are conducting the transaction. This means, you can either buy or sell the currency base. You can refer to the specific currency pair rate in order to find the price depending on what currency you like to use for selling or buying the base with.

Research Skills

In trading in the forex market, you should not trade on an impulse. You must be confident with your strategy and you can do this through research. In the past, you can do a background check on the hottest currency pairs by reading books, newspapers, and other traditional forms of information sources.

But with the advent of the World Wide Web, there are now countless sources of information that you can use for your research. However, not all of these sources are reliable and can guide you to become successful forex traders. In choosing a source to consult, make certain that this covers the currency pairs to buy or if it is time to sell your currencies based on different factors such as technical and fundamental analysis.

There are also reliable newspapers and publications that you can read, which includes interpretation of global news and how the current events could affect the forex market. Forex trading involves revisiting past basic economics, because politics can also affect the behavior of forex players. Hence, it is crucial that you are updated with significant non-financial news from around the world.

In order to develop a solid foundation in forex trading, you must be updated with important technical and fundamental developments in the industry. Successful forex traders usually have a thirst for information as well as the drive to look for all relevant data, which could affect the trade.

Many traders even maintain a monitoring platform to keep up with major news breakthrough that can have considerable impact not only in the forex market but also in the global financial scene.

Focus and Control

Focus is another important skill for forex traders, which can increase the more that you practice it. With the emergence of numerous online resources promising to guide you on forex trading, you should be able to develop how to identify and focus your lens on the actionable trends that could affect your trade.

There are forex traders that are only focusing on specific types of currency pairs so they can put all of their efforts in projecting the movement of the trade. By focusing on these currencies, traders can develop competitive advantage compared to traders who don't focus on their trades.

Meanwhile, a successful trader should also learn how to control their emotions and follow specific strategy or trading plan. This is crucial in handling risks in forex trades by taking profits at specific points or using stop losses. There are strategies in place that allow traders to lose a bit on bad trades but gain more revenue from ideal trades. Bad traders are usually affected by their emotions, which influence the strategic implementation of their trading plan.

Risk Management

Risk Management is a skill that you should master to safeguard your trading capital from losses. This must be integrated in your trading strategy as early as you can in your forex trading career. Risk management covers strategies such as risk to reward, scaling trades, and stop losses. Mastering this skill will allow you to obtain higher profits and prevent losing money.

For instance, many successful traders don't risk more than 2 per cent of their funds in a single trade. This will safeguard your account from any significant downturn and will allow you to safely trade using leverage.

Psychology

Successful traders are not only adept in the mathematics behind the forex trading platform. They are also masters of understanding the psychology of people behind the trade. Aside from observing the possible behavior of market players, a forex trader should also overcome psychological aspects such as greed and fear.

In forex trading, you should learn how to follow the rules of the game without allowing your emotions to distract your game plan. It is not easy to become a successful forex trader, but if you work through your plan and master yourself, you can win the game through skills and discipline.

Chapter 10 - How to Set-up Your Forex Trading Account and Begin Trading

"It's not what we do once in a while that shapes our lives. It's what we do consistently."
–Anthony Robbins

At this point, you may feel that you can now begin to trade in the foreign exchange market.

Make sure that you understand this Chapter so you can learn the important steps to set-up forex account and then begin trading currencies.

We have also included other important considerations that you must understand before you open up your forex trading account.

Gearing Up With a Forex Practice Account

For beginners in the forex market, the best way to gear up in this new opportunity is to use a practice account.

Many online forex brokers provide free trials so you can sign up with a trading account and immediately experience real-time price action without spending your own real money first.

In most practice accounts, you will be provided with a virtual cash that you can make trades. The risk will be zero and you can take advantage of the experience as you learn how forex trading works.

With a practice account, you will actually see how prices fluctuate at different times of the day and you can see how currency pairs may vary from each other.

While trading in a practice account, you should alongside monitor the news relevant to the currencies you are trading. This will provide you an insight on how the forex market will react to news releases.

Aside from evaluating the market movement, you may also start trading in real-time conditions in the market without the risk of losing your money and you can also try various trading strategies to see if they work in your condition.

You can also improve your own understanding on how margin trading and leverage works and you can experience managing opening positions and you'll get a chance using various orders.

Most forex brokers will allow 30-day trials when you can also access charts and other technical supplements.

Before you sign up for a full membership, try to open practice accounts first with different forex brokers. Explore different features and capacities of these platforms. Also take note that different forex brokers have different trading policies.

Setting Up a Forex Trading Account

Forex trading is quite similar to stock market trading because you have first to open your own trading account. Similar to the stock market, every forex account as well as the services you can take advantage of can be different. Hence, it is crucial that you look for the most suitable platform for you. In this Chapter, we will discuss the important factors that you consider when you are choosing a foreign exchange account.

Trading Leverage

When we speak of leverage, we refer to the opportunity to take control of bigger amounts of cash with minimal capital from your own pocket. The leverage level is directly proportional to the risk level. Take note that the leverage amount on a platform could be different according to the features of the account on its own. However, the most popular one is the 50:1 leverage. Some accounts could offer a maximum leverage of 250:1.

For example, a maximum leverage of 100:1 signifies that in each dollar that you hold in the brokerage account, you can use up to $100. For instance, if you have an account balance of $100, the brokerage can allow you to trade as much as $10,000 in the fx. This leverage could also define the total amount that you can hold in your account or your margin for trading a specific amount. In the stock market, the margin is often at 50 per cent and the leverage could be 50:1, which can be at least 2 per cent.

In general, leverage is regarded as a primary advantage of trading in the foreign exchange market, because this will allow you to create substantial gains with minimal capital. But leverage could also have extreme downsides when a trade is moving in the opposite direction, because the losses could also be big.

With this leverage type, there is always the actual probability that your losses are higher than what you have invested, even though most accounts have safeguard stops to prevent the account from hitting negative. As such, it is crucial that you take note of this when you open a brokerage account, and once you identify your preferred leverage, you could understand the involved risks.

Fees and Commissions

Another major advantage of forex platforms is that investing through them could be done through a commission, which is unlike stock market accounts where you need to pay a broker a certain fee for every trade. You are now directly dealing with market players and you don't have to pass through another layer such as brokers.

Every time that you enter a trade, it is the market makers, which can seize the spread. Hence, when the ask/bid for a forex market is 1.5300/50, the market maker can capture between the difference between the points.

In setting up your own forex account, be sure to take note that every firm has various spreads on currency pairs that you trade. Even though they are usually different by only several pips, this could be substantial when you are planning to do a lot of trading. Hence, in setting up an account, be certain that you are aware of the pip and spread of specific currency pairs that you are interested in trading.

Other Factors

You must take note that there are several differences between every forex platform and the programs or software that they are offering. Hence, it is crucial to review every firm before you make a commitment. Every forex trading company may offer various levels of programs and services including the fees beyond and above the actual costs of trading. Moreover, because of the less strict conditions in the foreign exchange market, you should find a reliable firm. When you are also not completely confident to trade with real cash, you can also try trading in practice accounts or demos.

How to Start Trading in the Forex Market

After understanding the most crucial factors in opening your own forex account, it is time to look into what specifically you could trade within the platform. The two primary methods in trading in the forex market includes the actual trading (selling and buying) of forex pairs, in which you short a currency and long another.

Another method is via buying the derivatives that monitor the fluctuations of particular currency pair. These strategies are quite similar to the common techniques used in the stock market. Basically, buying and selling the currency pair is the most popular method, much in a similar manner that many traders are buying and selling currency units.

In this setting, a trader may hope that the currency pair's value will change in a profitable way. If you choose to short a pair, it signifies that you are betting on the possibility that the pair's value will fall. For instance, let's assume that you want a short position for the USD/JPY pair.

You can make profits when the value of the fx pair goes down, and you will lose your investment if it rises. This pair will rise if USD increases its price against the JPY, therefore it is actually a trust on the JPY.

Another alternative is to use futures and options, which are derivative products, so you can make money from the currency value changes. If you purchase a currency pair option, you can gain the privilege to buy a pair on a specific rate prior to a setting of point.

Meanwhile, a futures forex contract could build the agreement to purchase the currency pair at a specific point. These trading strategies are often employed by more experienced traders, but as a beginner, you should be aware of them.

Order Types

In looking for a new trading position, you may have to use a market order or a limit order, which are actually similar when you are placing a new position in the stock market. A market order can provide you the capacity to acquire the currency at specific exchange rate that it is presently trading in the foreign exchange market. On the other hand, the limit order will allow you to identify a specific entry price.

If you are already holding an open position in the market, you may have to consider employing a take profit order, so you could lock in your gains. For instance, let us assume that you are already sure that the USD/GBP will react at 1.8700, but you are not completely certain that the price will rise any higher. You can use a take-profit order that will immediately close your position if the price hits 1.8700, which will lock in your profits.

The stop loss order is also a tool that you can use when you want to hold the open positions. This will allow you to figure out if the price could decline prior to the closing of the position and more losses could be accumulated. Hence, if the USD/GBP rate starts to drop, the investor may put a stop-loss, which could halt the position to avoid any further loss.

When you are also trading in the stock market, you will realize that the order types that you could enter in the forex trading accounts are quite similar. It is crucial to be familiar with these orders before you actually place your very first trade in the foreign exchange market.

Conclusion

Congratulations for finishing this book until the end.

At this point, you should already have enough understanding of forex trading and figure out if this is a suitable revenue channel for you.

Hopefully, the lessons that you have learned in this book will help you become a successful forex day trader and have a prosperous career.

As a summary, I would like you to remember the following pointers that we have discussed in this book:

- The forex market is the product of important historical events that result in designating USD as the primary reserve currency to replace gold. This is the reason why major currencies are always pitted against the dollar.
- At its core, forex trading is all about speculating the value of one currency against another. Similar to trading stocks or other financial instruments, forex trading is speculative with the hope that it will increase its value and you as a trader will make a profit.
- In the forex market, it is always important to be mindful of liquidity, which refers to the market interest level or the level of trading volume available at any point in time for a specific asset or security. The deeper or the higher the liquidity, the easier and faster it is to trade a security.
- Forex trading involves trading currency pairs with names that involve two different currencies. Currency pairs have nicknames or abbreviations that refer to the pair but does not necessarily involve the individual currencies.
- At any given moment, any number of real-world forces are at work in the forex market. This includes geopolitical events, interest rate decisions, and economic data.
- The primary economic theories found in the forex market are more about the parity settings. Basically, parity refers to the economic justification of the price at which the currency pairs must be traded according to important factors such as interest rates and inflation.
- In the stock market, fundamental analysis measures the true value of a company. A fundamentalist (one who mainly use fundamental analysis) base his decision to invest or trade in stocks according to the calculation.
- Many investors and traders in the forex market are using technical tools like indicators, charts, and trends.

- In starting your career as a forex trader, there are basic skills you need to learn. This includes analytical skills, research skills, focus and control, financial management, and psychology.
- Forex trading is quite similar to stock market trading because you have first to open your own trading account. Similar to the stock market, every forex account as well as the services you can take advantage of can be different. So, it is important that you look for the most suitable platform for you.

While this beginner's guide is only a small glimpse of all you need to know about forex trading, I hope that you have gained enough insight into this subject.

I also encourage you to learn more about the intricacies of the forex world and currency pairs that you want to trade. You must continue the best strategies that are suitable for you.

Thanks again, and good luck!

Book#3
Swing Trading Simplified

The Fundamentals, Psychology, Trading Tools, Risk Control, Money Management, And Proven Strategies

Introduction

Swing trading is a technique used in financial trading where the trader focuses on a longer—typically several days to several weeks—trading period than a day trader, and a shorter trading period than an investment trader. As its name suggests, the swing trader will generally focus on a single swing in the price trend whether that be in a positive or negative direction. This focus on a single swing in price direction allows the trader to concentrate on forecasting short-term price trending behaviors by using techniques such as price chart analysis, oscillators, and candlesticks.

In this book we will strive to educate you on the key principles required to be a successful swing trader in the financial market: Fund management, selecting the right security to trade, price forecasting strategy, and chart pattern recognition.

This book is designed for beginners who want to learn the skills of swing trading, with a primary focus on low risk as well as great technical strategies that will help you profit!

Chapter 1 - Introducing Swing Trading

What is Swing Trading?

As stated earlier, swing trading is a technique used in financial trading where the trader focuses on a longer—typically several days to several weeks—trading period than a day trader, and a shorter trading period than an investment trader. As its name suggests, the swing trader will generally focus on a single swing in the price trend whether that be in a positive or negative direction. This focus on a single swing in price direction allows the trader to concentrate on forecasting short-term price trending behaviors by using techniques such as price chart analysis.

Types of Financial Traders

There are three main categories for financial traders: Institutional traders, retail traders, and market setters.

Institutional traders work (as the name suggests) for large financial organizations that trade in heavy volumes. Because of their financial clout, they can have a huge effect on the market's direction.

Retail traders are smaller in size and make relatively small trades through a broker; this is the group that beginners like you will be classified in. As a beginner, you shouldn't need to concern yourself too much with either the institutional or the market setters, as you will be playing to different strategies to the big market traders.

Market setters are big-time traders who will make very large trades typically outside of normal business hours because they want to set the prices for stocks and indexes. However, as a beginner swing trader, you are unlikely to be affected by the market trend setters' influences, as you will likely be trading in lower cost stocks or options. However, if you are trading in currencies and derivatives, then market setters are an integral component of the system. This is because banks and governments will always be very influential in their currency's trading value being maintained between ideal thresholds.

There are also three types of traders: An investment or position trader, who takes a long-term position on a stock or currency, for example, expecting to make a long-term profit; a swing trader, who takes a medium-term position, which is typically days to weeks; and the day trader, who works for a few hours at most on any given day, and closes all trades at the end of each day.

Now, all three of these types of traders require distinct skills, strategies, and tools. As we are focused only on swing trading in this book, we will confine ourselves to the swing trading niche. However, it is well worth knowing what the key differences are between the three types. An investment trader will take long-term positions only after they have done extensive research on the financial instrument in question, such as the company's stock and its financial health. An investment trader typically works for wealthy clients or large institutions, such as fund and wealth managers.

Day traders, on the other hand, are a mix of institutional and retail traders, as these are the ones who trade on those short fluctuations in prices. Day trading requires incredible focus, heavy financial reserves, and nerves of steel. Day trading is a high-risk environment, as things can and do go wrong very quickly—of course, they can also go very right just as quickly, so it can bring very high rewards.

Finally, swing trading falls somewhere between the highly methodical, diligently researched, and knowledge-based decision-making in the field of investment trading to the highly dynamic, frenetic, high-risk, gut-feeling decision-making of the day trader.

Consequently, as a beginner swing trader, you can have the best of both worlds. What this means is that you will be spared some (but certainly not all) of the traditional research, stress, and high risk. However, you also do not have all of the investment security or potential high-profits, so you will also fall somewhere in between the other two trading disciplines.

Swing Trade Opportunities

There are many opportunities and potential markets for swing trading. Probably the most popular financial markets are stocks and shares, currencies, indexes, cryptocurrencies, and options. These trading entities are called *financial instruments*. However, there are many others such as futures, commodities, and many types of derivatives. A derivative is a financial instrument that accumulates its value from the components that it is built upon, such as a group of diverse stocks. In short, there are no limits to the number of financial instruments that are available for swing trading. After all, the money markets are continually dreaming up new trading instruments because that is how financial markets traditionally make their money and compete with the opposition.

In this book we will cover most of these financial instruments and their markets from the perspective of the beginner retail trader.

How Much Do You Need to Start Trading?

This is the first question that many beginners ask so it is important to get it out of the way early, as many beginners have unrealistic expectations. Unfortunately, the answer is often, "Well, it depends." The trouble is it depends so much on your own expectations, appetite for risk, and the time and financial commitment you are willing to make. Generally, a swing trader will need a minimum of around $5,000 to have any realistic prospect of longevity in the market. This is not as bad as a day trader's starting capital, as they would need cash reserves at a minimum of $15,000 to have any chance of lasting even a few months without being wiped out.

Now, this is where there is much debate, as some will have you believe that you can begin trading on some financial markets with as little as $100 to $1,000. This is true and feasible with trading indices and currencies since typically you are not actually trading anything you own, or even partially own—you are simply betting on the market direction. An example of this is with the hugely popular Forex market, where beginners can open an account and start betting on the performance of currency pairs with as little as $100. The harsh reality is that you are very unlikely to survive for very long with that amount of capital. Realistically, even on Forex or when trading indices, you will need a minimum of $5,000 if you want to still be trading in the market in six months to a year's time.

Another problem you will likely encounter includes having insufficient capital, where you will be limited with the types of financial instruments and the size of the trade that you can effectively work with. For example, in equity trading you can only afford the less popular stock, or on Forex, it will force you to take smaller positions in currency trading—but that will produce meaningless profits after commissions, at the same risk as a larger bet. In short, the more capital you have the more opportunity you have, and the greater the buffer against ruin should the market turn against you.

Many people are surprised at the size of the reserve funds required, but to buy a good position regardless of the financial instrument concerned requires a hefty investment and markets can change rapidly. For example, if you have the funds to buy premier stock such as Amazon, Google, Microsoft, or Apple, amongst many others, then you have a much greater chance of success. This is because these stocks have high volatility and high volumes of sales. So even if there is a sudden drop in price there will always likely be a buyer available, perhaps not at the price you want but reasonably close to it. On the other hand, if you are dealing in cheaper less popular stocks with low volatility and low volumes then you might find getting a buyer much more difficult. Something to always remember is that in contrast to how the movies depict financial markets you cannot cry out, "Sell, sell, sell!" and magically have a buyer at hand. The inconvenient truth is you can only sell at a price if there is someone willing to buy at that price. So, if you hold positions in less popular and falling stocks, particularly if they are in the same category, such as Tech, then you are likely (if you don't have sufficient reserves) to be wiped out very quickly indeed.

Furthermore, that $5k is your capital and your reserve so you must only take an ideal 1% to a 3% maximum position at any time. This is to conserve your capital and to make sure that losses can be recovered more easily. This will be covered under fund management in detail in its own chapter.

The harsh financial reality is that if you don't have $5k that is considered to be disposable income, then swing trading isn't likely to be for you. Certainly there are far better ways to invest your money, such as in investment trading. Having said that, if you do have ready capital that you can afford to lose then swing trading can be a very profitable way to trade in financial investments.

Chapter 2 - Fund Management

Preserving your fund is paramount to successful swing trading, and you must be diligent about understanding and handling basic fund management techniques. This is probably the single most important lesson that you can learn, as it can prevent you from being wiped out early on. Moreover, it can also be the difference with not just trading longevity but whether or not you make a profit.

The basic principles for diligent fund management are straightforward, but generally rejected by most beginners in financial trading. Swing traders are no exception, and far too many beginners start out taking on so much that they cannot possible sustain if the market turns against them. It's not unusual to see beginners investing 50% or more when buying into a position. Well, that is a recipe for disaster! So if you learn nothing else from this book, at least try to understand the necessity and basic concepts of fund management that we will describe in this chapter.

Basic Fund Management Principles

It is important that when you trade in the financial markets you don't overcommit the amount of money that you invest in each trade. This is necessary in order to manage risk because putting too much money on one position is very dangerous. This is because a poor trade can wipe out a large percentage of your brokerage trading account—your available capital fund—should the trade go the wrong way. It only takes a few poor trades without proper risk management to blow up your trading account entirely.

This is why experienced traders perform fund management in order to manage the risk. They will risk no more than ten percent, but you as a beginner should risk no more than three percent of your account per trade. It is recommended that you should actually go below that and invest one to two percent per trade at first, but feel free to do even less. The only problem is that buying suitable positions will become limited, especially with trading stocks, as they are traded in lots of 100 shares. This 1-2% limit will certainly curtail your opportunity for investing in premier stocks at that amount of capital per trade. For example, to trade in Microsoft at today's price of $134.36 would require an investment of $13,436 (100 x 134.36). Such a single trade would require, under best practices, that you have a fund capital of a whopping $1,343,600. And this is what can put many beginners off of using the 1% rule and instead they will trade at 10%—that means they only need a capital of $134,360, which for most is feasible for such a premium stock. The rationale being that premier stocks, even if they dive by 10%, will eventually rebound but it might take six to twelve months for that to happen. In the meantime, you are stuck with overpriced stock that will tie up capital for the duration of its recovery. This in itself, though not fatal to your position, will present you with missed opportunities, as your capital is locked up, so you are no longer in a position to seize the opportunity of buying other stocks that might in the interim become available at very attractive prices.

However, it is important to understand that it is not always the traders with the largest positions (and some of the largest profits) who will come out in front at the end of the day; it's often the careful trader who makes the best percentage trades, by using fund management skills, that will allow them to last for a long time in the market.

Fund management is a critical skill in financial trading, as everyone will certainly have their share of loss, which is especially true of beginners. The difference between experienced traders and beginners is that the former will invest while knowing there is always the possibility that the trade may go wrong and that the stock will move in the opposite direction of what they initially forecasted. As a result, experienced traders, or rather, *successful* traders, will know they have no control over where the stock prices move.

Consequently, successful traders will adhere to fund management and take a pragmatic approach by spreading their investments in smaller amounts over a diversified number of stocks. But it is also important that you diversify across categories. This is critical because the way the stock market operates is with stock categories seeming to work almost in synchronization, so if the category index should go up, nearly every member's investment in that category will follow suit. However, should the category index fall, then investments are likely to fall with it. Diversifying across categories enables a trader to hedge their bets against the risk of one stock taking a significant downturn, which will negatively impact the rest of the category as well as lock up a significant portion of their capital.

What is also important is that you do not trade with money that you can't afford to lose—for example, your pension plan. Financial trading does provide the opportunity to incur profit, especially when trading premier stocks, currencies, etc., however, whatever you may have read about financial trading, it is not free money and it's very risky. If your finances dictate that you cannot afford to lose your investment, then consider it to be a *very* high-risk endeavor. Remember that you can go a long way in trading with a mediocre trading strategy so long as you are careful with preserving your funds. It is almost guaranteed that you will likely go broke with a great trading strategy but poor fund management.

Developing a Trading Strategy

To recap, having a good trading strategy is not nearly as important as having a sound fund management policy. What's even better is having them work together in harmony. Ideally, as a beginner, you need the trading strategy to cover all trading fundamentals, such as discounting many of the prevalent myths regarding trading. You may have heard the phrase, "Buy low, sell high," which is fine if taken literally but it also naturally encourages beginners to seek out underperforming stocks in order to look for big wins. The fallacy here is that those underperforming stocks will typically stay that way, and what you should be searching out is affordable over-performing stocks. The experienced traders do not go looking for unknown under-performers; instead, they back proven winners. What this means is that the closer that a stock has to having a consistent long-term 52-week high, then the more likely it will remain that way. This is, of course, contradictory to the "buy low, sell high" saying.

However, it is not as simple as comparing the stock relative strength indicator (RSI) as if we would all be millionaires. You still need to know what to do when the market turns against you—and the stock's momentum changes direction. It is at this point that we need to have a strategy for knowing when to cut any losses.

Know When to Exit a Trade

Knowing when to cut losses by exiting a deal is just as important as knowing which position to take up in the first place. Failing to act decisively can result in runaway losses whereby you end up holding stock no one wants to buy. Remember, losses can take a long time to make good; for example, a 50% loss of capital takes a 100% gain to make good. Therefore, you should sit down and draw up an exit strategy, which clearly defines at what level of loss you consider acceptable, then set limits for your exit and stick by them.

Now of course comes the tricky bit, which is deciding how much to invest. We know that the best practices in fund management will restrict us to betting 1-3% of the trading account. But here is the problem: 1% may restrict both the stock you can buy and the potential losses, but profits will likely be less than what you were expecting—especially when you take commission into account. However, the maximum of 3% may be less of a constraint on trading and more profitable, but potential losses are much higher, so it really comes down to your own Risk/Reward appetite.

Know How Much to Trade

The Risk/Reward ratio is typically set at 2:1, 3:1—or for the gamblers at heart—sometimes even 1:1. But it's only a risk formula and to understand how it works in practice you need to look into the Risk of Ruin (RoR) formula. When we study the RoR in fund management we can see how critical it is in ensuring that the numbers go in your favor.

The RoR is a statistical model, which gives you an indication of the probability that you will lose all of your account based upon your win/loss % and how much % of capital (risk) that you put on each trade. This formula is absolutely critical to know; for example, if you decide to risk 10% of your capital per trade, and say you have a 2:1 Reward to Risk ratio (R:R), but you also have an accuracy rate of only 35%, then you may not realize that means you also have a 60.8% chance of losing all your money.

Risk of Ruin is basically the probability that you'll lose so much money you can no longer continue trading. This doesn't actually mean you will lose your entire capital fund, as the ruin point is subjective and based on your own personal risk appetite. Therefore, it depends a lot on what level of loss you would consider a state of ruin to be—it could be 15%, 50%, or even 100%.

RoR% with 1% capital at risk					
Win Ratio %	Payoff Ratio 1:1	PR 2:1	PR 3:1	PR 4:1	PR 5:1
Win Ratio 10%	100	100	100	100	100
Win Ratio 15%	100	100	100	100	100
Win Ratio 20%	100	100	100	100	0.0485
Win Ratio 25%	100	100	100	0	0
Win Ratio 30%	100	100	0	0	0
Win Ratio 35%	100	0.701	0	0	0
Win Ratio 40%	100	0	0	0	0
Win Ratio 45%	100	0	0	0	0
Win Ratio 50%	100	0	0	0	0
Win Ratio 55%	0	0	0	0	0
Win Ratio 60%	0	0	0	0	0
Win Ratio 65%	0	0	0	0	0
Win Ratio 70%	0	0	0	0	0
Win Ratio 75%	0	0	0	0	0
Win Ratio 80%	0	0	0	0	0
Win Ratio 85%	0	0	0	0	0
Win Ratio 90%	0	0	0	0	0

Now let us compare the RoR at 10% to demonstrate the difference.

Risk of Ruin Formula Using 10% Risk/Trade

ROR% with 10 capital at risk					
Win Ratio %	Payoff Ratio 1:1	PR 2:1	PR 3:1	PR 4:1	PR 5:1
Win Ratio 10%	100	100	100	100	100
Win Ratio 15%	100	100	100	100	100
Win Ratio 20%	100	100	100	100	46.6
Win Ratio 25%	100	100	100	30.5	16.3
Win Ratio 30%	100	100	27.7	10.2	6.1
Win Ratio 35%	100	60.9	8.2	3.53	2.33
Win Ratio 40%	100	14.2	2.5	1.24	0.888
Win Ratio 45%	100	3.41	0.761	0.426	0.329
Win Ratio 50%	100	0.813	0.226	0.141	0.116
Win Ratio 55%	13.4	0.187	0.0635	0.0438	0
Win Ratio 60%	1.73	0.0401	0	0	0
Win Ratio 65%	0.205	0	0	0	0

Win Ratio 70%	0	0	0	0	0
Win Ratio 75%	0	0	0	0	0
Win Ratio 80%	0	0	0	0	0
Win Ratio 85%	0	0	0	0	0
Win Ratio 90%	0	0	0	0	0

There are several Risk of Ruin calculators available online that you can use to calculate your risk.

Knowing How to Identify a Trade

This might seem to be a bit like putting the cart before the horse, since we've already discussed both how to *exit* a trade and how *much* to trade, before considering how to *identify* a trade. But that is really to ensure that you understand the importance of having an exit strategy as well as having sound fund management in place before you even think of entering into a trade. Surprisingly, despite this advice, too many beginners just jump in and start trading with no exit strategy, no fund management, and worse—no expectations of what profit they want! This is why we must take time in **identifying** our trades regardless of the types of financial instruments utilized. This is important because we must have profit targets set or we are likely to miss opportunities to exit if we stay too long or miss profit targets due to exiting too early. Remember, this is a balance between fear and greed.

Depending on the financial instrument you are trading, some of the tools you will use for identifying good trades will differ due to specialization. Nonetheless, along with specialist tools are a few common methods, such as financial charts, that are relevant to almost all of them. Reading charts is a skill that almost all experts agree on as being invaluable to identifying good trades, but they rarely occur. This is because basic chart analysis (i.e. looking for trends and basic historical performance data) is hugely valuable as is comparing recent trades. However, almost all the information that you can get as a beginner from analyzing a chart is readily available to you through other means. For example, you can find out the last highest sell/buy, the previous day's closing, the spread between buy/sell, the trade volume and trade interest, current open trades, velocity, and much more simply by reading the stock ticker. These are constantly updated throughout the day for most financial securities—currencies, stock, options, indexes, etc.—by the exchanges, so the information is pretty close to real time.

So understanding how to read a securities ticker is more important to the beginner than learning to analyze charts. This is so because the ticker contains all the information that you could possibly extract from your analysis of a chart, but with far less scope for error. Nonetheless, charts do have their uses, especially for identifying trends at a glance. And this leads us to another very important maxim of trading for beginners: Never bet against a trend!

Bet With the Trend

"Trade with the trend, always go with the flow" is sage advice that many successful traders adhere to. There is good reason for following this advice as a beginner. The best place to identify trends is by analyzing a chart, which incidentally comes with the ticker, or will be provided by the exchange or your broker's trading platform.

Example of a Ticker for Microsoft Stock, Showing a Six-Month Timeline

We will discuss tickers and chart analysis in more detail later in the book. For now, it's just important to understand the need to be prepared before you enter a trade. For example, in the above six-month example, it shows a steady upwards trend that might look pretty appetizing to the beginner (albeit one with a large trading account). But the devil is often in the detail and if we focus in on our time period of interest—a one-month timeline—then we will see somewhat of a different picture.

The takeaway here is to be careful, when judging trends, that you select the correct timeline for your prospective trade. Day traders, for example, use 5-minute charts, but a beginner swing trader should be looking at the 5-day or one-month timelines. As you can see, the one-month chart clearly shows a sharp fall in price on the 24th of June, which is absorbed within the general upwards trend in the six-month general trend sample. But that stock volatility could have also been seen more clearly in the 5-day trading chart (see below).

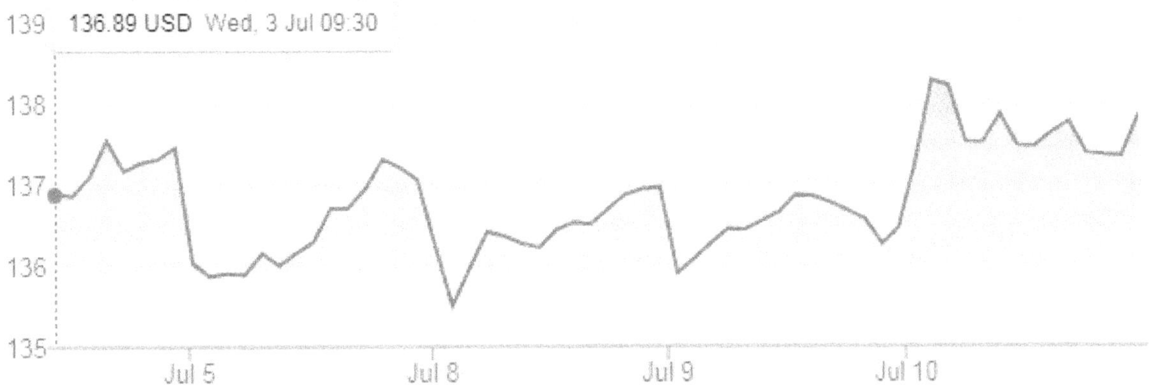

The intricacies of chart analysis will be covered in its own chapter later on, but for now let's focus on basic chart reading skills rather than in-depth analysis.

What we can clearly see from the 5-day ticker chart is the trading volatility, as the price is fluctuating between $135 and $138, which is a $3 movement over the five-day period. This means plenty of scope for profits—this would be a good stock to swing trade if you can afford it. If you cannot then don't despair as there are options, which are financial instruments that allow you to trade on premier stock at a fraction of the stock price. This is because you do not own the stock, you simply have an option to buy after a predetermined time at a fixed price. This reduces the cost of trading in premier stocks significantly. There is also the choice of indexes, where you might trade on a category or a portfolio of stocks, which in this scenario would include Microsoft.

Charts Can Be Ambiguous

Many a risk manager will tell you to focus on the trend and the results will follow. The problem is that trends are built upon historical data, so understanding them isn't something you'll find on the Internet or in books—but based on your own experience over the years.

It is crucial to find a trading methodology that suits your own trading instincts as it has to be a trading approach that is in line with your market beliefs. For example, if you have faith in historical trends, then making decisions based upon trends would lead you towards technical analysis and the analysis of chart patterns. However, should you have faith in market momentum, then the breakout trading strategy might suit you better.

Regardless, you must develop your trading strategy that will highlight what your trading plan should be:

- What are the ambitions for your trading?
- Which timeframes (a week, a month, etc.) are you going to trade?
- How will you set limits so you can exit your trades appropriately?
- How will you manage your trades?
- How much are you willing to risk on each position?
- Which markets and financial instruments will you trade?
- How will you enter your preferred trades?
- How are you going to execute your trades consistently?

This is where trading discipline will come into play, as there is no point in making a plan if you have no intention of seeing it through. One way to do this is to build up a sample of results based upon, for example, at least 100 trades so you can get a decent sample size, and then record and analyze the performance against your trading strategy. After all, there are few successful traders who do not record and analyze their trades. As in any discipline, whether it be sports or academia, if you want to improve then you need to know what you've done wrong. And the only way to find out is to record and analyze all of your trades!

Analyze Your Trades

If you have diligently adhered to your trading strategy, then it is likely that you have either become a consistently profitable trader or unfortunately an unlucky loser. Whatever the case, so long as you followed your plans then you are at a level where 95% of beginner traders will never be.

If you are still finding yourself on the losing side of the game then this is where you turn your losing experience and knowledge into valuable information. This is because now you will have a wealth of hard-earned experience and rich data within your trading charts, and all that additional market information that can help identify where you went wrong.

So, during your analysis, ask yourself these pertinent questions:

- Are there similar patterns that you can identify that are leading to losses?
- Is there any filter you could put in place to prevent a reoccurrence?
- Are you trading against the trend?

Just like with analyzing winning trades, you are likely to surface things that have a high probability of causing these wins or losses to occur repeatedly. Then it's a case of identifying the problems with your trading strategy. Now go back and tweak your trading plan and improve it until it becomes a winning one!

It's fine if you have a diversified equity portfolio. However, if you are trading Forex currency, for example, then it doesn't really help you. As a Forex trader you are a victim of circumstance since all the patterns in the charting world may be converging brilliantly. But that is not going to save you from a world leader suddenly making a political gaffe that sends their currency plummeting—along with your stake.

Know When to Enter a Trade

It's best to be conservative and once you have identified your exit price, your target profit, and of course your financial instrument of choice (which in our example was Microsoft stock), it will be time to plan your entry into the market.

Entering the Market

Now considering that we are interested in swing trading (taking a short-term position to leverage stock price volatility over a single wave of price fluctuation in order to lift profit), it is critical that we enter the trade at the optimum price. This is where basic stock ticker or chart reading skills come into their own because what we are looking for over and above the general trend is the points of resistance and support.

If you consult the five-day chart again for Microsoft stock, you will see there are peaks and troughs clearly visible, which are the price highs and lows. The lowest and highest points are called the *points of support* and *resistance*, respectively. What this means is that the market's (wisdom of crowds) belief is that the price should be no lower (support) or go no higher (resistance) and this is where we see these recurring ripples in the upwards trend. Remember, a very important thing a trade requires is a buyer willing to buy at a price and a seller will to sell at that price. So what we are seeing in these peaks and troughs is a reflection of market optimism and the health of the market. Since the price falls sometimes quite precipitously (i.e. on June 8th in our 5-day graph, to $135), this is where traders rush in to support the stock by placing bids to buy. This rush of trades to buy causes the direction to change and it climbs throughout the day to $137. At this point the market sentiment changes and they are resistant to buying at a higher price so it initially stabilizes before changing direction once more (and during June 8th it falls sharply to $136 before it is supported by traders willing to buy). The support and resistance points are very important to recognize so you can enter into a trade in a good position.

The process we've just explored are very sound methods for beginners to try before going on to the more advanced topics, such as chart and technical analysis. Many very experienced and successful traders use only the basic techniques we have described in this chapter.

Chapter 3 - Knowing What Financial Instrument to Trade

There is an abundance of financial instruments to choose from. Each market and exchange strives to create new and innovative products all the time, as they are differentiators in the competitive financial marketplace. However, we will only deal with the ones more suited for the beginner swing trader.

The Financial Market

The financial market consists of billions of people around the world who are trading a wide variety of financial instruments for one purpose: to make a profit. Such is the competition between exchanges that they have developed a vast variety of financial instruments to trade. Financial instruments basically fall into five broad categories: Indices, Equities, Commodities, Bonds, and Forex. Nonetheless, there are many factors that you as a beginner will need to consider before trading in any of these.

Factors in Selecting Financial Instruments

There are several key factors that a beginner in swing trading should consider when selecting a financial instrument to trade. There are a few common sense things such as personal experience, knowledge, or even just a keen interest in that particular instrument, that will always make trading (or at least the research) a lot more tolerable. We must not forget that research is critically important to success when working with almost all financial instruments, as charts and historical data can only get you so far. The art of forecasting, along with implementation, can assist with forming better trading decisions, which will in turn lead to knowledgeable predictions. Moreover, forecasting should not be guesswork, it should always be founded on research; that's one factor that separates the successful from the failed traders.

Regardless of the type of financial instrument, you should look for these general properties:

- **Liquidity** – This is a measure of the interest in and the ease of buying and selling the financial instrument at any given time. It's best to go for instruments that have high levels of liquidity because this makes them easier to trade and you can also enter and exit a position with ease.
- **Volatility** – This property in a financial instrument refers to its tendency to rise and fall sharply. That property is what enables profits in day and swing trading. High volatility allows traders to generate profits. However, with some instruments, such as

in option trading, a small difference in exit time during a period of high volatility can lead to high losses.

- **Low Transactions Costs** – Regardless of which financial instrument you choose, it must have low transaction costs, as that is the crucial property that allows you to generate profits on marginal trades. Brokers charge a different trading fee for different financial instruments and in swing trading, where you may be working with a portfolio of financial instruments on a high trading turnover basis, the commission rates per trade will be significant.
- **Availability of Research** - Research is necessary if you are going to survive and have a profitable trading career. Hence you will need a freely available flow of up-to-date information on the instrument you are going to be trading.

Top Five Financial Instruments

Forex

The Foreign Exchange (Forex) market is the largest market in the world and it accounts for more than $4 trillion in average daily volume. As a result, there is a large variety of financial instruments to trade. There is also a Micro-Forex and Mini-Forex, which allows you to trade small volumes and with less capital than the standard Forex, which makes them ideal for beginners.

You should be aware that the trading of foreign exchange is actually the trading of currencies. This instrument takes advantage of those changes in the exchange rates between different currencies. Therefore, currencies are paired and prices compared. By far the most popular Forex instruments are the currency pairs of the biggest economies such as instruments for the EUR/USD, GBP/USD, USD/JPY, and USD/CHF, amongst several others.

Forex instruments are popular to trade by beginners particularly because of their relative stability. There is also the advantage that Forex instruments are traded 24/5, which also makes them ideal for beginners who might also have full time jobs. Furthermore, many Forex brokers will provide a significant amount of leverage that makes it easy for beginners with limited funds to place a trade.

Forex instruments are also ideal for swing trading as they tend to offer high liquidity and they also tend to have high levels of volatility, especially with the major currency pairs. This makes it easy for traders to take advantage of short-term price swings.

One issue with Forex is that currency fluctuations come about through often indiscriminate and unpredictable global politics and events rather than through traditional financial metrics (trade, inflation, interest rates, unemployment), so volatility is practically assured. Unfortunately, this makes research and making knowledgeable predictions very difficult because currency rates are determined by market sentiment—and if the majority of the market doesn't care for the latest employment figures (a development with Brexit or the latest news regarding a US trade dispute), currency prices can fluctuate wildly within milliseconds. This lack of insight into why currencies can soar or plummet with seemingly little reason is what gives Forex its tremendous volatility, but it also makes it very risky. Despite this, it is still a very popular instrument for beginner swing traders and there is a wealth of information freely available. The only caveat would be the lack of research, and stay away from non-mainstream currencies unless you are an expert on those economies. Unfortunately, even if you are, you might find commission fees to be uneconomical.

Trading Forex

So, the Forex works by pairing currencies in order to make a direct comparison of performance of one currency in the pair relative to the other currency. It is based upon currency exchange rates, where we buy or sell currencies dependent on their relative value.

The exchange can be best demonstrated by considering how currency exchange actually works in practice. For example, if you are going on a trip to Europe and you require Euros then you would go to the bank and buy Euros by exchanging your US dollars. The bank, on the other hand, is in effect doing the opposite as it is buying your US dollars and selling you Euros at a stipulated sell price. Now when you return and you want to exchange those surplus Euros back to US dollars, you would go to the bank once again but this time you would sell those Euros and buy US dollars. The bank once again takes the opposite perspective, as it is buying Euros and selling US dollars at a stipulated buy price. However, currencies have different respective values so it is not a one-for-one exchange and this is why there are exchange rates. Regardless, in both directions the exchange is determined by the current currency exchange rate which fluctuates, albeit minutely, over the course of the day.

Therefore, with Forex the major currencies, such as the US dollar, Euro, Sterling, Swiss Franc, Canadian dollar, Australian dollar, and the Japanese Yen, are paired together and their respective exchange rates compared. Now, as a Forex trader, you are going to be betting on one currency in the pair outperforming the other. So if you choose to trade the Euro against the dollar (EUR/USD), then you would be betting that the Euro would strengthen against the US dollar. The way you make the trade is that you would select the EUR/USD pair, then you would either buy Euros if you thought the Euro would strengthen against the dollar, which is said to be going long, or you would sell the Euro if you believed it would weaken against the dollar, which is said to be going short. Remember, the strength or weakness of the currencies is relative to the paired currency—nothing else matters. So the way the Forex works is that you gain the difference in the movement of the currency price that you have bought if it has strengthened against its paired currency. Or you lose the difference in the movement of the currency price should the chosen currency weaken against its pair.

This may seem simple enough—after all, this is just currency exchange and you are betting that one will outperform the other—however, what you profit or lose depends on the currency price movement. As a trader you will watch the price fluctuate over the course of the day and exit the position when you want to collect your gains, or if you want to limit your losses. There are things like stop-orders and limit-orders which can automate this process and we will discuss them later. But for now, understand that what you gain or lose is the difference in the currency price at the time of the exit. As a trader you are effectively placing a bet on one currency against another by buying (going long) if you think it will strengthen or selling (going short) if you think it will weaken, depending on which way you feel the currency price will move.

PIPS

The problem here is that the fluctuations in price are typically miniscule; for example, $0.0016 or 0.14% for today's current EUR/USD trading figures. So instead of trying to work with these small amounts, the Forex has designated these tiny amounts as being measured using PIPS. A PIP is basically 1% of 1%, or most commonly the fourth decimal digit, so in our example for a currency rate change between the EUR/USD of 0.0016%, the Euro moved up 6 pips.

However, to properly evaluate risk and undergo sound fund management, we really do need to know the value of a pip in dollars, if we are trading dollars. Now for a US dollar account, where the dollar is the secondary currency in the pair (as with the EUR/USD or the GBP/USD), then the pip has a standard fixed dollar value.

The fixed pip amount differs depending on the type of Forex, for example:

- The fixed pip amount is $10 for a standard Forex lot, which relates to 100,000 worth of currency
- The fixed pip amount is $1 for a mini Forex lot, which relates to 10,000 worth of currency
- The fixed pip amount is $0.10 for a micro Forex lot, which relates to 1,000 worth of currency.

In the case where the USD isn't listed second then you will need to divide the pip values given above for each lot (standard, mini, micro) by the current USD/XXX exchange rate. For example, if you want to get the pip value for a standard Forex lot for the USD/EUR, when you are trading using your USD account, then you will divide $10 by the USD/EUR exchange rate. In the case where the USD/EUR rate is 0.89 then the standard lot pip value in USD is $10 divided by 0.89 or $11.23

Now what if you don't have a US dollar account?

Well, the same principles hold true for any currency—if it is listed second then it will have a fixed value. Let's say you had a sterling (GBP) account. The pip would be fixed at 10 pounds for a standard lot, 1 pound for a mini-lot, and 0.1 pounds for a micro-lot.

There will be times that you want to trade a currency pair that does not include your own account currency. For instance, you may have a USD account but would like to trade in the EUR/GBP pair of currencies. If that is the case then this is how you would figure out the pip value for any currency pairs that don't include your own account currency.

The key to working with a second currency is that it is always true that if you had an account in that currency the pip rate would be fixed. For example, if you held an account in the UK in sterling (GBP) then the EUR/GBP pip value is fixed at GBP10 for a standard Forex lot. Therefore, what you now have to do is convert that GBP10 into your own currency. So if your trading account is in USD, then you divide the GBP10 by the current USD/GBP exchange rate. Hence, if the current rate of the British pound against the US dollar is 0.7600, then the pip value is USD $13.16 (10/0.76). So we can see that the same principles hold true regardless of the account currency.

Now you are probably already realizing that if the price change movements are so small, as in our real-world example with $0.0016 (or 6 pips), then how can you possibly make any money?

Well, the answer is leverage...and lots of it! Basically, you borrow large amounts from your broker at current interest rates in order to make worthwhile trades. Forex trading does offer much higher leverage rates than with equity trading in that for an initial small margin a trader can control a substantial amount of money.

For example, if you intend to trade one standard lot of EUR/USD, which is equivalent to US$100,000, the margin you may require to put up is a margin of 1%, or US$1,000. So your margin-based leverage will be at 100:1 (100,000/1,000). You can see then that it follows that if you only contribute 0.25%, then the margin-based leverage will now rise to 400:1.

The standard formula for working out margin leverage is:

Margin-Based Leverage = Total Value of Transaction / Margin Required

The common values are listed in the table below.

Margin-Based Leverage Expressed as Ratio	**Margin Required of Total Transaction Value**
400:1	0.25%
200:1	0.50%
100:1	1.00%

50:1	2.00%

What you will find is that with Forex trading in the foreign currency markets, leverage is often available to beginners at rates as high as 100:1. What this means in practical terms is that for every $1,000 that you have available in your trading account, you will be able to trade up to $100,000 in value. This seems like being very high risk but leverage does not necessarily affect risk, as the trader always has the option to contribute more than the required minimum margin for any trade. This suggests that the real leverage, and not the margin-based leverage, is the biggest contributor to risk. For example, if you have a trading account with $10,000 available funds, and you open a standard lot ($100,000) position, you will be trading with 10 times leverage on your account (100,000/10,000). But if you were to decide to trade using two standard lots, which is now equivalent to $200,000 in dollar value with just $10,000 in your USD account, then your leverage on the account will now be 20 times (200,000/10,000). This is where high leverage levels become risky, as there is now the potential to amplify both your profits and your losses by the same amount. Indeed, you will find that the greater the amount of leverage you use then naturally the higher the risk that you will assume. This is because a highly leveraged trade that goes wrong will rapidly deplete your trading account and you will have greater losses due to the bigger lot sizes. There is no need to be frightened of using leverage since there is little option when trading Forex; once you become familiar with applying stop-loss orders and limit orders, there are loss controls in place. If you are taking a hands-off approach to swing trading and letting positions run without supervision or stop-orders in place, then you should be very wary of leverage. Otherwise, leverage can be demonstrated to be used very successfully and profitably in Forex so long as it is applied along with sound fund management.

Indices Trading

Unlike equity trading, when you trade a stock that you own or have borrowed, indices trading is different. For example, you buy or sell based on your opinion of how that index will perform against another group but without taking a position within the stock. This is more like Forex or option trading, but like Forex it is a zero sum game.

So what's an index? It is basically built upon a collection of likeminded companies that have performance levels within a category of stocks, such as Technology, whereby the index or the group serves as a benchmark for the market.

An index is derived through the following properties:

- A good index is transparent. You must know how many securities it holds and what diversity of securities an index should represent within a good portion of the economy.

- There is minimal turnover in the bundle of securities, as the index value is the aggregation of each entities value.
- The index is logical. This means that the underlying securities are selected by some objective measure.
- The index is relevant to the real world.

Tips for Choosing the Best Index Funds

When you decide that you are ready to invest in index funds, then you should get ready for some serious research. You should perhaps start with the type of investment that you need for your portfolio. If you need long-term growth, you may want to try equities. If you need financial stability, then you might want to consider trading bonds. But if you are looking for quick profits then perhaps go for trading Forex. Regardless, within these large categories of stocks, currencies, and bonds, you will still want some diversification. You may want to trade both U.S. and foreign stocks, and you want both large-company and small-company stocks.

Consequently, you may decide that you want an index mutual fund or an exchange-traded fund (ETF). It may be considered a secondary issue but an ETF may have lower operating expenses as well as costing less in commission to trade. An EFT is often your best option for long-term, buy-and-hold investment. However, and EFT is not your best option for investment. Where EFTs fail is when it comes to you requiring making regular contributions or withdrawals.

What about index returns? An index fund will only do as well as the aggregate of the component stocks value it represents, minus the expenses and commissions of the fund. Returns are also determined by the length of run—this means, in some cases, many years. There are cases where an index fund has returned profits in the past months or even in the last year or two. Such numbers are largely irrelevant as it often comes down to patience, fear, or greed.

Stock indices are a good way of trading on high-level instruments by using lower capital to predict the performance of a broader stock market segment or a portion of the market. These types of financial indices are comprised of selected stocks of companies that are typically from a particular industry sector or based on their market capitalization value. One thing to note is that the prices of stocks of larger companies tend to be weighted so that investors can compare potential profits on their investments. Generally, indices traders are likely to trade on the index price movement in the heavily traded stock indices such as the FTSE 100, the Dow Jones, NASDAQ, and DAX.

Now it is very important to understand how these instruments work as these are essentially a collection of individual but related stocks, which are often ranked by independent institutions like major banks. However, the individual index price movements and volatility are impacted much like currency by issues such as political factors, trade disputes, economic data (like employment figures), and big shifts in the currencies exchange markets. There is also the issue that as it is an aggregation of value of the portfolio of stocks, one major stock taking a nosedive could disproportionately impact the index performance.

Global indices markets are dominated by what are known as "benchmark Indices," and these have a disproportionate impact on an economy. Therefore, they are generally held as being reliable financial indicators of the economic health of an economic area or a particular country.

If you are contemplating trading indices then you should consider the heavily traded live markets since they have volatility and liquidity. These include:

- The FTSE 100 – This is the "UK 100" index of the highest-performing UK companies
- Dow Jones – Refers to "Wall Street's 30 of the US" biggest publicly-owned companies
- The DAX – This is "Germany's top 30" high-performing companies
- NASDAQ 100 – The "US Tech 100," which is an index that relates to the top 100 cap-weighted tech companies in the US
- Nikkei 225 – This is the Japanese index made up of the top 225 of the country's biggest companies
- CAC 40 – This refers to France's top 40 biggest companies by capitalization

The way that it works is that a stock index represents the performance of the country's economy or the entire world's stock market. S&P 500 is believed to be one of the most reliable indicators of financial health under the stock indices category.

The S&P 500 is considered to be a diverse index as it includes stocks of the top 500 companies. That is why the performance of the S&P 500 is a good indicator of the health and movement of the entire US stock market. On the other hand, the Dow Jones Industrial Average comprises stocks of 30 of the largest companies in the US, measured by market capital. The Dow Jones Index is a price-weighted index that allows for larger companies to have greater relevance in the index ratings.

The US stock market indexes' high level of volatility and liquidity makes them ideal financial instruments for beginners to trade. However, if you want you can trade Indices in other countries, such as the UK 100. Trading indices is just like spread betting or using a CFD trading account. So to get started all you have to do is find an index you are knowledgeable about. There are indices available from all around the globe for you to learn about as well. As a beginner it's important to understand which Stock Index is the best to trade and that you choose one you have a decent amount of knowledge about. Just like all the other financial instruments there is no substitute for research and analysis, which can help you identify the best trading opportunities.

Once you have done your research and you feel that you have identified a trading opportunity in your chosen index, you'll then need to decide which direction to trade in. That may mean that you buy (go long) or sell (go short), or do both by spread betting and CFD trading, which will allow you to profit from both rising and falling markets.

What Is a CFD?

Contracts for Difference (CFDs) came about from spread betting in the UK. They are an innovative and specialized over-the-counter (OTC) financial instrument that enables you to trade on the price movement of particular financial assets without you having to own them. The attraction of CFDs is that they enable you to trade freely without you actually having to buy anything or having any contractual obligation to own the underlying asset.

With CFDs you need to be aware that they directly relate to their price as a derivative of their underlying financial asset. You'll trade CFDs if you decide that the price of the underlying financial instrument, such as Bitcoin, is likely to go up in value. You can also trade in CFDs if you think Bitcoin is likely to go down in value. When trading using CFDs your profit or loss is going to be directly determined by the difference between your buying and selling prices.

This makes CFD perfect for beginners trading in equities, Forex, and commodities or other high-value trades. What's compelling about CFDs is that you can participate in trades at a fraction of the cost if you had to buy the underlying asset. Yet you will still reap the same benefits if you judge the movement in the market correctly. Keep in mind that CFDs are best suited to those knowledgeable in the particular field since research and knowledge are almost prerequisites to successful trading. Also, you must be very up to speed and diligent with fund management because there are often high amounts of leverage involved. But that can be lessened through diversification (avoiding trading all in one sector), known as *sector risk*. In addition, when trading CFDs the goal is always to maintain a 60/40 winning split; this might mean killing losing trades early and riding the wave of a winning trade. One thing to note is that CFDs are best suited to strongly trending markets regardless of direction, but keep your positions manageable to start with as they need to be carefully monitored.

Unfortunately, there are also some downsides to CFD trading. The first is that although they can make trading affordable they can also amplify losses if you are not careful. You must understand that trading CFDs requires research, focus, and diligence. CFDs are different in many respects to traditional trading due to wider spreads and price gaps, as well as the existence of overnight charges. The biggest risk involves margin calls—if you are not attentive then you can lose a lot more than just your account.

For example: Acme trades at $100 a share so you decide that you want to buy 100 shares for a cost of $10,000, as shares are traded in lots of 100 (100 x 100). If you were to decide to buy 100 CFD contracts with a 10% margin, that will provide you with 10:1 leverage for $1,000 from your broker. The price moves favorably in your direction to close at $112, and you close with a profit—disregarding commissions and fees—of $1,200, ($12 X 100 shares). But what if fickle fate had gone the other way and the stock had gone down $12? Your loss would also be $1,200 and that would exceed your invested capital by $200. Hence, you can now look forward to the expected margin call from your broker to refill your trading account.

When dealing with CFDs you need to be fully aware of fund management best practices to ensure you are always on top of any potential losses due to an unexpected swing in the market. So you must be constantly looking to lock in profits and minimize losses by trading healthy trends.

It is certainly not the goal here to put you off of CFDs; there should be nothing stopping you betting on the direction of indexes. This seems to be a popular choice for many beginners! Just make sure that you do not over-leverage your position and also pay attention to all of your outstanding positions. A better option may be just to trade on indices without using leverage. Let's say that if your research into the index of your choice determines that you want to buy (go long) or sell (go short) you can do so simply by betting on the direction you think the index will travel in. Therefore, should you decide that the market's overall trend is bullish (positive) and that the price movement of your index will rise, then you will choose to buy. On the other hand, should you decide that the market may be turning negative and the price movement is more likely to drop, then you would open a sell position. The only downside is that profits without sufficient leverage are often very unattractive.

Placing Your Indices Trade

The first thing we need to understand is that an equity index is really just a benchmark that measures the relative price performance of several equities bundled together and listed on the particular exchange. The relative value of an index is typically described in a number of points. Each index is calculated differently, but it will usually be the aggregation of the current values of all of its individual component stocks. Because it is often weighted, this will mean that a company with a higher capitalization, or *cap value*, will have a disproportionately greater impact on the index value.

The interesting thing about trading indices is that you don't actually *trade* anything—instead, you will bet on the changes in price just like you would with trading currencies. To do this you'll forecast the direction of the price of an index, open an appropriate position, and see which direction its price goes. If you are correct then you will earn money!

Trading Indices

Interestingly, though many will know all about Forex, many beginners don't know how the stock indexes are traded and often assume they are traded like individual stocks. You don't buy all of the underlying stock in an index, you simply own a small proportion which makes it far more economical to trade. So the instrument has significant value that will allow you to trade just like with any other instrument.

There are several factors you should be aware of when you start trading indices. First, study the financial assets that compose the index. Contemplate whether the equities that comprise an index belong to one or several market sectors. The answer will help you avoid placing too much emphasis on a specific sector and allow you to diversify, which could possibly enhance the value of an index.

Another thing to be aware of is to regularly check the changes to index listings. After all, the stocks that comprise an index can change due to mergers, acquisitions, or even closure. But remember that the companies with the biggest capitalization will have a disproportional effect on the indices value. After all, a company's market capitalization is the total value of its issued shares assessed by the market value. An index will naturally be affected by the individual share prices of all the companies. For example, in the scenario whereby a company's market capitalization drops, their stocks will probably no longer meet the criteria to remain on the index. In this scenario it is likely that the company will be replaced with another one that now has a larger market capitalization. When a stock within an index changes, the capitalization changes as well, and this will obviously affect the final value of the index. This is an important point, as it is necessary to track any changes in the index listings by following individual company financial statements and looking out for breaking news for companies that are in the index.

Equities

In contrast to betting on or trading in stock indices through CFD, you can instead trade in individual company stocks, which are called *equities*. Stocks or equities are a very popular financial instrument. Stock or equity trading means that you actually purchase stock in a company so you have part ownership of it, depending on the number of shares you buy. Stocks are popular financial instruments but they are typically traded in units of 100, which makes trading popular premier stocks difficult for beginners or those working with a restricted budget. Nonetheless, stock trading is very popular because the markets have high volumes and high levels of liquidity, which makes entering and exiting positions easier. Also, they have large price volatility—the fluctuation in price on a daily basis. Volatility provides the opportunity to take advantage of frequent price movements.

Volatility, volume, and liquidity are key factors to look for when choosing stocks to trade. However, for beginners, the stocks of some of the biggest companies are naturally going to be out of their financial scope. But if you do have sufficient capital, these premier companies are the best and safest for swing trading. This is because stocks like Apple, Microsoft, Amazon, and Google, for example, have very high liquidity and volatility due to their huge trading volumes.

As a beginner you should be looking for more affordable stock to trade, at least at the beginning. You'll need to learn about the things that can affect stock prices. This is pretty straightforward since companies are based primarily on measurable data, such as their quarterly earnings. Earnings have a large effect on the company's share price because they are a key indicator of the financial health and the long-term prospects. It's best to identify when the companies whose stock you are trading will release their figures for their quarterly earnings—this will be a time of potential huge price volatility over a short period of time (the day of release) and you might be better as a beginner to avoid this and wait until the market settles down. Of course, this is also a time for huge potential profits if you can call it right! For example, if your research shows you that the quarterly earnings will be very positive then you would do well to buy that stock; on the contrary, you might want to sell if your forecasts are pessimistic.

Similarly, unpredicted stock price movement can also be generated by the release of market analysts' stock ratings, as they do have an effect on a company's share price. Analysts performing detailed market studies do in-depth analysis of companies in each sector. Consequently, this analysis is used to provide recommendations on how traders should trade the stock; depending on the reputation of the analysts, these reports may trigger large price swings. It's always a good idea to follow and keep track of the major analysts' stock market surveys.

In a similar way, breaking industry news can also affect the price of individual stocks. But more importantly, there might be a domino effect that will consequently affect all of the companies in a sector. The impact can be seen quite clearly if you follow indices. For example, if the overall sector of Technology's trend is up or down, most (if not all) of the individual Tech companies in that sector will follow suit. This is especially true if a major cap-value company releases better-than or worse-than expected quarterly earnings, or—the dreaded profits warning. It is thus essential to keep on top of the industry news when it comes to trading equities as financial instruments.

Equities trading is much harder to trade both long and short; to trade short you will need to borrow stock from your broker, called a *margin account*. As a beginner swing trader you really do not want to be doing this...only experienced traders want to use margins in equity trading because things can go horribly wrong very quickly.

The issue is that to make money on a bearish market in equities, you need to borrow stock from your broker and this means setting up a margin account. Now, what you are essentially doing is borrowing stock. Let's say you borrow at $10 a share. That's $1,000 dollars that you can trade in the expectation that the price will fall. So if you intend to borrow and then sell that stock, then buy it back again later at the lower price and pocket the difference. This is what is known as short selling.

Short Selling

The problem with going short in equities is that you are dealing with actual stock. This is stock that you have borrowed at a certain price. The goal here is that you trade the stock at the current market's falling price in the hope that the price will continue to plummet and then you can buy it back at a much lower cost just before the price rises. Then you return the borrowed stock to the broker when the price recovers, minus the charges, and pocket the profits. If the price reverses and goes up instead of down, you will have to buy back the stock that you borrowed at the now higher price and accept the loss.

Despite the high risk, many experienced traders do go short, but it is considered to be a risky endeavor for a beginner.

Commodities & Futures

Commodities such as crude oil, agricultural produce, and precious metals also provide a way for people to trade in the financial markets. Commodities have been around for a long time and are the basis of future trading, and as financial instruments they also provide diversification from equities or stock indices.

Commodity trading was originally introduced as future trading in agriculture as a form of price guarantee for both the farmer and the dealer. The concept behind commodity trading is well established. If you want, you can buy and sell various types of commodities through future contracts on exchanges. Now, few people today who participate in future trading want to end up with bushels of wheat or the barrels of oil they are trading in. So today's future contracts are bought and sold on the financial markets. These financial instruments are classified into four general categories: agriculture, energy, precious metals, and industrial metals.

Within the precious metals category, the most popular and highest volume traded financial instrument is gold, silver, platinum, and copper. With energy, the highest volume and popular financial instrument is crude oil followed by natural gas and petroleum. In agriculture, the most popular instruments are in agricultural meat products such as cattle feed, pork bellies, and lean hogs. Other popular futures in agriculture are in soybeans, corn, wheat, coffee, cocoa, and rice.

As mentioned, traders are in the future market not because they want to own the underlying assets, such as pork bellies and soy beans, but due to the attractive price volatility and profit potential. Therefore, these types of financial instruments become very attractive to use with CFDs because they allow you to trade on the price difference between buying and selling in financial assets including Futures, Cryptocurrency, Indices, Shares, and ETFs—without you having to own or have a contract on any of them.

Now that CFD provides you with a much more cost-effective way to trade in the commodities market, this will potentially benefit you in profiting from the forces of supply and demand that drive price volatility in the market. In commodities, a lower supply on a given commodity typically results in higher prices, especially when coupled with a high demand. Though generally commodities are thought of as being agriculture and oil, it is gold that is the most traded financial instrument within the commodity sector. This is because gold has a sound reputation with commodity traders and is viewed as being reliable and dependable in the way it conveys value.

But that is not the only reason gold is a popular instrument, as professional traders also turn to precious metals when hedging their positions against things like high inflation, or particularly during periods of currency devaluation. Crude is another popular financial instrument since oil output prices fluctuate during times of political or environmental instability, which has a huge effect on prices around the world. This volatility allows traders to take advantage of the volatile price changes.

Another more traditional instrument is in grains and other agricultural produces, which tend to be extremely volatile and perfect for trading during summer. Recent extreme weather conditions, along with a growing population, puts pressure on a limited agricultural supply and this subsequently provides opportunities for price swings.

Option Trading

The way that option trading came about was when people wanted to bet against the price shift of an instrument without having to actually own the underlying instrument so that it has its provenance in future trading. For example, you could enter a contract with the owner of an equity or security with an option to buy at a later time at an agreed price, and trade for a fraction of the price. What happens is that you enter into an agreement that is time-limited whereby you say the price will go up or down on a certain date. You at no point own that stock, you simply have the right to trade. The difference with Options and Forex is that you have obligations. If you buy an options contract the price will be predetermined and so will be the exit date. You as a buyer have no obligation to buy the instrument and you can trade as long as there is sufficient time left on the contract. However, should you as a buyer renege on the contract and don't want to buy, you will lose—or rather, forfeit—your entire contract price. On the other hand, should you go short and sell an instrument, then you are obliged to sell at the contract price. So going short on options is very high-risk.

Now the reason that many traders go for options is that like Forex there is large leverage, what means that you can trade well above your account balance. In equity trading, options are very attractive as you no longer need to buy the underlying stock and you simply enter into a contract to buy. You could trade in stocks such as Apple, Microsoft, and Facebook at a fraction of the outlay, but most importantly, reap all the benefits.

The way it works is that you enter into a bargain with stockholders in premier companies and then agree on an initial contract price as well as a finishing and exit date that will allow you to trade the stock as if it was your own. Should you bet correctly, at the time of exit you'll discover the price has risen so you either buy the stock at the agreed contract price or return it and take the profit. However, should your bet falter, you are under no obligation to buy the stock at the agreed contract price, but you will lose your contract deposit.

The big issue with option trading is when you attempt to go short and sell in a falling market. When you take up a short (selling) position you are then obliged to sell if the trader wants to buy the stock at the agreed contract price. Then you are in deep trouble because you will need to go to the market to buy the shares at a typically much higher price in order to fulfill the contract.

Time is a very important factor when buying an option; the longer the time period that the options remain valid, the higher the price. This is because the probability is also higher that your prospective position will reach the strike price. However, the problem is in getting the expected price movement to coincide with the time span of the option. This is critical because even if you speculate the market movement successfully, it may come about too late, and the option will likely become worthless and expire. When you are evaluating which option to buy you must expect to pay more. Essentially you are buying yourself more time for options that have longer expiration periods. Typically, the price and the validity of an option will range from a few weeks to up to two years. Nonetheless, an option's valuation is volatile as time decay will play a major role (basically the option loses some of its value every day) but its value also fluctuates due to the performance of the underlying stock price.

When you buy or call an options contract, your rights allow you to:

- *Buy a specific quantity, typically 100 shares of the underlying stock (exercise your rights).*
- *Buy the 100 shares in the stock by a certain date (expiration date).*
- *Buy the specific quantity of stock at a specified price (strike price).*

We can see from this that the value and the price of the call option rises when the underlying stock price goes up because the price of the rights you bought through the option is a fixed strike price; however, the underlying stock is hopefully increasing in value over time.

On the other hand, should you sell or *put* an option, then it gains value when the underlying stock falls in price. When you hold an option you have the following rights:

- *Sell a specific quantity, typically 100 shares of the underlying stock (exercise your rights).*
- *Sell the 100 shares in the stock by a certain date (expiration date).*
- *Sell the specific quantity of stock at a specified price (strike price).*

The right to sell a specific quantity (100) of stock on a certain expiration date at a specified strike price is very beneficial in a bear market. When prices are going downhill, your option retains its value. For example, if you hold a put option with a strike price of $100 then you own the rights to sell that stock back to the contract writer (seller) at $100 on the expiry date. Now the thing to remember here is that the contract is between you and the option writer. This makes them obliged to buy the stock from you at the strike price (in this case $100) regardless of the stock's current value. The Option writer is of course betting that the stock price stays above $100 but stock markets are notoriously fickle and volatile. This means that just about anything in the way of bad news may push the stock price below $100, say to $90. Should that be the case, then you will find that the Put Option you are holding has become much more valuable. This is simply because the Put Option writer will be obliged to buy the underlying stock from you at $100 even though its current market value is now only $90, effectively losing out to the cost of $1,000 (100x10).

Regardless of whether it is a call or a put option, the direction of the movement in price must occur before the option contract expiration date or it will simply expire and unfortunately become worthless.

Another issue with options as opposed to Forex, Indices, and Equities is that many brokers do not like beginners entering the market as it is considered to be high risk, so leverage is hard to get.

ETFs and Government Treasuries

Exchange Traded Funds (ETFs) are investment funds that follow the price movements of selected commodities, indices, or bonds. As ETFs cover a wide spectrum of underlying financial assets—for example, they could form a portfolio including stocks, currencies, bonds, futures, commodities, and even real estate—you are only buying a share in a specific bundle of securities. Therefore, when you buy an ETF, you are actually buying shares in a portfolio that is tracking the price performance of the specific underlying financial assets.

Why trade in ETFs?

You might want to consider trading in ETFs rather than in equities or indices because when you buy ETFs you have something tangible you can trade, like stocks. Consequently, ETFs can then be traded on the market, as the market is viable. As a result, their price does fluctuate during trading which provides price volatility and the opportunity to profit. Furthermore, ETFs also provide you with an easy route to diversification and the added benefit of reducing your risk. This is because they only track the performance of underlying indices. You might want to consider trading in some of the biggest and liquid ETFs such as:

- SPDR S&P 500 (ARCA: SPY)

- S&P 500 VIX Short-Term Futures
- ETN (ARCA: VXX)
- Russell 2000 Index Fund (ARCA: IWM), and
- PowerShares QQQ Trust (NASDAQ: QQQ)

You will probably find that in your country the government's treasuries are among the best and safest financial instruments to trade due to their built-in safety net. They come with much reduced exposure to financial risk. There are precious few other financial instruments that come with a guarantee of financial returns, as treasuries or bonds have. Consequently, they have remained a popular financial instrument over generations of income-focused investors as they have an excellent proven record for high returns.

US Government Treasury securities come in three basic categories. First, there are the T-bills, which take the shortest time to mature (between 4 to 52 weeks). Second, there are the T-Notes, which are the middle-range government bonds as they take a minimum of between 2 – 10 years to mature. Finally, there are the T-Bonds, which are for long-term investors since they take up to 30 years to mature.

Cryptocurrencies

Cryptocurrencies are defined as being encrypted decentralized digital currencies that are transferred between individuals. These currencies are not physical, tangible objects and exist only in the electronic format, so it is really a digital asset that exists and remains as data. This means they are not backed up by anything of real value, such as gold or some other precious object. They are also not controlled, or most importantly, *supported*, by a central bank. As a result, they make poor retail currency due to their notorious instability. For example, in late 2017, should you have used Bitcoin to purchase a laptop for $1,000 then in only two weeks that laptop had effectively cost you $12,000 due to Bitcoin's soaring value during that time. However, they have remained of interest as a currency because they found a way to transfer money at much lower transaction times and costs compared to using a bank.

The concept of cryptocurrencies is that of an immutable digital ledger. This process is called a *Blockchain*; it is public and is distributed across the network, so everybody that has the same Bitcoin has a copy of the ledger that holds a history of all its transactions, which creates a community of trust. This makes each Bitcoin individually identifiable as it is based on a very complex mathematically-derived code.

Bitcoin is not the only digital currency but it is by far the most popular and influential cryptocurrency, especially in trading. However, there are a range of altcoins which are considered alternatives to Bitcoin and growing in value and market share. Therefore, you could consider trading in some of the other top ranking altcoins. These include, in no particular order: Litecoin, Ethereum, Bitcoin Cash, Bitcoin Gold, and EOS, to name a few.

How to Trade Cryptocurrencies?

The initial way that cryptocurrencies were traded was through individual traders setting up a Bitcoin wallet and then buying some Bitcoin using tangible currency. Then the cryptocurrencies would be exchanged on a cryptocurrency exchange site for either tangible currency or for the altcoins of choice.

There were many issues with this, especially with security, as the trader was responsible for securely maintaining one or more digital wallets. The exchanges themselves became prime targets for cyber theft and hacker attacks. Today, it is more likely that you will trade using CFD or through a secure broker platform where a wallet is not required.

Factors to Watch While Trading Cryptocurrencies

The cryptocurrency market is very unstable and suffers from unexplainable periods of volatility. The market also changes rapidly as new cryptocurrencies emerge and others fall away. On the plus side, many online retail stores have started accepting Bitcoin and other digital currencies as a form of payment. As a result, many banks are starting to realize that cryptocurrencies may have the potential to change the financial world.

Nonetheless, there are several different factors that drive the price of cryptocurrencies up or down. To start with, just like with Forex or any other financial instrument, the higher the demand then the higher the price will be. The purchase of the coin by traders buying on speculation can also affect the demand and the price. Media reports discussing the growing currencies performances will also have an effect on the price of digital currency and Bitcoin in particular.

Which Financial Instruments Should a Beginner Swing Trade?

For the beginner, selecting the ideal financial instrument to trade will depend on several key factors, with the most important being personal preference. Choosing an instrument that you have an interest in will make trading and keeping up to date with research far easier than trading in something you have no interest in. The next biggest challenge in finding a suitable financial instrument is available funds. Unfortunately, the capital and the size of your trading account will dictate to a great extent the type of instrument you can trade. This is because trading in the financial markets was never really meant for the small independent trader on a budget. Instead, it was (and still is) heavily skewed towards the large institutional traders. For instance, if you are to invest in government bonds, you are likely going to need a significant amount of capital available to you compared to say, the Forex markets, where leverage is always on offer even to the beginner.

Another thing to consider is the time of day that you will be trading because when it comes to swing trading, some financial instruments tend to be volatile and liquid at different times of the day. Therefore, if you are holding down a full-time job and only able to spend time trading out with market hours then that will obviously have a large effect on the types of instruments available to you. For instance, if you are betting on movement of currency pairs pegged to the dollar, you will typically find the greatest volatility and liquidity during the New York trading session. Similarly, the same movements in GBP and the Euro will occur during the London and Frankfurt stock exchange sessions.

Nonetheless, the Forex market is turning out to be the go-to place for beginner swing traders and for those looking to launch a career in the investment and financial markets. The Forex market boasts of a daily turnover of more than $4 trillion, making it the highest liquid market, which is ideal for opening and closing trades quickly to take advantage of small price movements.

Another thing favoring Forex is the low capital requirement, which is another key reason why people are trading Forex instruments compared to other securities. Remember, you can start betting on micro and mini Forex with as little as $100 up to around $1000, as that would be safer to start with. Nonetheless, you can open an account and swing trade on a wide variety of Forex instruments.

Conclusion

In this chapter we discussed financial instruments and which ones might be better choices for the beginner in swing trading. We saw that the financial markets do provide a wide variety of instruments that you can trade in. However, that does not mean that every instrument is necessarily suitable for the beginner. After all, there are some where expert knowledge is required (such as with futures trading in agriculture, or precious metals) and others require large capital (such as in equity trading and dealing in government bonds). It is crucial to your market longevity that you research and understand the inherent behavior of a financial instrument. This also means understanding the factors, which are very likely going to affect its price. So you should never decide on a financial instrument until you have gained sufficient knowledge of all the market conditions and other things that can affect it. One of the worst things you can do as a beginner is choose a financial security just because it is popular, and then not carry out thorough research on its behaviors, as this is a sure way of losing money in the financial markets.

Chapter 4 - Learning the Fundamentals of Financial Trading

In this chapter we will take a look at how you get started in trading and you will learn about the mechanics of making a trade. First of all, we will cover how you find a broker since you will need them to make the trades on your behalf. Finding a suitable broker requires that you research the online options that match your trading style. Some brokers will gladly welcome beginners in Forex or Index trading with open arms, but are reticent in accepting high-risk options or futures traders. Second, we will examine the types of orders that you can make and it is very important that you are able to distinguish between them before you start trading. This is because they work differently and if you use the wrong one for the wrong purpose it could cost you a lot of money or opportunities. Third, we will examine entry and exit strategies, as these determine how profitable you can be.

Choosing a Broker

The type and style of the broker that you choose is ultimately up to you. What we would suggest is that you shop around online and find a broker that suits your trading requirements. Every trade requires that you pay a commission. This in itself can turn a marginal win into a loss. So be careful when selecting a broker and check out their commission on every trade. One thing to keep in mind is that when you trade multiple orders it might seem to you to be a single trade but to the broker these are often individual trades that increase commission on every single transaction. That can ruin your profit.

Another aspect that you should be aware of is when you start off trading on the broker's simulator, things may not be what they appear to be. We will discuss this in more detail later in the chapter but remember that the simulator is just that—it is not real market conditions.

The broker's simulator is there to encourage you to play, so of course the odds are on your side and you will appear to be a natural trader. Just remember, fund management is the core skill in trader longevity so adapt your strategy in such a way that you ignore stop losses and profit captures when playing simulators or paper trading, as they are certainly not guaranteed in real-world trading.

Understanding the Types of Orders

Basic Order Types

A financial order is a transaction that can be executed by your broker in several different ways. In swing trading you will need to be aware of the different types of orders that you can place.

You'll be placing orders regardless of the type of security, such as Forex or equities trading, using specifications that you will set. There are some very important nuances between the types of orders that you must know before the order is placed.

Many of these different order types are based around expected prices:

- **Market orders** are orders used to buy and sell at the best market price available. This is the best price on the exchange at the time the order is placed. These are the most common type of orders. The issue with this order is that if you are not careful of when you enter a trade, you may pay over the odds for your position. For example, if you place a market order for 100 Microsoft stock, that order will be fulfilled if there are shares available at the best price at the time, which let's say is $145 per share, and that might be more than you are prepared to pay.

- **Limit orders** are the other type of orders to buy or sell but only at a specific price or better (higher for a sell order, lower for a buy order). In this case you are specifying an exact price or better from your perspective for the security. With a limit order, the broker will only execute the order if that price or condition is met. For example, if you place a limit order at $6.00 when the stock is trading at $6.05 but you expect the price to fall and it drops to $6.01, your order will still not be executed as this is at a higher price than you specified. Limit orders makes sure you don't pay over the odds for stock in a rising market but they also can lead to missed opportunities.

- **Stop orders** are a special type of order which is deployed to buy or sell once a security hits a specific price. These are event-driven orders that remain dormant until they are activated by a price reaching a specific limit. Stop orders are usually entered to limit losses from a position by ordering an automatic close (sale) if a particular price is hit. The thing to remember with stop orders is that they are used differently than limit orders, as they continue to be executed if the stop is hit. For example, if you place a stop order at $6 to close out a call position currently priced at $6.50, it will be executed as soon as the price hits $6. However, it will also continue to be executed even if the price falls to $5 or below. This is because once it meets its triggered price event it reverts to working just like a market order. So you may well start selling stock at prices you are not happy with!

- **Stop-limit orders** are another special type of orders, which are a combination of stop and limit orders. This type is used in the same manner as stop orders but with the caveat that the order will only be executed when the stop price is triggered—at the limit price or better.

- **Trailing stop orders** are another combination of order types. They start out working like a standard stop order because they are orders to buy or sell once a security hits a specific price. However, unlike stop orders that continues to execute after the trigger price is met and will do so at the best available price, the trailing stop orders can be set to move with the market. This means that they will continue to fulfill the orders at the best price but only within thresholds that you set. Trailing stop orders are typically set as a percentage above or below the securities current market price.

So you now have a selection of order types that you can use for specific trading scenarios. The objective is to now choose the correct one for each trading situation. For example, you will always (and this cannot be stressed enough) set stop loss orders to prevent runaway losses.

But what stop order do you use? If you were to set a market stop loss order, what would happen is that should the market turn against you, a buy or sale would be triggered that would allow you to bail out at the best available price. That might be what you want as you will get the best available price on the market. Of course in a plummeting bearish market that might clean you out—remember, there has to be a buyer when you are selling, in which case the price may well fall very low before a buyer is found.

This is why traders use limit orders as they stipulate a price to buy or sell but it also has its problems. For example, you may set the limit stop orders on your current security price at a dollar below or above the current price depending on which way you are trading. However, as the financial market is infamously volatile, the price might jump across your trigger price. For example, if you set a bullish limit loss order at $5.90 for a $6.00 security and the trade goes against you and the price tumbles quickly, you might miss the opportunity to exit the position if you aren't following the news. Nobody is interested in buying at that price since it has quickly fallen beneath the market valuation. Yes, you will retain your stock, but its value may continue to plummet down to $3 dollars or even crash altogether. A similar scenario is if you set your limit stop order on a bearish market and prices reverse, then you may well miss the opportunity to be bailed out. This is simply because prices can change very quickly and you need someone to buy at the price you have set. If there is no one willing to buy at that specific price you could be in big trouble.

This is one of the biggest differences between paper trading, simulators, and real-life trading. In paper trading and simulators there is no real concept of a market (an available partner in trade). Many simulators just accept your stop loss as being guaranteed. But in the real world, it doesn't work that way. Remember that you can only sell if there is someone willing to buy. This is hugely important to understand because your simulator may lead you to believe that a stop loss will mitigate your losses, but in the real world that stop loss is not a guarantee—it's a only a defensive strategy.

Exit Strategy

It is not just enough to have a stop order lose points; you will also need to use trading orders to lock in profits. This is generally termed as being an *exit strategy*. For example, you may want to limit losses at $1 should the market go against you. However, when the market trend is favorable, you might want to cash in on your profits. You can do this again by placing stop orders or any variety at the target price. What would happen then is that you would sell in a bull market to claim your profit. Of course, you might not want to do that if the market is extremely bullish, and you may want to ride the trend instead. After all, you are a swing trader! But what you can do is lock in profits using limit stop orders on say 50% of the position and leave the other 50% to ride the trend.

The previous method of splitting your strategy can be a great way to lock in profits but it also can leave you feeling underwhelmed. Should your 50% of riding stock rocket you will be cursing yourself for being so conservative. But if the price suddenly reverses then you have come out a winner. There is no decision that is correct because nobody has a magic ball that can see into the future. However, best fund management practices would always suggest playing it safe and taking what you have.

Chapter 5 - Performing Fundamental Chart Analysis

A beginner's guide to reading charts was briefly covered earlier but in this chapter we will go beyond simple trend pattern spotting to actually surfacing some of the secrets within trends that are revealed via chart analysis. I think we all understand that trends go either upwards, downwards, or for traders—most infuriatingly sideways. When you complete this chapter you should have a better understanding of how to profit from all three scenarios. Depending on the direction of the trend, we can use specific trading techniques to benefit from the situation and make it work for us.

It might seem counter-intuitive but we can equally profit from a falling market as we can a rising one. Most astonishing is we can make as much profit if we know what we are doing in a stagnating, sideways trend, where there is neither up nor down movement worth mentioning. To enable us to do this we need to understand how to do basic chart reading.

There are four basic techniques when reading a financial chart whether it is a Forex currency or an equity ticker chart, as they share the same criteria:

- The first, as we have already mentioned, is the trend—and never bet as a beginner against an established trend.
- The second is to identify and highlight the points of support and resistance; these will be stronger in a sideways market so are critical to scope and study.
- The third is to identify the changing average over a period such as ten, twenty or thirty days for swing trading, but much shorter for day trading and of course much longer if you are in the game of investment trading.
- Finally, the fourth is to decide upon either using the relative strength indicator (RSI) or the moving average convergence-divergence (MACD).

The last point addresses trading signals, which are relatively simple indicators that just about every simulator will provide automatically for you. However, they are not a panacea for financial trading but they do give you a heads up on how the market has been recently behaving. The use of the past tense is crucial here, as these indicators are developed via historical data, so they can only tell you how things have developed up until now. But please, understand before you spend hours scouring charts; they cannot give you any reliable indication of how things will pan out in the future—nothing can.

Having said that, charts do seem to surface trends that do appear to often repeat themselves so are considered by many experienced and successful traders as being oracles. The problem is what effective timescale you can use to reveal these obscure but repeatable patterns. After all, a chart for five minutes is radically different in its shape than one for one month when all the price volatility gets ironed out over time. Similarly, a chart covering five days may be a happy medium. Furthermore, they may be a good timeline for swing trading but could contain just too much information within those smaller price fluctuations. Even plotting out the support and resistance levels can be wasted time, as they are deemed relatively ineffective under certain trend conditions, as we will see next.

Support and Resistance

After identifying the direction of an existing trend (whether it is trending upwards, downwards, or sideways) the next indicator to try and get from a chart is the support and resistance levels.

Support and resistance levels do play an important role in chart reading at a basic level and that is because they do reveal the levels of current market optimism. It really goes back to asking the crowds as to what the consensus of opinion is for the overall value of the instrument you are tracking. As we noted earlier, support levels appear when an instruments price falls and then the market as a whole rallies around to shore up the price by buying the stock. Similarly, the resistance threshold is the level met when the market thinks an instrument's price is overheated and starts to sell to bring it back down to a more realistic level. Hence support and resistance levels are significant indicators to market sentiment.

The problem is that we have strong and weak support and resistance points. In a strong bear or strong bull market the support and resistance points are almost irrelevant because they are breached with regularity. But in a sideways market, where the price direction is neither becoming a bull or bear but is still relatively volatile, then the support and resistance indicators are pure analysis gold. Many experienced traders still swear by support and resistance levels even in full-on bull or bear markets that are trending sharply, when they are setting their next stop-loss and limit orders.

Moving Averages (MACD)

The Moving Averages indicator is a moving average of the price over the time period. For swing traders you can look at 5-, 10-, or 20-day moving averages to get an indication of the trends over those periods. Where moving averages become advantageous is when they work alongside support and resistance points; they can identify and confirm strong support and resistance points when the two coincide. Furthermore, once you activate MA on your charts they are dynamically updated so you don't have to perform any more manual support and resistance points. Dynamic MA will detect them for you as it tracks the price line across the graph. The support and resistance points can be identified easily where the MACD curve intersects with the trending price line. Many Forex and equity swing traders look at these moving averages as key dynamic support or resistance points and will buy when the price is at a support level, and sell if prices rise and intersect with the moving average curve. What is beneficial here is that the MACD and price line curves can be seen in almost real time, as the intersections are displayed dynamically with only a few seconds delay.

One thing you should remember is the revealed support and resistance points used with MA are no different from the normal support and resistance lines. This means that the price won't always bounce perfectly from the moving average curve and it may go a little bit past before retracting back in the direction of the trend.

However, there are times when the price will break through. What some swing traders do is activate two moving averages on their charts, let's say a 10-day MA and a 20-day MA, and only buy or sell once the price is in the middle of the space between the two moving averages. Swing traders refer to this sweet spot as "the zone."

Relative Strength Indicator (RSI)

The relative strength index (RSI) is a commonly used indicator that shows the momentum and magnitude of recent price changes. It is used to evaluate overbought or oversold conditions in the price of a stock or in the case of Forex currencies or indices amongst other underlying assets. The RSI is displayed as a line graph that displays movement between two extremes and as such has a relative reading from 0 to 100.

However, to make sense of the RSI, we need to understand that the interpretation of the indicator suggests that an RSI value of 70 or above will indicate that a security is becoming overbought. On the other hand, an RSI reading of 30 or below indicates an oversold or undervalued condition. What this means is that in the case of the former, the instrument is perhaps overvalued and may well be a prime candidate for a market price pullback. In the case of the latter, the suggestion is that the instrument is undervalued and so is also prime for a re-evaluation—but this time towards the rising price.

Consequently, when using the RSI as a trend indicator, you can consider the price and so the RSI will rise when the trend reveals a larger number and size of positive closes (i.e. it is on an upwards trend). Of course the RSI will fall when the number and size of losses increase over the same period. As such, the RSI is typically used to compare bullish and bearish price momentum and so it displays the results alongside a price chart, typically at the bottom. But like most technical indicators, the market trend signals it produces are perhaps only reliable when they are judged against a large pool of sample data like in a long-term trend. However, in equities trading, where you are dealing with tangible stock with inherent value, it is still a very popular metric but not so valuable in Forex trading where value is transient.

Things to Note

The thing about trends, patterns, and support and resistance levels is that they are indicators of past performance. Many market influencers use these to shape the market, but beginner traders entering the market with limited funds will have almost zero influence on the market. What we mean by this is your decision to sell or buy based upon a pattern that you have identified at a prescient point, no matter how knowledgeable, your actions will have zero effect on the trend. You are always following the trend set by the large institutions, those that *do* have the resources and the intent to trade large and control the market trend in their favor. No one has ever claimed this to be a fair market—it certainly is not!

Chapter 6 - Reading Financial Charts

Some of the most useful and easy-to-use indicators for technical analysis are right in front of you in the charts. As we have just seen in the last section, trends are very important and as a beginner you should always go with the trend. However, identifying a trend is not always as easy as it first appears; although they can be upwards, downwards, or sideways, they are not always cemented in that direction. This means that you might need to take a look at longer-term charts to see if you can visualize a trend in the price movement.

There are other tools that are typically freely available to you when reading charts and one of the most useful is the moving averages. These are simply a trend line built using the average price over a time period. Moving Average (MA) lines can be automatically generated by the chart software by selecting a range of time periods, typically in the range of 5, 15, or 60 minutes, which are of interest to day traders. Or for swing trading you can use the daily 5, 10, 20, or 50 day trend lines—but there may even be MA up to 200 days.

What makes moving average so popular amongst traders in equities, Forex, and other financial instruments is because of its simplicity. In most broker platforms, or on many price charts, you can generate them automatically. However, like all indicators, moving averages does have its time and place and are best used in a trending environment.

The way the moving average indicator works is that it is based upon statistics. The moving average is the arithmetic mean of a set of data over the time period of interest. Now when used with swing trading chart analysis, the data set we will use will usually be represented by the end-of-market closing prices of stocks for that particular day. You can just as easily use separate moving averages for low and high daily prices or even plot two or more moving averages at a time. For example, you could use a 10-day and a 20-day, and many traders do this when calculating resistance areas or zones. You could also, if you want, plot an average of midpoint values, but you would probably have to do this yourself by summing up all the daily lows and highs and then dividing them by two. Also, like we said earlier, you use a moving average on a shorter timeframe; for example, day traders will use the daily or 5-minute charts.

Now if you are out of luck and the charts you are analyzing are fixed, as some do not dynamically generate the data for you, then you are going to have to plot the moving average manually. Doing this is very straightforward. Say you want to make a 10-day moving average, then to do that you would just simply add up all the last 10 days' closing prices and then divide by 10. The same method is true for any time period (i.e. add up the last 20 days and divide by 20 for a 20-day moving average).

Now we have our 10-day moving average for the day so the next day you would do the same thing. But the numbers now have changed, as they have all moved down one day and what was the last day's price (day 10) is now replaced by yesterday's price. The data shifts in this manner with every new trading day, hence the name "moving average." This is actually called a simple moving average and as we will see shortly there are other more sophisticated types of moving averages that we can use.

As a swing trader you'll use moving averages to surface and follow trends typically in closing prices. Hence, its purpose is to establish the beginning of a trend, follow its progress, and highlight any changes in price direction over the given period. This makes using moving averages very handy for spotting where a price reversal occurs.

However, unlike technical analysis, the simple moving average cannot indicate the start or the end of a trend. They use historical data so can only confirm a trend; it cannot anticipate what will happen tomorrow. Hence, they will highlight a reversal sometime after it has already occurred. Moreover, the number of days or the time period you select affects the value of the trend. This is because in swing trading, when working in days, the fewer days a moving average contains, the better it can surface and highlight a trend's reversal. This might seem at first a bit counter-intuitive since the longer 20-day chart has more data to work on. However it is because of the amount of historical data that makes the longer-term moving averages less useful at spotting outliers. This is simply due to the fact that more data smooths out any anomalies which strongly influence the moving average. Hence, a 5-day moving average generates the signal of a trend reversal sooner than the 20-day average. However, there is another issue; if we select fewer days for the moving average then we will lose accuracy and the falser signals we will likely get.

The solution to this is to use a combination of several moving averages. Many traders do use this method of plotting two or three timelines for the moving averages. What they are looking for with this method is to identify when all of them are the same thing at the same time. When there is consensus amongst the timelines this gives a trader the added confidence to open their position. Nonetheless, you should not discount the moving average's lag behind the trend because it cannot be completely removed.

Understanding the Trading Signals

You can use one or several type of moving average to generate your trading, buy, or sell signals, and it is this simplicity that makes moving averages so popular. Now in most cases you will be using charting software that plots for you the moving average as a line directly onto the price chart. In the case where you are using a single moving average line on a chart, the trading signals you are interested in are produced where the prices intersect the moving average line. The indicators are easy to understand:

- Should the price cross above the moving average line, this is an indicator that implies the start of a new upward trend and should be interpreted as a signal to buy.

- If the price crosses below the moving average line and the market also closes down in this area, then this implies the start of a downward trend and indicates a signal to sell.

However, when you are using multiple moving average lines, things are a bit different. Remember that you use multiple moving averages when you want to eliminate the anomalies and the "noise" in prices and especially to remove any false signals, also known as *whipsaws*, which a single moving average can be vulnerable to. Therefore, when reading the moving averages indicators you will look for behaviors that indicate a firm buy or sell signal such as:

- When using several moving averages, a buy signal will occur when the shorter of the averages crosses above the longer time period average. For example, when the 50-day moving average moves above the 200-day moving average, this is a strong buy signal.

- On the other hand, when there is a scenario where the 50-day moving average moves beneath the 200-day moving average, then this is a strong sell indicator.
- Using similar logic and techniques, you can also deploy a combination of three averages if your charts allow for this feature; for example, you could trace 50-day, 100-day, and 200-day moving averages on the same chart. In this scenario, a bullish trend will be indicated if the 50-day average curve is above the 100-day moving average, while simultaneously the 100-day moving average remains above the 200-day moving average. You can consider it a buy signal when any lower period moving average crosses above a longer period moving average curve.
- You can also consider it to be a bearish downward trend if the 50-day average curve moves lower than the 100-day average, while the 100-day average is still remaining lower on the chart than the 200-day average.

When you use a combination of three moving averages at the same time this considerably reduces the amount of false signals produced due to short-term pricing fluctuations. However, there is a downside as it also limits your potential for profit. Using three moving averages on a trading signal requires correlations between all three moving averages and this takes longer to show. This means that you will probably only identify buy or sell points after the trend is firmly established. This lag is the unfortunate thing about moving averages but there are some other cons that you should be aware of.

Despite the lag, spotting potential trading data is always present when using moving averages. The reason why they remain so popular is that they adhere to several basic rules of trading. Firstly, once you have identified an entry point as either a buy or sell, using moving averages encourages you to let your profits run while cutting your losses. Secondly, as moving averages generate their trading signals based upon historical data, they in effect force you to trade in the direction of the market, not against it. Thirdly, as opposed to other forms of technical analysis, which are highly subjective techniques, moving averages are quantifiable. Therefore they can be used to generate trading signals according to clear trading rules. What this means is that a lot of the guesswork is taken out of your trading decisions.

Unfortunately, a significant failing when using moving averages is that they are only useful when the market is trending strongly. If the market is not noticeably trending upwards or downwards then using moving averages is of only limited use to you. For example, in times of price volatility but in sideways trending markets when prices fluctuate in a limited range then they do not work at all. Moreover, that is not the exception as these market conditions can occur just as often as upwards or downwards trends (about a third of the time). Building your trading strategy on moving averages alone would not be a very complete strategy since relying on moving averages alone would be foolish and very risky. Consequently, many swing traders recommend combining moving averages with another indicator that is responsible for measuring the overall strength of a trend.

Moving Average Types

Popular types of moving averages are the Simple Moving Average (SMA), which we have already covered earlier, the Exponential Moving Average (EMA), and the Exponentially Weighted Moving Average (EWMA).

Simple Moving Average (SMA)

As we learned earlier, the simple moving average is calculated using the arithmetic mean of all the days in the sample and is the simplest and most commonly used type of moving average. Basically all you need to do is add up all the closing prices for a given period—10 days, for example—which you then subsequently divide by the number of days (10) in the period. However, this primitive method has two basic flaws: It doesn't account for any of the data out with the selected period (a 10-day simple moving average is only interested in the data from the previous 10 days). The SMA simply ignores all the older data prior to this period. Secondly, the SMA also allocates equal weight to all the individual data in the data set.

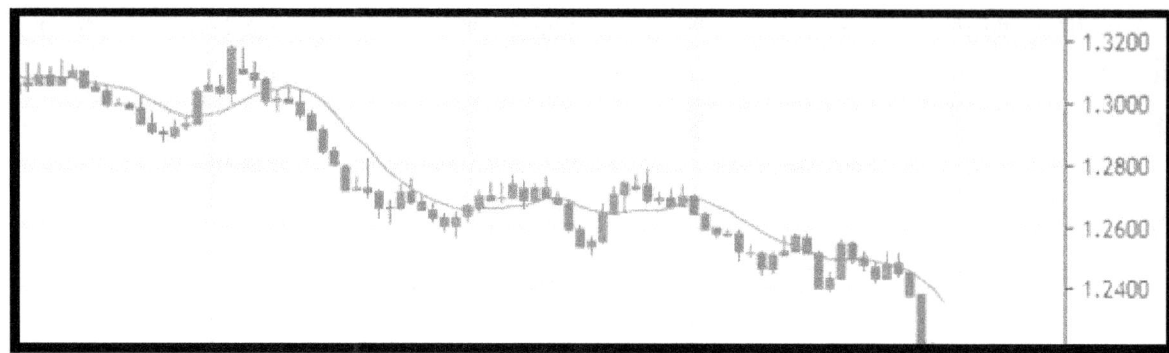

This means that the SMA calculation applied the same relative importance to each day in the period. So in a 10-day moving average, a price from 10 days ago will consider it equal to a price from yesterday (at a weight of 10%). Now the problem there is that the consensus of many traders is that the recent data should carry more weight than older data. The benefit would be in reducing the average's lag behind the trend.

Exponentially Weighted Moving Average (EMA, EWMA)

The solution to the SMA perceived failings was to build an indicator that solves both of the problems associated with the simple moving averages. Firstly, it solves the problem of relative weighing of each data point by allocating more weight in its calculation to recent data. It also takes into account all the historical data for the particular instrument albeit to a much lesser extent.

The EMA, EWMA type of average is named after the fact that it calculates the moving average using weights that decrease exponentially as the data gets older. The slope of this decrease can be adjusted to the needs of the trader.

Oscillators

Another very well-known type of financial indicator used in trading charts is the category of indicators that are referred to as *oscillators*. This category of indicator is typically displayed at the foot of the chart to represent things like trading volume. As such they are popular because these indicators can draw attention to a possible change in the trend, which the moving averages miss. This is because oscillators are most effective where moving averages are least effective (for example, during times of sideways trending markets). Also, oscillators let traders predict possible changes in trends before moving averages can.

Oscillators typically take the form of either bar charts or line charts that are drawn under the price chart for the particular instrument. Oscillators get their name due to the nature of the specific indicator as it tends to oscillate with the metric it is measuring within a certain range. This means that you can analyze the current market situation by studying the oscillator indicator's current position within this range. Oscillators usually move in a sine curve between its two high and low values. This relative position allows you to quickly assess the strength of the indicator.

Purpose and Use in Technical Analysis

Oscillators are primarily used in trading as leading indicators. Their purpose is to alert you of possible new start positions of a new trend or an imminent reversal. When you are analyzing oscillators it is important to consider two things. First you must watch the current position of the oscillator on the sine wave and compare it to the recent trend of the oscillator's values compared to the corresponding price line. This is important as the current value of the oscillator describes the current strength of the trend. This is of value because if you remember, moving averages cannot do this; it can only provide you with historical data on a trend. With oscillators, on the other hand, they can give you a picture of future trending patterns as they can measure momentum.

If the oscillator values are rising, then the trend is gaining momentum and the prices are changing more quickly. If an oscillator's values are dropping, then the prices are probably now changing at a slower rate and so the current trend is losing strength, which can forecast that a reversal will soon happen.

Secondly, you can also use oscillators to detect imbalances in the market. For example, if the instrument is gaining too much momentum and the price is rising sharply, then the oscillator value can be an indicator that the market is overbought. If this occurs you will see the price level is rising too quickly compared to the previous periods. If this is the case then it is highly probable that such a steep rise will be followed by a short-term price correction. At the very least it will result in a loss of momentum in the price trend that will constrain the price rise for some time to come. Similarly, if the oscillator dives quickly then it is indicating an oversold level. In this case it implies that the price is falling too quickly. In this scenario it is probable that the decline will ease up or stop completely, and remain that way for some time. In both cases, overbought and oversold, it can be followed by a trend reversal.

You can use oscillators to detect divergences between the indicator and market price or volume. In this scenario, for example, if the market price reaches the next high and this is higher than the previous high, what you can do is compare the path of the oscillator, MACD. This type of oscillator tracks the difference between moving averages of price for several time periods; if it stops lower than the prices line’s previous high then this likely indicates there is a bearish divergence in the market. This implies that prices are starting to rise slower and with less momentum than in earlier periods. Consequently, you can consider this to be a good indicator that the current trend is losing momentum and backing. When you discover this type of divergence it usually precedes the start of a downward trend.

However, in this case of divergence, the oscillator does not provide you with any clear entry or exit signals. Hence, to get precise trading signals, you will have to use the oscillator in conjunction with other indicators such as moving averages or from signals derived from the study of chart patterns.

Using Trading Signals

As you can see, using oscillators in order to generate trading signals is highly advantageous. The most successfully-adapted trading signal are those when the oscillator enters either the oversold or the overbought zones. This range can be identified since most times it starts when the oscillator's value matches a specific value. Typically, this oscillator's specific metric value can be changed to take into consideration the current market conditions and your needs.

For instance, if you were to use the oscillator indicator of Relative Strength Index (RSI) (this indicator, like moving averages, is commonly available on charts) then you may look out for it crossing above the value of 70. This may well imply that the market is overbought and thus provide you with a clear early signal to close your long positions. In addition you can also take this as a clear notification to start moving into selling short. Conversely, should the RSI cross below the value of 30, it means that the market is perhaps being oversold. This implies that you should cover your short positions and start buying.

Interestingly, many successful traders wait until the RSI breaches the overbought/oversold level for the second time in succession before they are confident in opening positions in opposite direction to the current trend. Like moving averages and other indicators, oscillators often also tend to suffer from noise and they can generate false signals. However, the frequency of false signals can be easily reduced by modifying the critical values. In our example here you could change the RSI thresholds from 70/30 for overbought and oversold respectively to 80/20. This is a tradeoff; although this will effectively reduce the number of false signals, it also reduces the total amount of all signals. What this means is that we will detect and act upon a trend reversal later than if you were using the less stringent thresholds.

Another very popular signal used by experienced traders for opening a position with confidence occurs when the oscillator breaches its midpoint value. So in this scenario you are looking out for when the oscillator's path crosses into the other half of its scale. The rule of thumb is that if the oscillator's value climbs above the midpoint value, but is still below the overbought area, then this can be considered a reliable indicator that the upward trend should continue. On the other hand, if the oscillator's value falls below the midpoint value, but has not yet reached the oversold area, then it too can be considered a reliable indicator that the downward trend should continue and the price should continue to fall.

One oscillator used for such purposes is the MACD, which has a scale of 1 to -1 and a midpoint value of 0. In this case, if you are monitoring the MACD and it decreases from 1 towards -1, it crosses the midpoint value, which implies a reversal, and the recent price gains will be replaced by short-term price decreases. Hence it generates a sell signal. Conversely, if the MACD later climbs from the -1 area to the value of 0.5 it again crosses the midpoint value but this time it generates a buy signal. However, when you use this signal, it's recommended not to open positions against the trend's overall direction.

Pros and Cons

Oscillators are often most reliable in periods when there is no clear trend in the market, when prices are moving sideways usually in a narrow band between the strong support and resistance levels. Under such market conditions the oscillators can yield quite precise buy and sell signals by identifying the oversold or overbought levels.

However, problems come when the market moves strongly in a certain direction. If this is the case then the support (or resistance) will typically be breached and consequently start a new trend. Unfortunately, under these conditions, oscillators are worthless as they almost always will generate erroneous overbought or oversold signals. Nonetheless, during these periods the oscillator's values may remain in these positions on the scale for some time. This can catch traders off guard and these signals can lead to large losses. Consequently, it is considered wiser that during a price breach of a support or resistance level to ignore the oscillators completely as the new trend emerges. Nonetheless, later on when the trend is nearing its end you can start to monitor the oscillators once again. This is because they will become worth watching, since they offer interesting information about possible divergences within the trend. If you recall, earlier we revealed that spotting divergences in the trend early on can help us to detect any potential reversals. This is especially true if the trend is reaching the overbought or oversold levels. One other rule of thumb is that the signals generated by oscillators are more reliable the more mature a trend.

Popular Oscillator Types

MACD (Moving Average Convergence/Divergence)

The MACD oscillator is one of the popular and widely used trend-following indicators that you will come across. It combines the very useful complimentary properties of a moving average indicator with those of an oscillator. In addition, it uses the difference between several exponential moving averages to plot the trend. The most commonly used periods for the moving averages trend line used in MACD are 9, 12, and 26 days. However, you are able to adjust it to use your own preferred time periods.

The way that the MACD is plotted is by using two lines:

1. The first line that is plotted will be the actual MACD line. This relates to a 12-day exponential moving average of prices minus a 26-day exponential moving average of prices

2. The second line is the Signal line, which consists of a 9-day exponential moving average of MACD values

When the MACD is plotted on a chart it is typically plotted either as the two lines, the MACD and the signal, or as a histogram of the difference between these two lines. The histogram is gaining more popularity as it is easier to read in this format, and is believed to be easier to see any divergences between the MACD and the price. Regardless, the real value of the MACD is that a buy signal is indicated when it crosses above the zero line. Conversely, a sell signal in generated when it crosses below zero. Therefore, as this is the place where the two lines (MACD and signal line) will intersect, it makes the analysis much easier to spot.

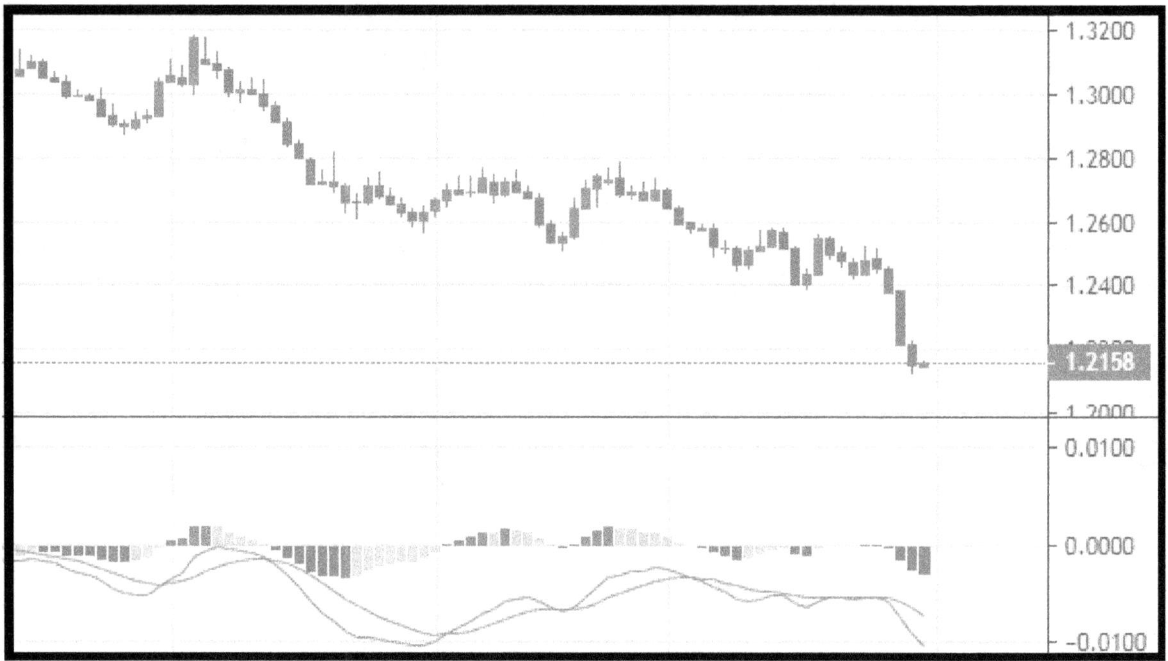

The trading signals that MACD generates are based upon simple logic:

- In the case where the MACD line rises above the signal line, this will indicate a buy signal.

- In the case whereby the MACD line drops beneath the signal line, then a sell signal is indicated.
- When the MACD line crosses above zero, it yields a buy signal.
- Conversely, when the MACD line crosses under zero, it is considered a sell signal.

Moreover, you should also look out for when there is a steep rise or drop of the MACD line relative to historical values. This could also be considered a strong indicator of an overbought or oversold state in the market. Nonetheless, unlike most other oscillators, MACD's values are not standardized, and that's why there is not a clear rule of thumb regarding how high or low a MACD rise or fall needs to be in order to be considered overbought or oversold. That's why you will need to do a comparison of the current MACD's values to historical values that you used in the past.

The Relative Strength Index (RSI)

The RSI is a popular oscillator, which measures the rate of increase or decrease in price of a stock over a certain period. As an output, the RSI generates a buy or sell signal when it reaches a level associated with a security considered to be at an overbought or oversold level. The relative strength indicator works on a scale of 0-100.

As the RSI is a very common oscillator, it is commonly available with brokers graphs and charts, and even with stock tickers.

The RSI formula is:

RSI= 100 - (100/ (1+ RS))

Where: RS= (average daily price increase / average daily price decrease)

When calculating the RSI it is typical to use a period of 14 days when making the calculations. However, like other oscillators, when you use a shorter period the more sensitive RSI becomes to price changes, which also leads to further increases in the number of false signals produced. Regardless, when you want to calculate the RSI manually, what you do is add up all the points by which the price increased during the uptrend days and then divide the total by the number of days (14). Generally, the RSI indicator tells you that:

- If the RSI rises above the 30 level, this is a buy signal.
- If the RSI falls under the 70 level, then this a sell signal.

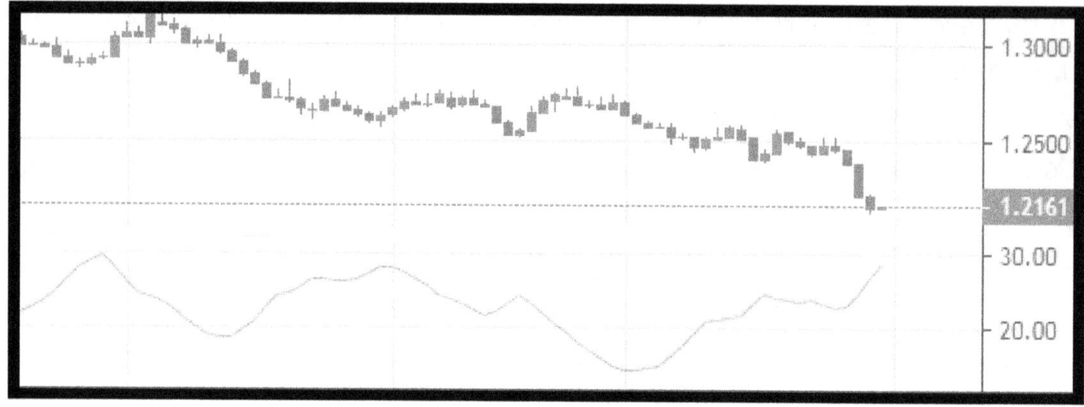

RSI, unlike some other oscillators, has the advantage of being standardized. What this means is that its range of values is contained between 0 and 100. Hence, when you are using RSI it is relatively easy to read the level and then determine any overbought and oversold areas. The typical values are considered to be at over 70 for overbought and under 30 for an oversold condition. Despite this, as we have seen, some traders like to change those thresholds in order to eliminate any false signals. Consequently, they tend to prefer to change the values to 80 and 20.

Another thing about RSI is that it is also used for finding divergences. This is the case when the RSI moves in the opposite direction to price. If this is the case then there is the probability that a price reversal in about to happen. Moreover, crossing the middle value of 50 in either direction is sometimes considered by some traders to be a price reversal prediction signal.

Stochastic

The purpose of the stochastic indicator is to assist in attempting to evaluate where the current price is relative to the last few days. When using stochastic, the premise is that if market prices are rising, closing prices for every day will tend to be near the upper boundary of the price range for the last few days. On the other hand, if prices are dropping, then the closing prices will tend to be closer to the lower boundary of the last few days' price range.

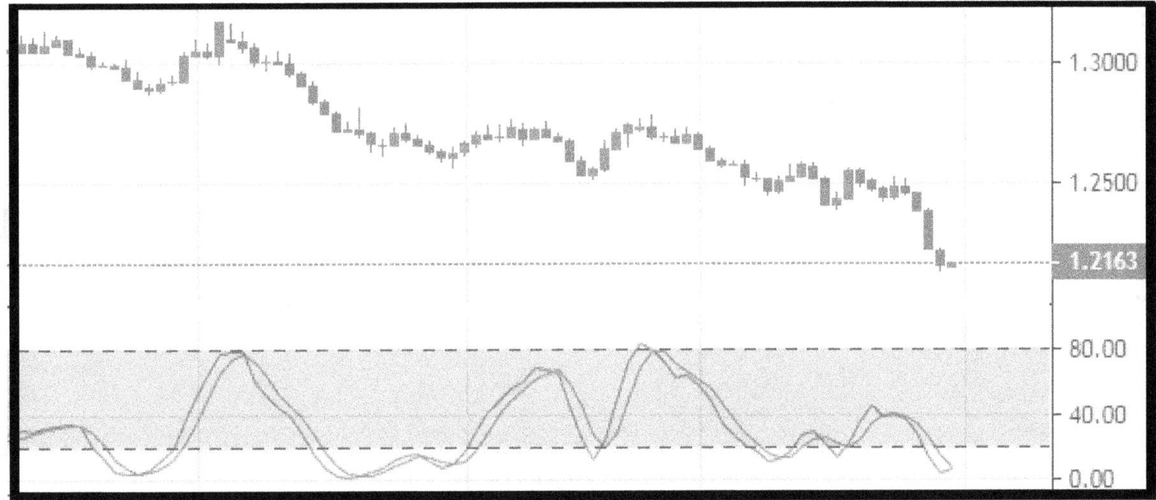

Again, a medium range of 14-days price range is used to avoid any extra sensitivity or false signals.

There is also a fast stochastic version which uses a smaller timeframe; this is popular with day traders. In fast stochastic you simply replace the last 14 days values with the last 14 hours or 14 minutes values. This is, of course, more of value in day trading.

In addition, there is also another version of this indicator called full stochastic. In this case the full stochastic differs in that it uses three lines. All versions of stochastic work in the same way in that the stochastic values will range between 0 and 100. In cases where the stochastic crosses over 80 it means that the market is overbought and thus indicates a sell signal.

A buy signal is implied by the stochastic crossing under 20 as this is a strong indicator of an oversold market.

Average Directional Index (ADX)

The purpose of the ADX oscillator is that it is used to measure a trend's relative strength. Its computation is not easily explained and beyond the scope of this book. But suffice to say that it is based on the relationships between changes of prices during each trading session. ADX consists of two lines:

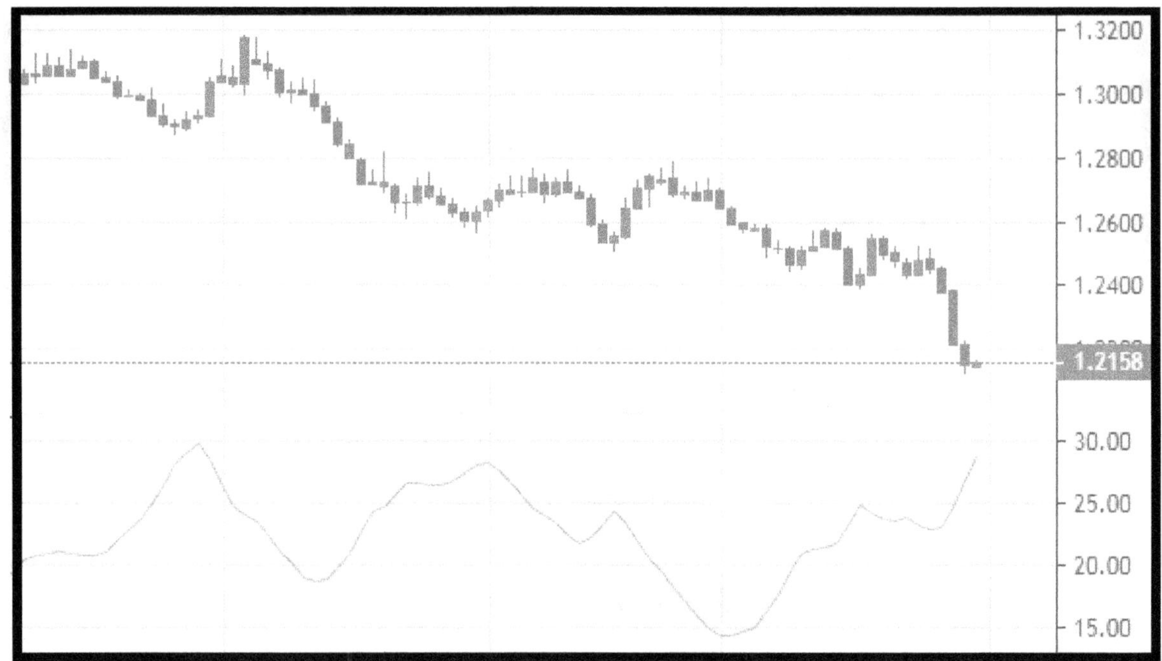

The way it works is that ADX calculates two trends—one based upon the upward trend which is called the +DI line. A second -DI line is also calculated and this represents the downward trend. The ADX indicator itself shown in the diagram above is the difference between these two lines.

Fortunately ADX is not so complicated to use as it is standardized and its values are limited to between 0 and 100.

In general, ADX follows some basic rules: If the ADX's values are rising, then the trend is bullish and gaining momentum. However, should the ADX values be falling then the trend is losing momentum.

Very generally, ADX values greater than 40 represent a strong trend, and values under 20 indicate lost momentum, which more likely points to a sideways trending market and a period of consolidation.

ADX can also be used like MACD to show a divergence between trend and price. This can be seen when the price strikes a new high while the ADX is instead decreasing. However, this divergence is not considered to be a strong trading signal—indeed, it is typically thought of as just an indicator that the current trend is beginning to lose momentum. Nonetheless, sometimes trades will be initiated in the opposite direction based upon ADX. But this isn't something recommended for beginners. However, experienced traders will initiate trades against the current market trend when ADX shows the +DI line intersecting with the -DI line.

ADX is popular because it is an easy way to determine the strength of the trend, albeit with some unavoidable time lag. ADX provides traders with information that gives them the highest chance of successful trading with or against the current market trends.

Chapter 7 – Reading Candlestick Charts

Candlesticks have been used in trading charts going back all the way to the 17th century, when they were first recorded as being used by Japanese rice traders. An updated version was introduced into the US around 1900, but many of the principles were very similar:

- The "what" or rather, the *price action*, was still considered to be more important than the "why" (news, earnings, and so on).
- All the known price information is reflected in the candlestick.
- Buying and selling pressure caused market movement; this is based on fear and greed.
- Markets do fluctuate due to the levels of relative stress applied by buyers and sellers.
- The market price may not reflect the actual value of the underlying security.

Candlestick Formations

When you first create a candlestick chart, you must have a basic data set that contains price data related to the date, the opening, highest, lowest, and closing price values for each time period you want to display. Some charts also include volume but that is unnecessary for a pure candlestick chart.

The way that the candlestick is represented on a chart tells you all about the prices and even sometimes the trading volumes. The shape of the candlestick determines several key pieces of price data. The body of the candle can be hollow or filled in, it can also be of varying length with upper and lower thin lines called *shadows* or sometimes *wicks* and *tails*. These shadows represent the highest and lowest prices. The highest price is represented by the wick, or the tip of the upper shadow, and the lowest price by the tail at the bottom of the lower shadow. The earliest candlesticks were in black and white but today's charts use red and green respectively. Hence the naming of many early candlestick formations refer to black (filled-in) and white (hollow) objects.

Now, the color and shape of the candlestick varies depending on price movement. So for example, should the stock, index, or currency close higher than its opening price, a hollow or green candlestick is drawn. The length of the candle's body is determined by the difference between the lower opening price and the higher closing price. On the other hand, should the traded instrument close at a lower price than its opening price, a filled or red candlestick is drawn. In both cases, the top of the body always represents the higher price and the bottom of the body the lower price.

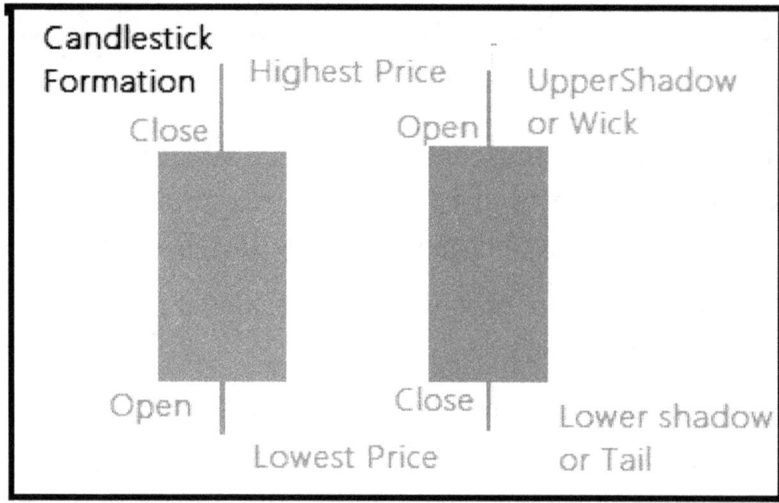

Each candlestick is designed to provide a simple representation of all of the price action. You really need to understand the candlestick formation as then you will be able to see the relationship between the open and close price as well as the high and low prices.

The thing to bear in mind is that the relationship between the open and close provides important trading data on market sentiment and trading pressure. For example, you will be able to tell immediately that a hollow or green candlestick indicates buying pressure. The filled-in or red candlesticks show selling pressure. In addition to the body being hollow/green or filled-in/red, the longer the body indicates the strength of the buying or selling pressure. But if there are very short candlesticks, with little or no body, that look like a cross, then this indicates that there is no price movement in both directions and this is likely to represent market indecision or consolidation.

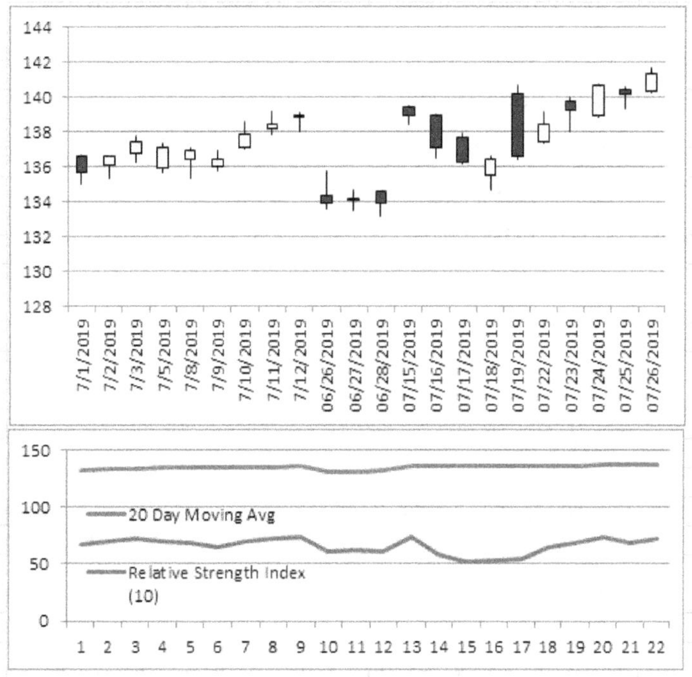

If you look at the candlestick chart above you can see that a hollow candlestick shows buying pressure. Moreover, the length of the hollow candlestick tells you how much further the closing price was above the opening price. This is a strong indicator that prices advanced significantly from open to close and it was the buyers who were more aggressive and won the day. Nonetheless, although these hollow long candlesticks are generally seen as being representative of a bullish market sentiment, a lot will depend on their position within the chart. For example, the presence of a long hollow candlestick can mark after a period of extended price declines, a potential price turning point, or a future support point. But it is not always a messenger of good news because if a long hollow candlestick is present after a period of extended buying then this could well signal excessive bullishness and that the instrument is likely about to be overbought.

Conversely, the presence on a chart of long filled-in candlesticks represents a strong selling pressure. The longer the black/red candlestick body, the further the closing price was below the opening price. This condition indicates that prices declined significantly from the market opening and sellers were the most aggressive. After a long period of upward price trending the presence of a long filled-in candlestick can be prescient in detecting a trend reversal or mark a future resistance level. After a sustained period of price decline, a long filled-in candlestick can also indicate panic or capitulation.

There is another type of candlestick formation that you should know about and these are called the *Marubozu Brothers*. They are more potent indicators of market strength but like the others they represent price direction using black (red) and white (green) bodies. Interestingly, the Marubozu candlesticks do not have upper or lower shadows, as the high and low are matched and therefore represented by the open or close prices. For example, in the case of a white Marubozu, this forms when the opening equals the lowest price and the close price equals the highest price. In this scenario the Marubozu indicates that the market buyers are very in control of the price action from the opening trade to the closing trade. On the other hand, a black Marubozu is present when the opposite market condition is true and the opening price equals the highest and the close equals the lowest price. This indicates that market sentiment heavily favored the sellers as they controlled the price action from the first opening trade to the last closing trade.

Long and Short Shadows

It is not just the candlestick body we need to concern ourselves with, as the shadows at both ends hold pertinent information. For example, the upper shadows, or wick, represent the trading session's highest price and the lower shadow, or tail, represent the trading session's lowest price. Hence, any candlesticks with a short shadow or wick will indicate that the majority of the trading action was confined near the open and close. Any candlesticks that have long shadows or wicks indicate that prices extended well past the open and close.

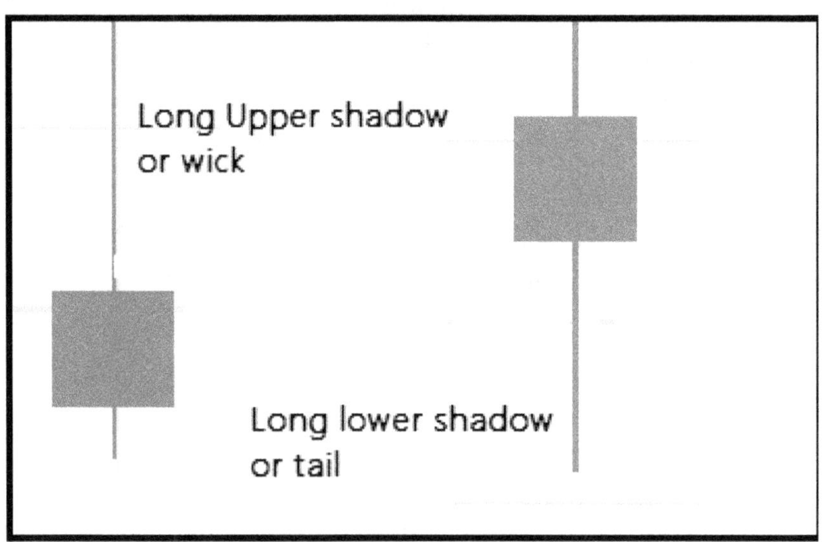

Similarly, if you find candlesticks with a long upper shadow, or wick, and short lower shadow, or tail, then this indicates that buyers have dominated during the trading session. This is due to the contrast of an earlier strong high price during the session and a relatively weak close price, which resulted in a long upper shadow. This means that bidding prices during trading was higher, but then sellers managed to drive prices back downwards from their earlier highest prices. Conversely, you may find that candlesticks with long lower shadows and short upper shadows indicate that it was the turn of the sellers to dominate during the trading session and they succeeded, albeit temporarily, to drive prices lower. However, once again the market changed and this time it was the buyers who later made a successful resurgence to bid prices higher and claimed lost ground by the end of the session. In this scenario the strong close is represented by a long lower shadow or tail.

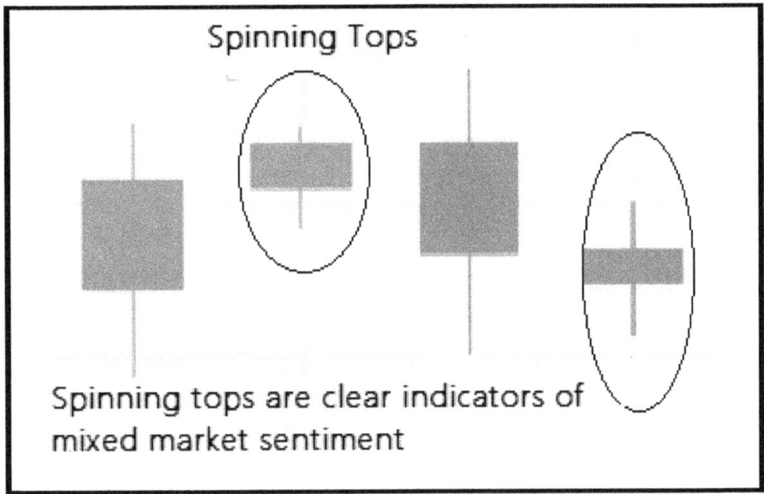

Candlesticks with a long upper shadow or wick, as well as a long lower shadow or tail, combined with a small body, are called *spinning tops*. Previously we saw that the presence of long shadows at either end where representative of a reversal of market sentiment in some direction. However, in the case of spinning tops, these represent market indecision. This is because their small body, regardless of color, shows that there has been very little movement from the opening to closing prices. Further, the shadows at both ends indicate that both buyers and sellers were equally active during the trading session. However, it also shows that despite there being little movement in opening and closing price, there was significant movement in both directions. Despite this, neither buyers nor sellers could gain an advantage and the final result was a stalemate. The presence of a spinning top after a long advance or after a long white candlestick indicates weakness and indecision among the buyers, and a potential change in trend. The presence of a spinning top following a period of decline or after a long black candlestick means indecision and weakness among the sellers and a potential change in trend.

Doji

The Doji candlestick represents when a security's open and close prices are virtually equal. Typically, the length of the upper and lower shadows will vary, and consequently the resulting candlestick will look more like a cross, an inverted cross, or even if the shadows are small and equal, a plus sign. Alone, the Doji candlesticks are considered to be neutral patterns as there is neither a bullish nor bearish bias. As such, the Doji convey a sense of indecision between buyers and sellers.

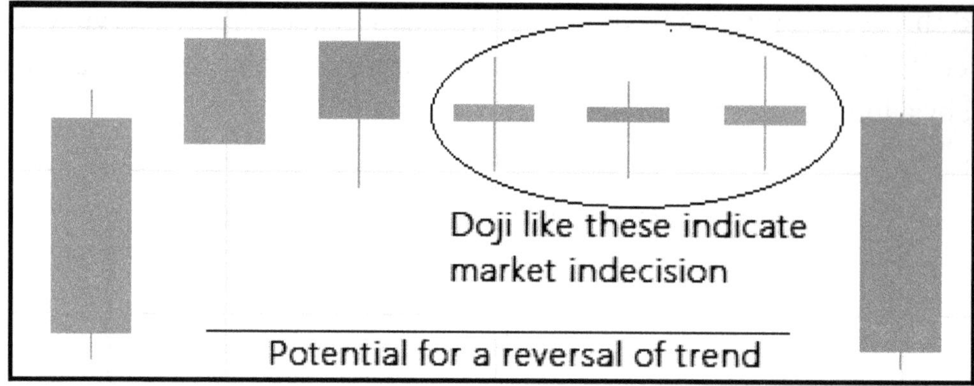

Regardless, when determining the robustness of the Doji you will need to depend on the price, any recent volatility, and previous candlesticks. Relative to previous candlesticks, many traders say that a Doji that forms among candlesticks with small bodies would not be considered important. On the other hand, a Doji that forms among candlesticks with long bodies would be considered significant.

Doji and Trend

As we have just seen, the actual relevance of a Doji depends almost entirely on the preceding trend or the preceding candlesticks. For example, if a Doji is present after an upward trend, or after a long white candlestick, then the Doji signals that the buying enthusiasm is beginning to weaken. Similarly, if the Doji appears after a period of decline, or after a long black candlestick, then its signals can be considered an indicator that the selling pressure is starting to weaken. This is because in both cases the Doji indicates indecision and that a potential change in trend may be possible. A presence of a Doji does not mark a reversal since it is not a strong enough signal. Furthermore, the length of the shadows on the Doji also indicates the level of indecision. The greater the length of the shadows (or *legs*, in the case of the Doji), the greater the range of trading has been in both directions. However, neither side was able to overpower the other so the level of indecision remains high.

What Candlesticks Don't Tell

Candlesticks unfortunately cannot tell you everything as they do not reflect the sequence of events between the open and close prices. They really only tell you the relationship between the opening and the closing price. The high and the low prices are also provided but they do not relate how those prices came about. For instance, there may have been many swings back and forth during the trading session before the final high and low prices came about, but simple candlesticks cannot relate this information to you.

Candlestick Positions

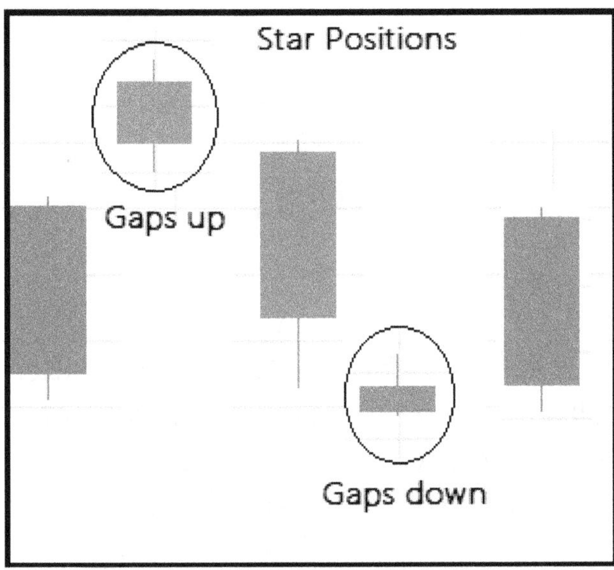

Star Position

A Star position is said to be when a candlestick gaps away from the previous candlestick and may not even appear to be connected to the current price trend (i.e. it is situated a lot higher or lower). Typically, in a Star position, the proceeding candlestick will have a large body and the following candlestick, which is in the star position, will have a small body. The Star position is dependent on the previous candlestick form, as the Star position candlestick is said to gap up or down (i.e. take a higher or lower position in relation to the body of the preceding candlestick). Typically, the two candlesticks can be any combination of white and black and the candlestick in the Star position may be a Doji or a spinning top, or some other formation that has a functional small body.

Hammer and Hanging Man

As we can see in the diagram above, the Hammer and Hanging Man look exactly alike, and this is why pattern observation is so ambiguous. But they do have different information on the ongoing trend based on the preceding price action. This is because both have small bodies (black/red or white/green), as well as long lower shadows coupled with very short or non-existent upper shadows. Hence, most single and double candlestick formations, including the Hammer and Hanging Man, require confirmation before taking trading action.

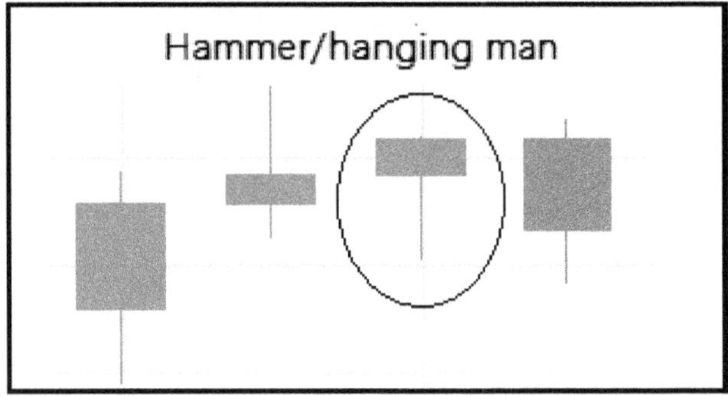

However, after saying that, you can consider the Hammer to be a bullish reversal pattern should you find it just after a sustained price fall. In addition to being an indication of a potential trend reversal, Hammers may also identify prospective support levels. So after a sustained decline in price, the Hammer's candlestick could signal a bullish revival.

Furthermore, the low of the long lower shadow will indicate that the sellers have taken the initiative and driven prices lower during the trading session. However, the strong finish that results in the pattern also indicates that the buyers recovered to end the session on a high.

Now you might think this is sufficient market intelligence to act upon as the low of the Hammer shows that there are plenty of sellers active in the market. Therefore to drive prices higher would require more buying pressure which would also require more trading volume. But before you trade you should seek confirmation. That could come from the presence of a long white candlestick. This is because Hammers are indicators of selling peaks, and heavy volume can serve to reinforce the validity of the reversal.

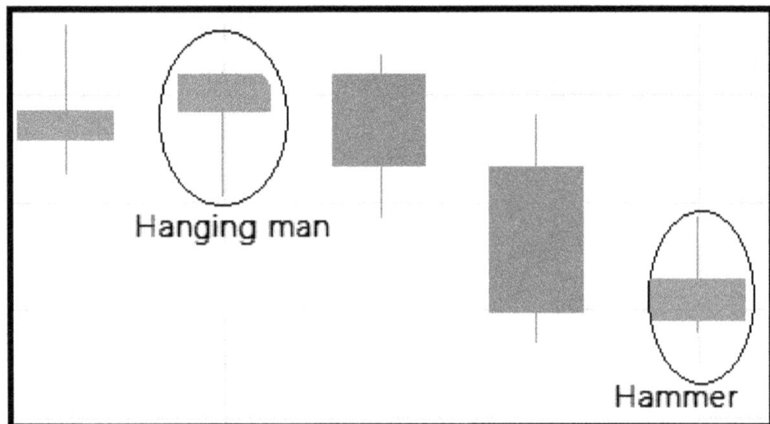

On the other hand, the Hanging Man is a bearish reversal pattern that indicates a top or resistance level has been met. This most commonly comes around after it emerges following an upward trend. In this scenario, the emergence of a Hanging Man signals that selling pressure is starting to increase. In this case, the lower shadow confirms that sellers are gaining confidence and starting to force the prices lower during the trading session. Regardless, that the buyers regain the initiative and once more drive prices higher by the close, the appearance of that large amount of selling pressure should raise concern. As with the Hammer, a Hanging Man requires further other bearish indicators for confirmation before any price action. Such confirmation may come from seeing a gap down or long black candlestick on heavy volume.

Inverted Hammer and Shooting Star

Similar to the Hammer and the Hanging Man formations are the Inverted Hammer and Shooting Star. They look exactly alike but they also contain information that is only viable based on previous price action. Both the candlesticks have small real bodies and it doesn't matter whether they are black or white, with long upper shadows or small lower shadows. These candlesticks mark potential trend reversals, but they also require further confirmation before taking a price action.

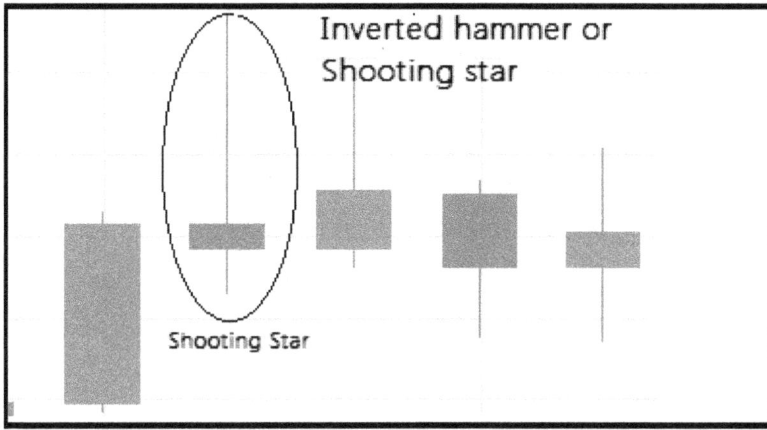

As we discussed earlier, the Shooting Star is a bearish reversal pattern that appears after an upwards price advance and somewhere above the body of the previous candle. A Shooting Star can mark a potential trend reversal or a new resistance level. The Shooting Star candlestick emerges when the price gaps higher on the opening, then climbs during the trading session, and subsequently closes well down on the previous highs. Consequently, the candlestick has a long upper shadow and small black or white body.

Indeed, after a large advance, which is demonstrated by the tall upper shadow, the ability of the seller to rally and subsequently force prices down may be a warning. You must be careful that the sellers are not through yet and to confirm a substantial reversal, with any confidence, the upper shadow should be at least two times the length of the body. This is enough to provide a bearish confirmation and it can also take the form of a sudden gap down or a long black candlestick supported by heavy volume.

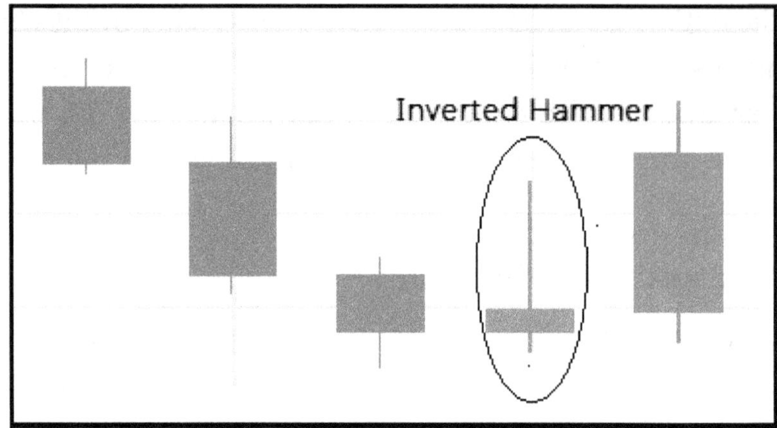

Finally, let us look at the last of our individual candlesticks called the Inverted Hammer. This candlestick looks just like a Shooting Star, which is why pattern recognition requires careful study, but it forms only after a decline or downtrend. The Inverted Hammers represent a potential trend reversal or new emerging support level. The reason for this is that after a sustained fall in price, the long upper shadow in the Inverted Hammer indicates much more buying pressure during the trading session. You could surmise that the sellers were not able to sustain this pressure on the buyers but they did enough and the prices subsequently closed well off of the session highs to create that long upper shadow. Because of this failure, it would seem that the market is still not confident enough to go bullish so further confirmation is required before further price action. Nonetheless, the appearance of an Inverted Hammer that is followed by a gap up or long white candlestick with heavy volume can act as that sought after bullish confirmation.

Long Shadow Reversals

Sometimes you will come across pairs of single candlesticks in a reversal pattern. These are typically made up of a long body paired with a small body candlestick. In this case one may have a long shadow and the other a short shadow. In most cases where you see this pattern, the long shadow should be at least twice the length of its body, regardless of whether it is black or white. In this scenario you would look at the location of the long shadow and any preceding price action to determine the classification.

For example, if we consider the Hammer and Hanging Man formats, then you will see that they consist of identical candlesticks with small bodies and long lower shadows. However, in the second example, the Shooting Star and Inverted Hammer also contain identical candlesticks, and also with identical small bodies and similar long upper shadows. It would take consideration of the preceding price action to provide further confirmation on whether the trend will be bullish or bearish in nature.

Most traders do agree that when they see the Hammer and Inverted Hammer forms after a decline then this tends to indicate a bullish reversal pattern. On the other hand, if you spot a pattern whereby the Shooting Star and Hanging Man form a pattern just after an upward trend, then these are patterns that will typically suggest a bearish reversal pattern.

Blending Candlesticks

Another thing that you can do with candlesticks is that under certain circumstances you can blend consecutive candlesticks together to form one aggregate candlestick. This method of blending candlesticks together actually captures more fully the essence of the ongoing trend and it can be achieved using the following technique:

- You calculate the opening price of the first candlestick
- Then you match it with the closing price of the last candlestick
- By doing so you discover the high and low of the combined pattern

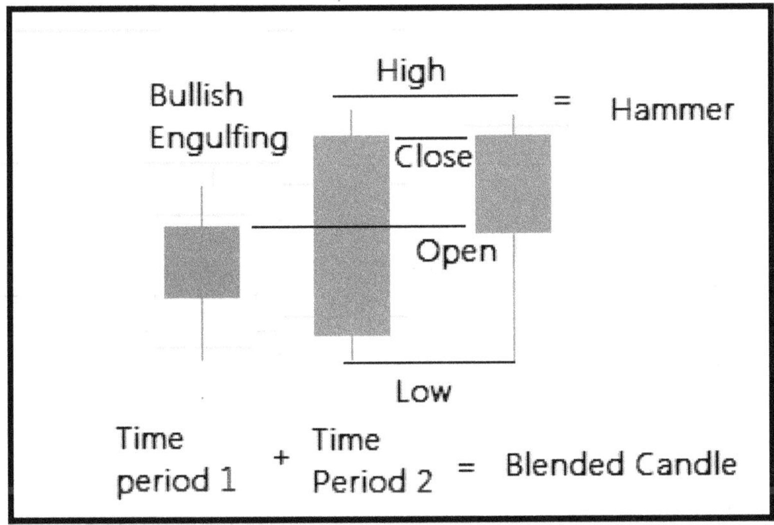

In the diagram we can see how we can blend the candlesticks of two contrasting candlesticks to form a Hammer. In addition we can do the same thing to make a Shooting Star.

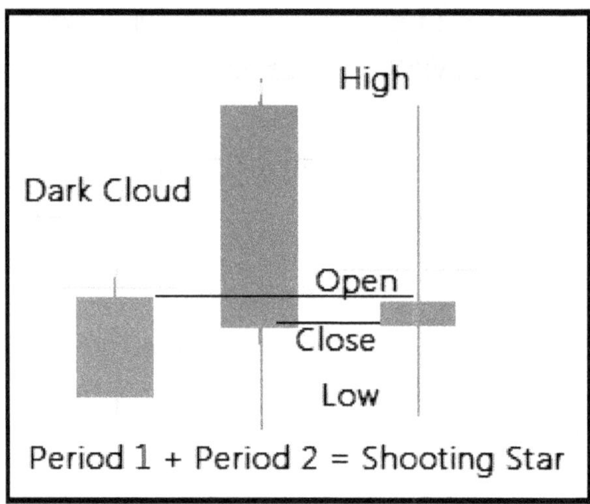

By doing so we can see that binding the candlestick patterns together we can reimage a form whereby the long, upper shadow of the Shooting Star indicates a potential bearish reversal. Nonetheless, as we have witnessed with the Shooting Star, Bearish Engulfing, and Dark Cloud Cover Patterns, they all requires more bearish indicators as confirmation before we make a price order trade.

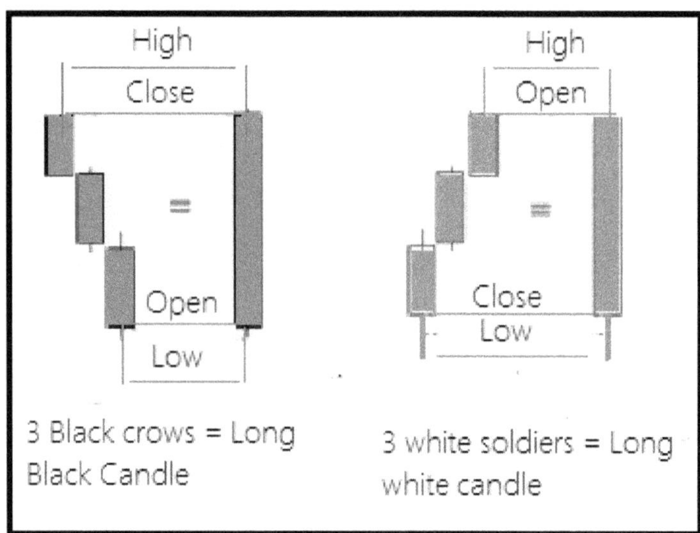

Moreover, we can also add more than two candles to amalgamate a trading position. In this case you would search for and identify more than two candlesticks that have similar form. If these can be detected then you can easily blend them together using the same guidelines of: open from the first, close from the last, and use the high/low of the pattern. By blending these common characteristic candles together, you can become accustomed to trading using the Three White Soldiers, which form three smaller-bodied candles to create a long white candlestick, and then blending the Three Black Crows, which in turn reveals a long black candlestick from three single smaller-bodied candles.

Chapter 8 - Chart Pattern Analysis

Indicators and oscillators are not always the best things to use when trying to judge trends or reversals. Sometimes you need to just go naked and use the price to guide your direction. Many traders do feel this way and have abandoned the high-tech oscillators and indicators for more subjective discovery of patterns within trends. The premise here is that even in Chaos theory, mathematicians believe that they can identify recurring patterns amongst the chaos. Traders have latched on to this possibly optimistic claim so have spent years analyzing charts in order to find these recurring patterns that could be the holy grail in trading.

Here's the list of chart patterns that they have uncovered and believe reoccur prior to or during significant changes in trend behavior. We will take a look at some of the main patterns, but be aware there are many more that we cannot possibly cover here.

Double Top & Double Bottom

Double top or double bottom chart pattern are indicators of an imminent trend reversal. The double top is a reversal pattern that comes about after an extended upward trend has tested but failed to break through a resistance level. After hitting this level the first time, the price will fall back slightly, but then it will rebound in another concerted effort to push the price through the resistance. However, should it fail to break through, then you have what is known as a double top. The "double tops" are the peaks or buying pressure which are formed when the price hits the resistance levels.

Double Top

In the chart above you can see where two peaks or "tops" formed at the resistance levels after a strong upwards push. With a double tops pattern it is often the case that the second top does not match the high of the first top. This can be considered an indicator that the uptrend is lacking motivation and that a reversal may be about to follow. This is because the pattern is showing you that the buying pressure is almost exhausted. When trading using the double top pattern, you would ideally place your entry order just below the neckline as you are anticipating an imminent reversal of the price trend.

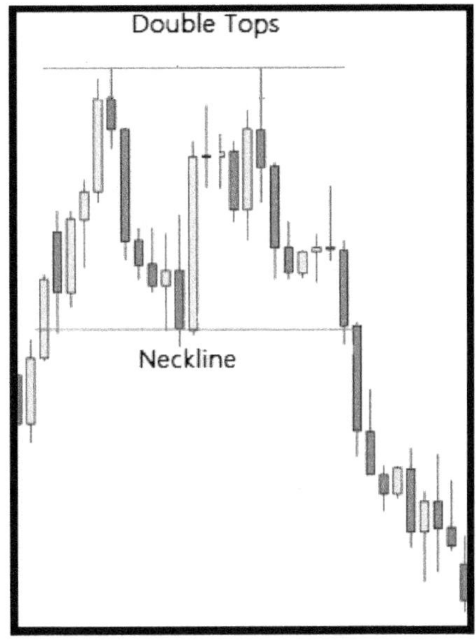

Double Top Breakdown

If you look at the chart you can see that the price breaks up through the neckline and makes two attempts to break through the resistance. After the second attempt the price drops below the neckline then falls away sharply. The double top pattern shows a lack of buying pressure, which indicates a trend reversal formation. In this case you will likely see a strong down trend. You will want to look for double tops after a strong uptrend.

Double Bottom

Similarly we see the same pattern, but in reverse with the double bottom. This is also a trend reversal pattern. It indicates the end of a downtrend. The double bottom occurs after an extended downwards trends when the price "bottoms" and fails to break through the support floor.

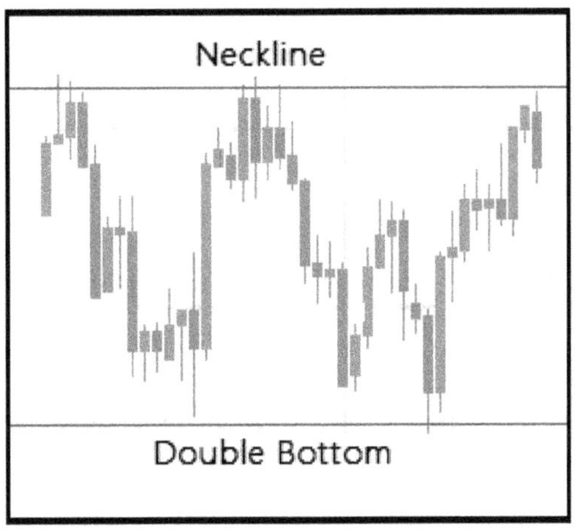

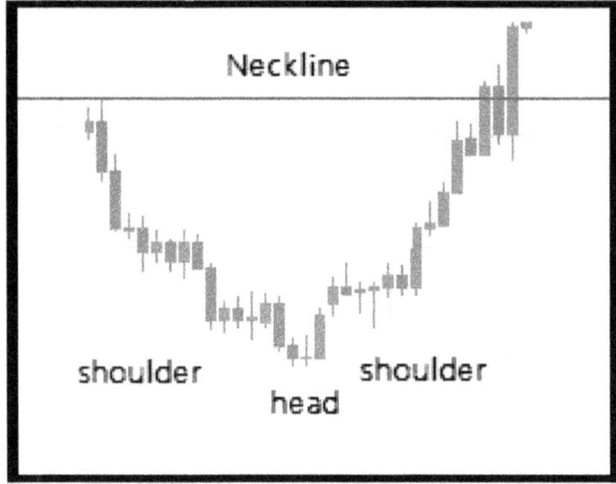

Wedges

When you see a wedge pattern it indicates consolidation and a stall in the current trend. This is because wedges can be either continuation or reversal patterns.

Rising Wedge

A rising wedge is formed when prices find themselves constrained during a period of consolidation between upward sloping support line and the falling resistance levels. In a rising wedge the slope of the support line is steeper than the slope of the resistance lines. This indicates that there is sideways trending with higher lows forming faster than the higher highs. When you see prices consolidating like this there is often a big breakout either to the top or bottom. Either way, the important thing is that if you come across this wedge-shaped trading chart pattern, you need to be prepared to enter a trade.

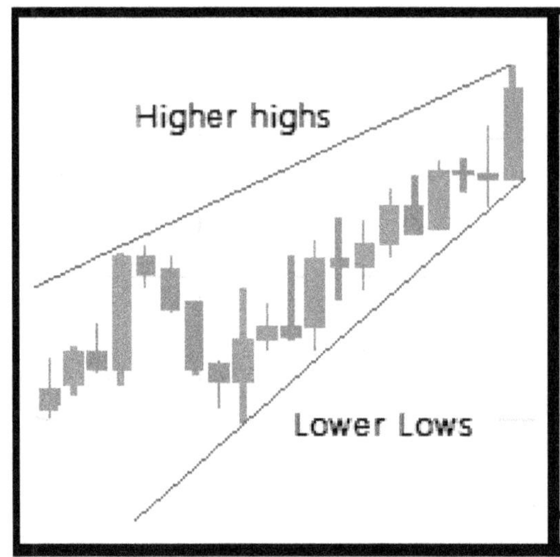

In the diagram above you can see a rising wedge form at the end of an uptrend.

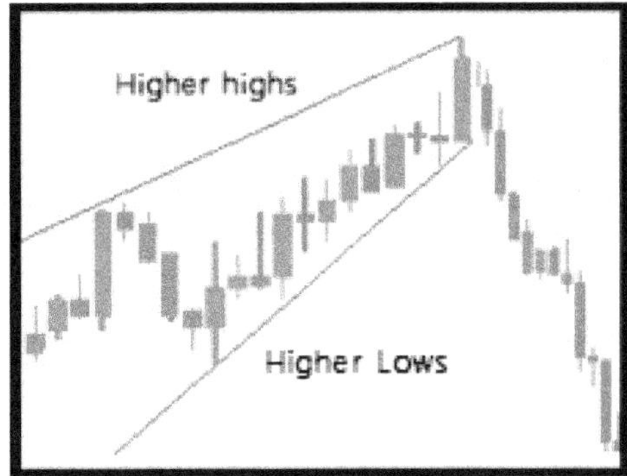

Just like in the head and shoulders and double tops/bottom, in the wedge pattern the price movement after the successful breakout will be around the same size as the height of the formation. One other thing for you to note is that typically a rising wedge that is formed after an uptrend will lead to a reversal, i.e. a downtrend. However, the opposite is not true as a rising wedge formed during a downtrend typically will produce further consolidation of the downtrend. Therefore, you should consider the rising wedge to be a bearish pattern.

Falling Wedge

The falling wedge can either be a reversal or continuation pattern that is considered to be bullish in nature. When it acts as a reversal pattern it forms at the bottom of a downtrend. This should indicate to you that there is likely a reversal to an uptrend to follow. However, it may also act as a continuation signal. In this case it will be formed during an uptrend, and this indicates the upward price action will continue after a pause.

1.

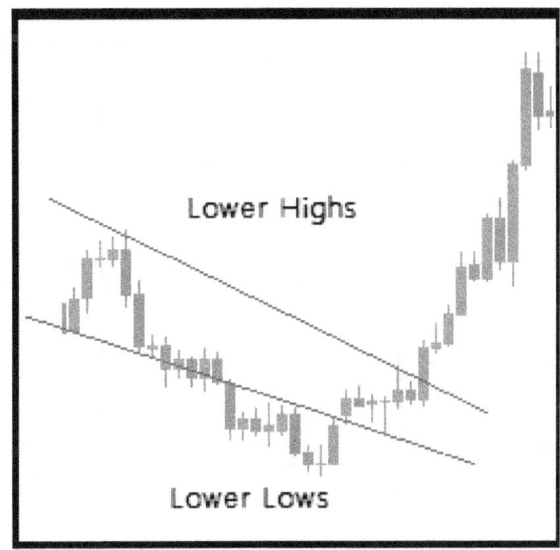

Rectangles

A rectangle is a chart pattern occurring when the price trend is moving sideways and is constrained by parallel support and resistance levels. A rectangle pattern indicates a period of indecision by both the buyers and sellers. The rectangle is formed due to the price testing but failing to break through the support and resistance constraints. However, it is only a matter of time before it breaks out whether it is to the upside or downside.

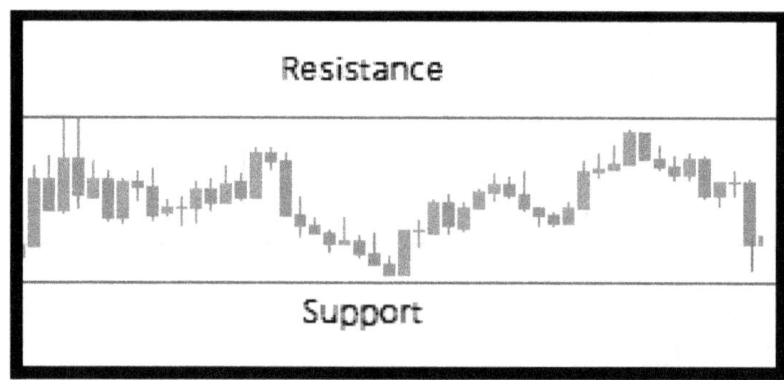

In the example above, we can see that the price was constrained by the support and resistance levels which are parallel to one another and forcing the trend sideways.

Bearish Rectangle

In the case of a bearish rectangle this pattern will be formed during a period of price consolidation during a downtrend. This often occurs when the seller pressure weakens but is still motivated. In the example below, the price consolidates and trends sideways but it does eventually break out through the support level of the rectangle chart pattern and continues to trend downwards.

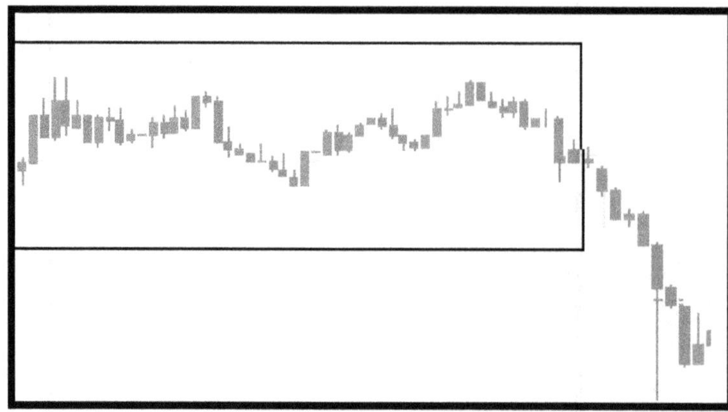

Bullish Rectangle

There is also a bullish rectangle and this occurs after an extended uptrend when the price pauses during a period of consolidation.

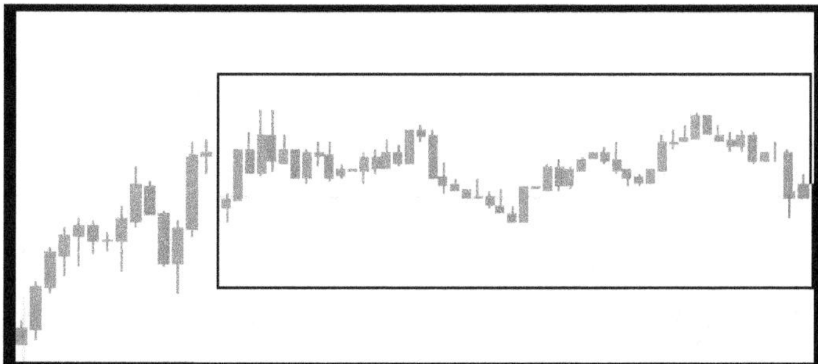

Because this is a bullish pattern you can assume that the price will eventually break through the resistance levels and resume the upwards trend.

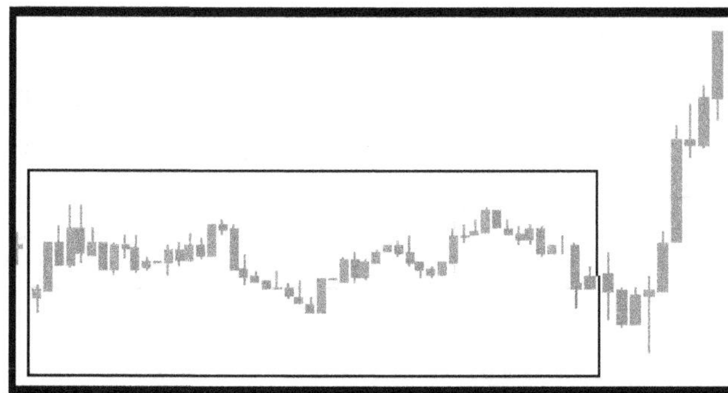

Similar to the bearish rectangle pattern example, once the pair breaks out, it will usually make a move that is roughly proportional to its formation.

Symmetrical Triangle

A symmetrical triangle is a pattern, where, as the name suggests, the slopes of the price highs and lows will come together to form a triangle. What this pattern indicates is that the sideways trend is making lower highs and lower lows. This means that neither the buy or sell pressure is high enough to force the price enough to form a clear trend. This is also a type of trend consolidation.

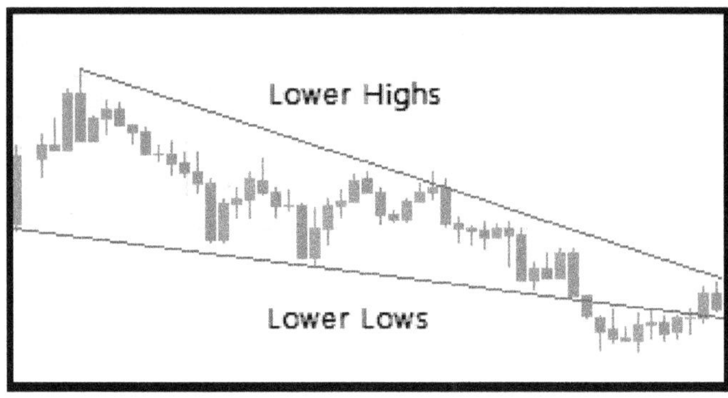

If you consider the chart above, you can see that neither buy nor sell pressure is sufficient to push the price in one direction. As the two slopes begin to converge this typically indicates that a breakout will follow. However, there is no indication of a direction, only that one side of the market will prevail. This is not as bad as it seems because as we are assured a breakout in either direction, we can place entry orders above the slope of the lower highs and below the slope of the lows. This means we can catch the breakout in whatever direction the market moves.

Ascending Triangle

This type of triangle pattern occurs in charts when the resistance level is horizontal and there is a succession of higher lows creating a rising support slope. This comes about when buying pressure is not sufficient enough to break through the resistance. However, the buying pressure is sufficient enough to gradually push the price up as you can see by the succession of higher lows.

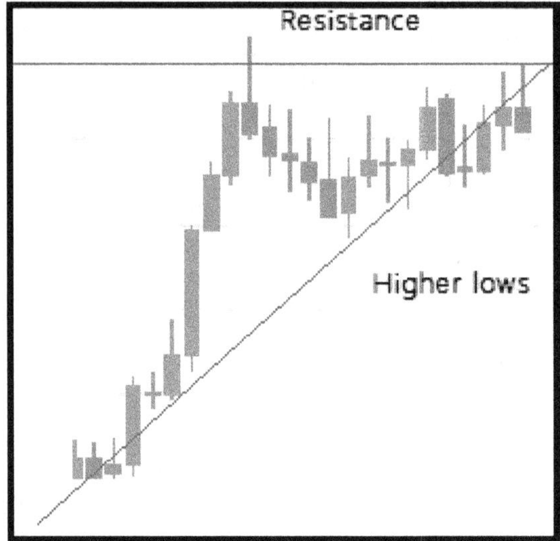

If you consider the chart above, you can see that the buying pressure is increasing due to the presence of those higher lows. By gradually increasing the pressure on the fixed resistance level, this will eventually force a breakout. The consensus of opinion as to the direction is that the buying pressure will prevail and the price will break out through the resistance. However, sometimes the resistance level proves to be just too resilient, and there is simply not enough buying pressure to break out.

Of course, you can still catch the breakout by trading on both directions. In this scenario, you would need to set an entry order above the resistance line and below the slope of the higher lows.

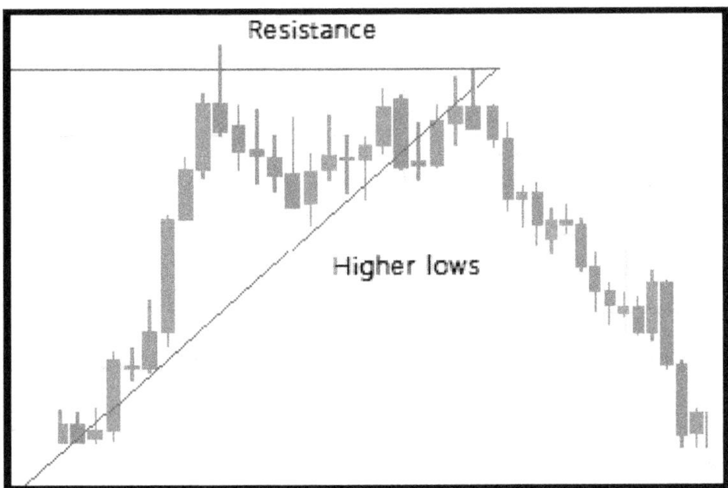

In the diagram above we see the scenario where the buying pressure became exhausted and the price collapsed. Again, like the other patterns, the breakout was proportional to the pattern formation. This is shown in the diagram above that the fall was approximately the same distance as the height of the triangle formation. This is a pretty good rule of thumb for all the patterns.

Descending Triangle

A descending triangle forms where there is a string of lower highs that form the upper line. The lower support line is a price that selling pressure cannot seem to break through.

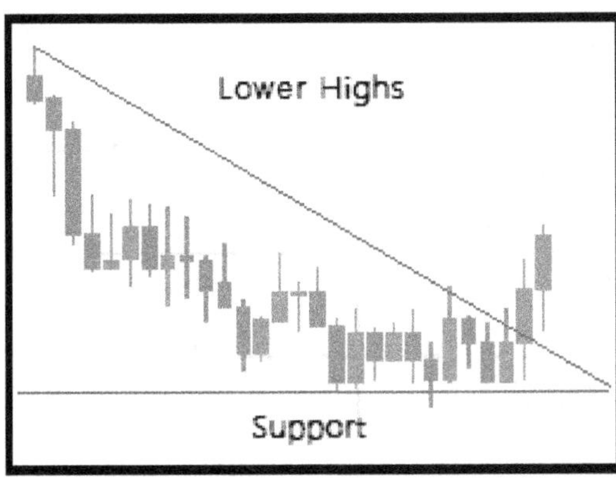

In the chart above, you can see that the price is gradually making those lower highs, which indicates that there is more selling pressure than buying pressure. This should indicate an imminent support breakthrough and a sharp drop in the price. However, in some cases, as shown in the diagram, the support line will be too strong and the price will fail to break through. In this scenario, you could place your entry orders just above the upper resistance line (the lower highs) and just below the lower support line.

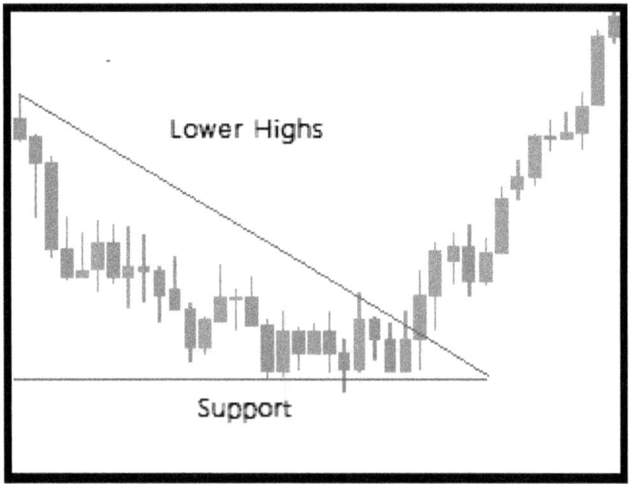

In this scenario, we see that the price failed to break through the support level and bounced upwards, ending up breaking higher than the triangle pattern.

Trading Using the Chart Patterns

In this section, we'll discuss how we can use chart patterns to effectively trade. After all, it is not enough to just recognize the patterns—you need to know how to take advantage of them!

In short, the patterns we have introduced in the book can be categorized into one of three main groups: Reversals, Continuations, and Bi-lateral patterns.

Let's summarize the chart patterns we have just learned and categorize them according to their behavior. The first group is the reversal patterns and these are:

- The double top and the double bottom
- The head and shoulders and the inverse head and shoulders
- The rising and falling wedges

To trade these reversal chart patterns, you simply need to place an order beyond the neckline of the pattern formation because you want to catch the reversal as early as you can and in the direction of the new trend. Now you will need to set a target that will be roughly the same as the height of the formation.

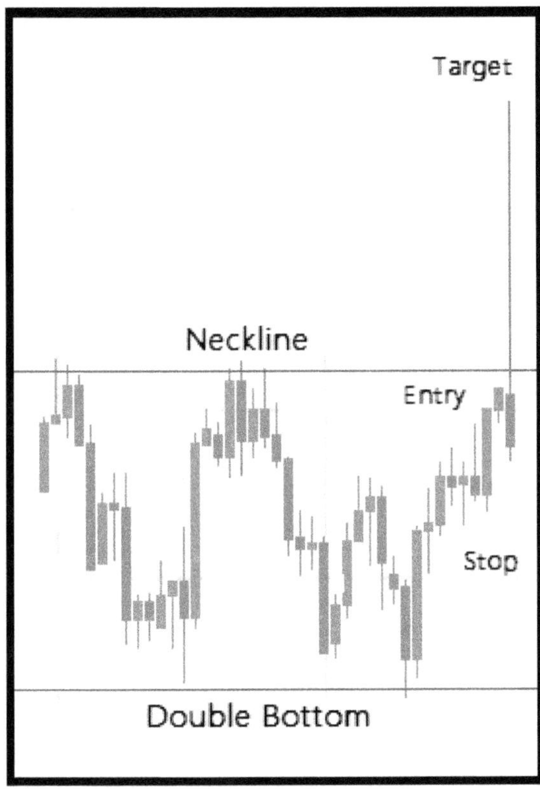

For example, as shown in the diagram above, if you are trading on a double bottom, you would be best to place a long order (remember, you want to catch the uptrend) at the top of the neckline. Then you could go for a target that's just as high as the formation itself (i.e. the same distance from the neckline to the bottoms). Now we need to insert our stop orders and this is best done around the middle of the pattern formation. For example, you can measure the distance between the double bottoms and the neckline, then divide that distance by two and use that figure as your stop size. This methodology works for all the reversal patterns.

Continuation Chart Patterns

When we consider the category of continuation patterns we need to remember that these are chart formations that indicate that the preceding trend will continue after a brief pause. These patterns are also known as *consolidation patterns* because they show a pause in the buying or selling pressure before the trend resumes, moving further in the same direction as before. We have covered several continuation chart patterns, namely rectangles and pennants, and wedges can also be considered a continuation pattern.

Regardless of pattern, you will trade continuation patterns using the same method. For example, when you are trading using rectangles or triangle patterns, you need to follow the direction of the ongoing trend and place your order either above or below the formation. When considering a target you should set this to at least the same dimensions of the chart pattern for wedges and rectangles. For continuation patterns, stops are usually placed immediately above or just below the actual pattern's formation lines as shown below.

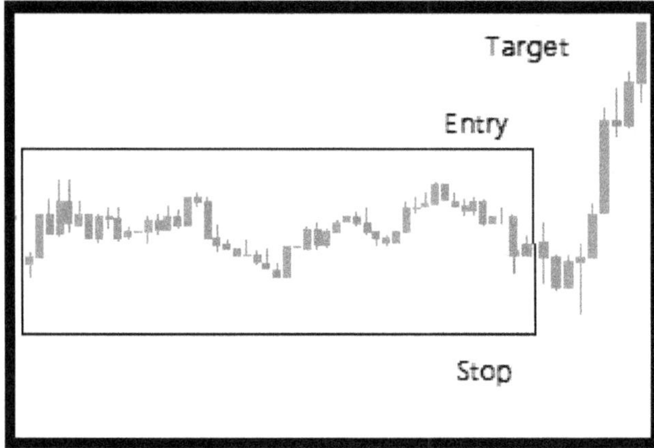

As an example, when trading a bullish rectangle, place your stop a few pips above the top or resistance of the rectangle.

Bilateral Chart Patterns

Bilateral chart patterns are a bit more difficult because these patterns do not indicate the trend of the breakout, so the price can move in either direction.

This is where triangle formations come into play. With triangles, the price can easily break either upwards or downwards. There really is no telling which way.

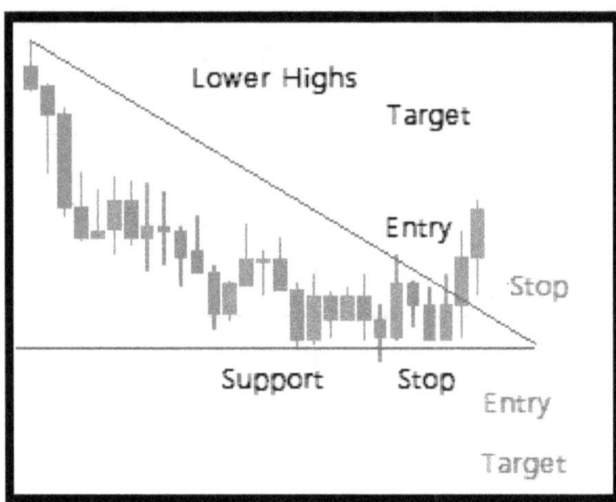

As the triangles do not indicate to us which direction the breakout will occur, we need to cover both options. This means that we will place trades for both long and short trades. When trading triangle or other bilateral chart patterns, you might consider placing one order on top of the formation and another order at the bottom of the triangle's pattern lines. You can reverse the order for your stop orders as shown in the diagram above. Now, only one is going to get triggered and you will then need to cancel the other one. The only issue with placing orders close to the pattern formation line is that you could be caught out by a false break. So perhaps you might want to give yourself some leeway by not setting your entry orders too close to the top or to the bottom of the pattern's formation.

Table of Chart Patterns

CHART PATTERN	TREND BEHAVIOR	INDICATOR/SIGNAL	NEW TREND DIRECTION
Double Top	Uptrend	Reversal	Down
Double Bottom	Downtrend	Reversal	Up
Head and Shoulders	Uptrend	Reversal	Down
Inverse Head and Shoulders	Downtrend	Reversal	Up
Rising Wedge	Downtrend	Continuation	Down
Rising Wedge	Uptrend	Reversal	Down
Falling Wedge	Uptrend	Continuation	Up
Falling Wedge	Downtrend	Reversal	Up
Bearish Rectangle	Downtrend	Continuation	Down
Bullish Rectangle	Uptrend	Continuation	Up
Bearish Pennant	Downtrend	Continuation	Down
Bullish Pennant	Uptrend	Continuation	Up

Chapter 9 - Technical Chart Analysis

In this chapter we will look at some sound beginner trading strategies and finish off with a more advanced swing trading example. The chart patterns that we will be trading are easy to identify and trade. So you can try them out the next time you are looking for entries into individual stocks.

T-30 Chart Pattern

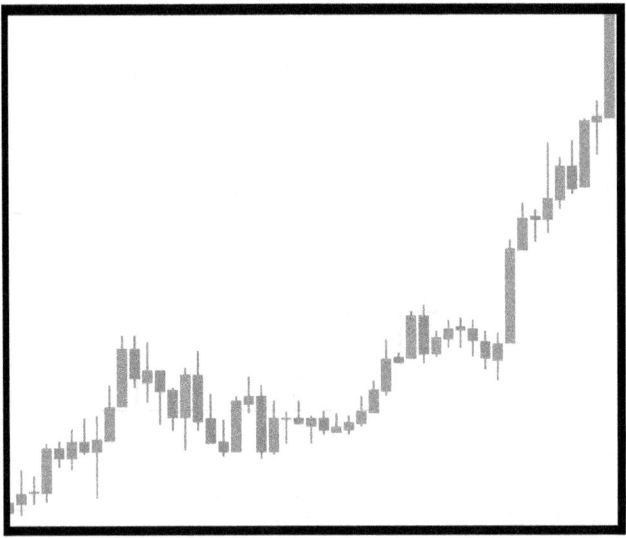

This is a very suitable chart pattern for beginners to use when they start out trading. This is simply because it is easy to recognize and easy to trade.

The name T-30 refers to a "tail" that slices down through the "30" period EMA (exponential moving average) shown on the diagram above. This will look like a Hammer candlestick pattern on the chart. A T-30 doesn't need to have a Hammer, it just needs a long tailed candlestick of any color. Interestingly, it doesn't really need the 30-day EMA; it is sufficient enough to use the preceding support levels, whereas having the 30-day EMA makes it easy to spot the pattern since it's an easy reference to visualize.

However, there are a couple of caveats when you are trading any kind of tail or Hammer pattern. One is that although for the T-30 you may not strictly require a perfect Hammer, or even an EMA what you will need is higher volume than the previous day.

How to Trade This Pattern

Ideally you want to enter the trade on the day of the Hammer (tail), preferably near the end of the day. The only thing that you need to see is that it is at a support level and that volume is rising. That indicates that the demand is increasing and this is all the confirmation that you need.

The Stop Loss Order

Now you will want to consider where to place your stop loss orders. There are two options and each has advantages and disadvantages.

You could place your stop loss just under the low of the Hammer. The advantage to this is that your stop loss point is a good distance from your entry price and that you are relatively safe from getting stopped out prematurely. The disadvantage is that the distance it is from the entry price means that your losses could be higher if the trade goes against you.

The second option that you have is to put your stop under a support area nearer to the real body of the candle. The advantage is this makes your stop position much closer to your buy price. The disadvantage of course is that you may get stopped out prematurely by market noise.

Taking Profits

When you are trading Hammers, you will most likely find out that the stock will trend sideways for several days. This is what you want as a swing trader so be patient, as you are already in the trade and are just waiting for others to join you. However, be prepared after those days of low volatility and volume for the trend to move in your favour. Then you can safely begin to trail your stop to exit or to lock in profits.

Swing Trap Chart Pattern

The swing trap pattern comes about through traders getting trapped in a trade when the market reverses. This forces many swing traders to accept a loss. If you look at the chart below you can see that the stock has a short period of consolidation as the market takes a breather before it breaks down and then reverses.

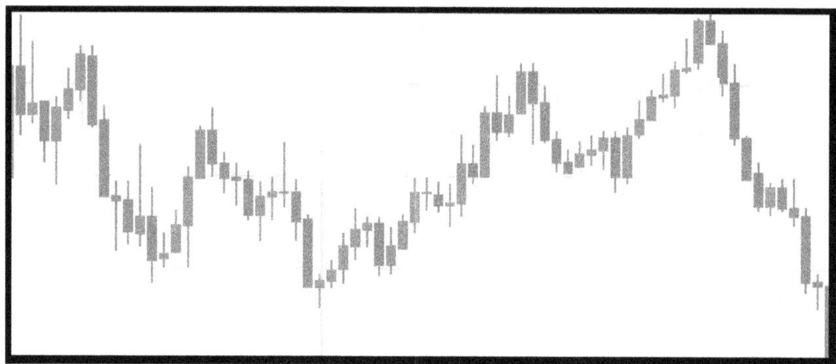

It is because of this quick reversal that swing traders get caught on the wrong side of a position. However, when this happens and losses occur, stocks also rally. This results in some potentially large movements in price.

The Setup

If you consider the following chart you may think, like most of us, that this trend is sideways and consolidating. However, since it is in a general uptrend, it may likely break out soon.

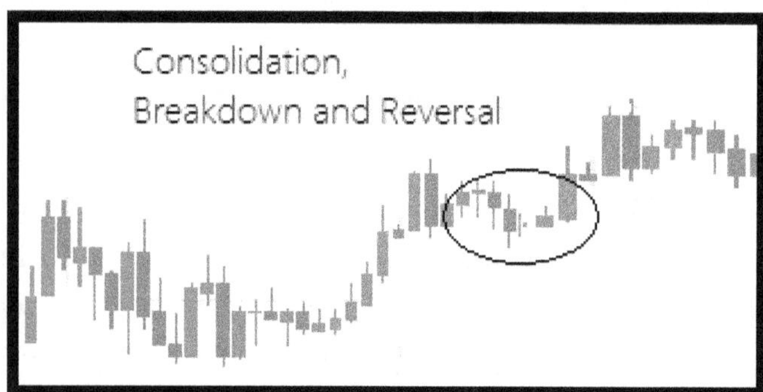

As this is the common belief shared by most of your fellow traders, there will be buying pressure building inside of the consolidation in anticipation of a breakout. You should be waiting for the breakout; there is nothing to do with this stock except wait for a breakout or trade both directions.

This is because it could break out in the opposite direction if not enough buying pressure can be mustered. For example, look what happened the following day:

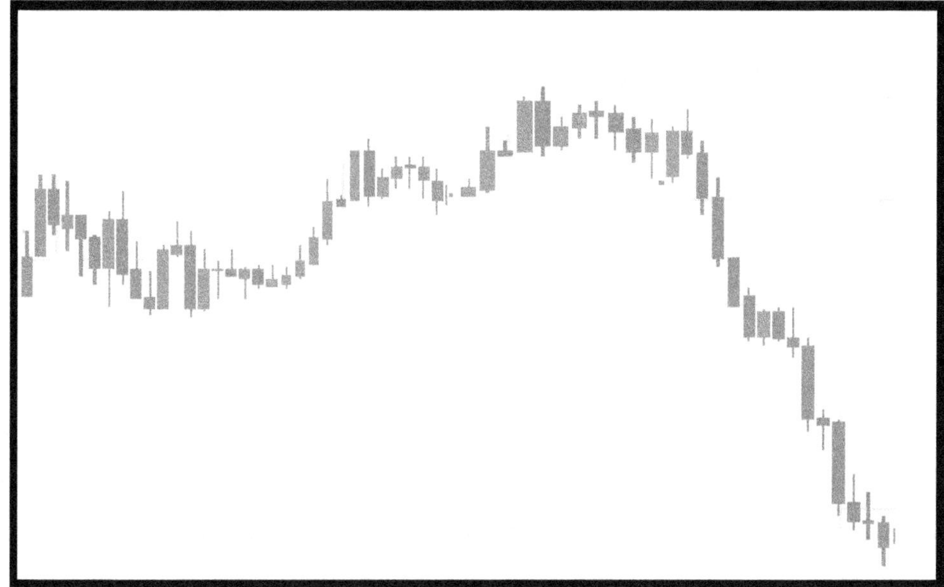

Well, the stock broke alright but not in the direction expected, as it broke down through the consolidation because some traders have been aggressively shorting this security.

What is interesting is that this chart looks bearish. But look what happens over the next few days:

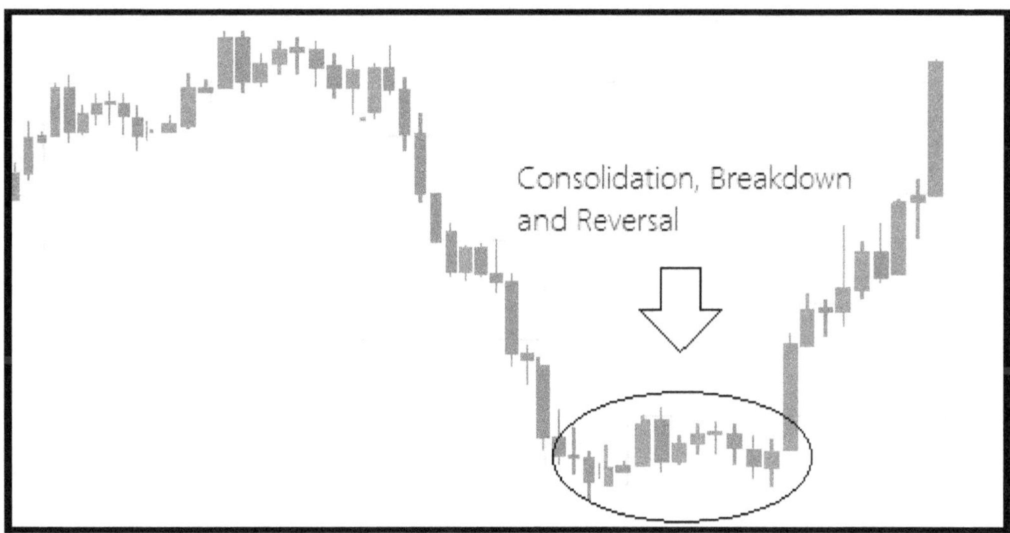

This sudden reversal came about because the trend could not break through a strong support level. Consequently, the short traders lost their momentum during the consolidation phase because there are no new sellers coming in to strengthen the trend and to move this stock downwards. This meant that with all selling pressure about exhausted, this stock can rally and now reverse its trend and move higher.

How to Trade This Chart Pattern

There are three important components you should recognize when trading this chart pattern:

- A consolidation phase
- A breakdown
- A strong reversal candlestick

In short, you are looking out for a consolidation trend followed by a breakdown causing the chart to look bearish or bullish, and finally a strong reversal pattern. Ideally, you want to enter the trade on the day of the appearance of a strong reversal candle. You want the candle to be a strong indicator so make sure it closes at least halfway relative to the breakdown candle.

Bear in mind—when you set your price targets you want to see movement above or below that sideways trading pattern (consolidation). That is where the potential price surge will occur.

Trading tips

- The longer the consolidation pattern persists then the more potential there is for a price surge.
- The reversal candle must be a very strong indicator of a change in trend.
- Volume is not important when trading this pattern.
- This pattern shows up increasingly when the overall market trend is down.

This is an important chart pattern for swing trading but be careful with those stop losses because you are a beginner trading against the market trends. So remember diligent fund management and your exit strategy when trading this pattern as these are the two components of successful swing trading!

Conclusion

As a beginner in swing trading you must understand the two key concepts that will make you a successful trader: fund management and trading strategy. Within this book we have strived diligently to pass on the information that you need to accomplish both these tasks. Remember—always use a strategy and don't just gamble because you will eventually lose. And *always* protect your capital!

If you follow the instructions in this book you may well turn out to be a successful swing trader. I wish you all the best and happy and profitable trading.

Book #4
Options Trading Simplified

Beginner's Guide to Make Money Trading Options in 7 Days or Less!

Learn the Fundamentals and Profitable Strategies of Options Trading

Chapter 1 – Getting Started in Trading Options

An old Chinese proverb says that every journey starts with a single step. And here you are starting out on day 1 of your quest to learn all about trading options and making money in 7 days or less! Options are complex there is no getting around that and there is a lot to learn in such a short time and it's difficult to know where to start. But as this book is aimed at the beginner – someone new to options and financial trading then starting with the basics is as good a place as any. So today on day 1, we will introduce you to the basic concepts and theory of Options, what they are, how they work for us and why we trade them.

By taking this journey one step at a time we will build your knowledge, chapter by chapter, with each subsequent chapter building on the concepts learned previously. By approaching the journey one step at a time you will learn and become comfortable with some of the complex theory, concepts and principles of options trading but importantly also learn the practical skills you will need to thrive in the Options market.

In This Chapter

You will learn:

- About why people are trading Options
- What are options?
- How did options come about?
- Comparing Options to other Financial Instruments
- Learn some of the key definitions
- Learn how options operate in theory and in practice
- How options are ultimately valued

Introducing Options

In financial trading, an option is a contract between two parties that gives one party – the prospective buyer - the choice between committing to a trade on a specific asset at an agreed price and at an agreed date and alternatively backing out of the trade. Therefore we can consider an Option to be a financial instrument that allows you the buyer to speculate on the market with low or at least identified risk. For example, as a beginner you may wish to test the water and so buy a stock option – this is a contract based on the underlying shares of a company - with a view to buying the underlying stock at a set price at a later predetermined date. The beauty of the Option is that should your assessment of the market be correct you can exercise your right to buy the shares or take your profit.

However, should your assessment be wrong and you have misjudged the market trend then you can simply walk away with no obligation to buy the stock. For example, a call option would let you select an Option today that is set at a fixed price which will be available to you at a future date. This means that you can assess the current price of the stock and then choose an option with an attractive future price, which you feel will maximize your profits. But, importantly, you are under no future obligation to buy the underlying stock – you can walk away for any reason.

Options are certainly not just tools for learning trading as institutional traders will use them regularly for what is known as Hedging where they buy options – importantly not the underlying stock - as insurance against a turn in their market position. This gives Options several unique characteristics which makes them valuable tools for insurance against risk.

Moreover, trading in Options is not just about hedging and insuring against risk it is also a very powerful way to make money if you know what you are doing. Unfortunately many rush in without fully grasping the technical details of Options and subsequently make large losses. This is simply because options are at first complex to grasp and even though they may well be based upon stocks and shares the mechanics of trading is very different.

This common perception of complexity and higher risk makes a lot of beginners and intermediary traders avoid trading in options. But it doesn't have to be that way because trading options is actually a good place for beginners and intermediary traders to start out because if done correctly it can limit losses and risk while at the same time increasing the potential for profits. However, we must not underestimate the difference in the levels of knowledge and skills that are required to successfully trade in options.

What Are Options?

An option is defined as a contract between two parties, which gives the holder (buyer) the right, but not the obligation, to buy or sell the underlying asset at an agreed fixed price at an agreed time in the future – or in some cases at any time before the contract's expiry date.

Options as we saw earlier were designed to allow institutional investors to mitigate risk and act as tools for ensuring against market unpredictability. Thus the Options contract was originally used to buy insurance against potentially catastrophic price movements that would have led to huge losses. But their inherent characteristics soon made Options attractive to traders as speculation tools in their own right. To see how Option became fashionable with traders we need to take a deeper dive into what makes up an Option contract.

An option is a contract based upon an underlying asset, a derivative, which means that an Option's value is derived from the underlying asset. In financial trading the underlying asset is usually stocks or a commodity, but it also can be the value of a market index or interest rate. Indeed in contract law it can be practically anything.

Options in Common Law

Options can be best explained and easiest understood using examples from everyday contract law as Option contracts have been in place since trade began. For example, suppose you want to buy a house or a new car, but you don't have a mortgage or finance at hand. In this case you would perhaps agree with a price with the seller and a date for completion of the sale. However the seller is going to want a deposit in return for this sales contingency, which gives you the right to buy at the agreed price at a future date or walk away from the sale if you change your mind. The deposit is compensation to the seller for providing you with the right, but not the obligation, to buy the car or house at the agreed price and date. If you renege on the deal and walk away, you will lose the deposit as that is the price of that option.

This is the basis of financial options, and if we consider the transaction through the lens of a financial trade we can substitute many of the technical terms to make the metaphor more transparent. So for example when you go to buy a house you agree to a price (strike price) and a date (expiry date) and a suitable deposit (premium) as part of the sales contingency (the Option contract). Then on the expiry date you will exercise your right to buy the house (stock) at the strike price or walk away (let the option expire) losing your deposit (premium).

Don't worry too much about some of the terms, such as strike price and premium all the trading jargon will be explained soon enough. What is important just now is that you understand that with Options trading you are dealing with a contract, the right to buy rather than the asset itself. But because that contract has inherent value, as it derives its value from the relationship between the strike prices, which is fixed in the contract, relative to the current market stock price. And if the contract is deemed attractive to others in the market then it also becomes a tradable asset in its own right.

Why Options Exist

An Option is considered in finance to be a derivative as it derives its value from an underlying asset. A stock option is similar to a contingency on the sale of a house or a deposit on a car but it involves the stock market rather than a private agreement.

For example, an Option - **MSFT 2019 Mar 39 call** - gives you the right to buy Microsoft at $39 per share at any time before the expiration date in mid-March 2019. If Microsoft is trading above $39 per share, you can exercise the option to buy and make a quick profit. The term, Exercising the option, is when you – the option holder - take up your contractual right to buy the shares at the agreed price – typically then to sell the stock on the market at the higher price for a tidy profit.

However, should the stock not perform as expected over the lifetime of the Option contract and the stock is selling below $39, then you would just let the contract expire as it makes no sense to buy a stock at a higher price than market value as you could buy the stock cheaper in the open market.

When an Option contract expires it means the value of the option is worthless and thus the loss to the buyer is 100% of the cost of the Option – the (deposit) Premium.

To get a better understanding of why they came about it is best to look at how they are used by taking a closer look at their use in practice.

Options as Insurance

As we touched on earlier Institutional and fund managers use stock options as a form of insurance. They want to protect themselves against any market turn-around and potentially damaging losses by having in-place a hedge bet, which is a counter-balance position. In effect they will be placing a bet that works in the opposite direction to the desired position of the asset they wish to protect thereby nullifying any adverse market movements. This works because with Options they are guaranteed a method to buy or sell stock at a specific price, but with no obligation to buy, before or upon a certain date.

So, for example, should they wish to protect the value of a portfolio, of let's say, their very expensive Amazon shares (that they own). Then they could do so by buying a relatively cheap Option that worked in favour of falling Amazon stock prices – i.e. its value increases as Amazon prices fall. In this way, even though their prized Amazon portfolio dropped in price their Option would be increasing in value and vice versa so together they would counter-balance any price fluctuations in the market.

This form of Hedging is often performed in order to protect against risk to a position or an asset. Institutional stock traders have always had in place complex and often costly methods of risk management. However, it was only in 1973 when there was the standardization of stock options that it finally made risk actually manageable and very cost effective.

Using options in this way allows institutional investors to ensure against price changes and is known as hedging. Institutional traders are willing to pay the price, known as a premium, to obtain this insurance.

Trading Options Basics

Learning Options trading is not trivial but it can be very rewarding if you learn the basic principles well and stick to good trading practices. The most important thing to learn as a beginner, as with all forms of financial trading, is the necessity of protecting your capital. The most profound way of doing this is by only paper trading – or using a test simulator – when you first start out. It is vital that you test your strategies and trading tactics with virtual money before you ever trade with real money.

Options trading, though is still deemed to be complicated and very risky, it is actually a good place for beginners to start out financial trading as it provides several safety nets. For example, in Options trading, a beginner, if they follow the correct strategies, will find that their risk and losses are limited but their potential profits are unlimited. This is simply down to the nature of Options in so much as you as a beginner will be trading in contracts called premiums rather than buying the underlying stock. Hence the extent of your losses is limited to the price of the premium – don't worry we will explain all this in detail later – for now it is enough to know that when trading options we can show you how to limit losses and risk while chasing unrestricted profits.

As this book is targeted at beginners it would be helpful first to give you a high-level summary as to why trading in options is advantageous. And the best place to start is to explain the mechanisms behind Option trading and how they work.

What is Options Trading?

When you trade in options you are trading in a contract based upon an underlying asset – typically a stock in a company. An Option is a contract that gives the holders the right but not the obligation, to buy or sell an asset in the future at a price determined today.

That definition is hugely important to understand as it is the basic concept of Options Trading – basically you are buying the right to buy the underlying shares but are under no obligation to do so. So should the price go against your position you can simply walk away albeit you will lose the cost of the option but no more. Hence, despite the common belief of it being a high-risk pursuit, trading in Options is much less risky than buying stocks outright where losses and profits are unlimited.

However there is another attractive characteristic of trading in Options and that is due to the fact that you can as a beginner trade safely in high-value stocks that would generally be out with your budget. This is because when you buy an Option you are not actually buying the stock but the future right to buy at a fixed price. Therefore, the option is priced at only a fraction of the actual stock price.

This means that you can buy an option in high volume, volatile stock such as Apple, Amazon, etc., which would give you the control over 100 shares for perhaps $100, whereas to buy 100 shares of these premier stocks would set you back thousands of dollars. Remember, as there is no obligation to buy the shares you can simply take your profit and walk away – no questions asked.

Indeed as there is no obligation to exercise the Option itself it also becomes a tradable asset – and this is what came about. Instead of traders exercising their rights to buy the underlying asset many simply bought the Options to trade on the open market. However for every deal there must be a buyer and a seller – so other traders soon began writing Options in order to fulfil the market demand. Hence the flourishing market in Options we see today.

Options are extremely flexible so are used as both a form of insurance and as a source of speculative profits. The value is largely derived from the value of an underlying asset or financial instrument, but it also has additional components such as time till expiration, and a locked-in price that provides additional value. So the value of the Option is not solely determined by the current value of the underlying asset or security as there are several other factors that come into play.

Moreover Options provide the beginner the right level of entry into the market if they have only limited funds and trading knowledge. Furthermore, the beginner can despite their lack of experience and trading skills also trade well above their budget and leverage their account to trade diligently in a low risk and high reward strategy. But Options are not just attractive to beginners with limited funds for in financial trading Options provide ways for experienced traders to add options on individual stocks, indexes, and exchange-traded mutual funds (ETFs) to their investment portfolio.

Nonetheless, the best reason for a beginner to start trading in Options and an intermediary level trader to add options to their trading or investing strategies is that Option trading allows you to both manage risk while at the same time allowing you to optimize profits. And because there are so many different methods and techniques to trade in options there is a wide market for both buyers and sellers – i.e. just about anyone can benefit from trading them, so let look at some traditional examples.

If we contemplate the traditional buy and hold strategy for stocks, which is a good example, as that is the way that long term investors operate. In this scenario we can consider it to be akin to you owning (real estate) apartments and then taking income as rent through properties per month for long periods to generate year-on-year income.

Now this is a good way to generate long term safe income. However this patient strategy may not work so well when you want short term profits and large gains. In which case, the way to generate quick returns would be to rent out your apartment short term at higher rates via Airbnb. In which case, a financial trading metaphor would be to shift away from trading in stocks and mutual funds to invest in writing (selling) short term Options based upon your stock portfolio.

Comparing Options to other Securities

Options are a form of financial derivative, and all that means is that it derives its value from an underlying security. For example, a common type of Option is the Stock options - which this book focuses on – and they derive their value from the underlying company stock's market performance. However Options can and are traded using other derivatives such as commodities and exchange-traded mutual funds (ETF):

- **Commodities and futures**
  The provenance of financial Options are in the trading of Commodity and Futures contracts as these were agreements between two parties typically farmers and traders looking for a future price for their next harvest crops. The futures markets developed to help traders hedge and speculate on commodities, especially in the agricultural market. The options market in turn evolved from the futures market, hence, the similarities and the shared concepts. But, because commodities and futures deal with a physical asset there are slight differences as to how they work. The seller of a commodity or futures option is still obligated to buy or sell stock. However, exercising the contract is different as commodities and futures contracts set the price for delivery of a specific quantity of a physical item – a bushel of wheat, for example - to be delivered to a particular location

on an agreed date. There is nothing similar in stock options as there is no need for a physical delivery of anything. Commodity options are options listed on such things as corn, oil, gold, or interest rates.Futures on the other hand are options trading on the underlying value of futures contracts, typical futures on commodities and currencies. Futures contracts are therefore derivative contracts – their value is derived from the underlying commodity/asset - that give holders the obligation to buy or sell an asset at a specified future date for a specified price. Where there is a similarity between stock options and commodities and futures contracts is that they lock in the price and quantity of an asset and have predetermined expiration dates. But in both cases, they are in themselves tradable assets, which means you can trade away your rights and obligations if you wish to exit the contract early.

- **Equity options**
  An equity option is an option based on the price of a share of stock of a company. However options are not available on all stocks but some do not have options attached to them. It is up to the exchanges to determine whether or not to offer an option – based upon perceived demand – it is not up to the companies that issue the stock.

  Most equity options are priced at 1 contract per 100 shares. Equity options are what most people think of when they contemplate Options.

- **Index Options**
  The concept behind trading options in indexes is that if you can buy an option on a stock of a particular company within a sector say technology then why does the exchange not make available an option on that market sector as a whole? That's the idea behind index options you can bet on the sector performance and not have to drill down to a specific company.

  The result has been a proliferation of Index options based on the performance of different market indices. There are options on the S&P 500, NASDAQ, and FTSE. Trading in indexes has become a very popular alternative to trading in stock options as they can represent a collection of diverse assets. This means that a trader can spread their investments across several sectors of interest. The index works by pooling together several stocks in the same sector or across diverse sectors and the performance aggregate is used to measure the price of the group. There are many indexes and these include stocks, commodities, and futures as they are all used as components of an index. But an index is just a logical category a convenient grouping of other securities so you can't buy an index directly. Instead, you buy a security that tracks the value of the index.

An example of such an option would be one that tracked a particular ETF that owned the stocks in a particular index such as Standard & Poor's (S&P) 500 Index.

- **Exchange traded funds (ETFs)**
  ETFs are mutual funds that have become very popular trading vehicles as they can be traded like stocks on an exchange. Most ETFs are designed to track an index or an underlying sector so technically ETFs are not derivatives. However they are often referred to as quasi-derivatives. This is because unlike other indexes they can be traded and also because they are not necessarily holding exactly the same securities of the index that they are tracking. For example, some leveraged ETFs use swaps to mimic the action of the underlying index while adding leverage. ETFs allow you to trade on their underlying indexes, directly or through options. One of the most popular and well known ETFs is the S&P 500 SPDR (SPY).

- **Stocks and bonds**
  Buying a company's stock gives you part ownership in that company, whereas buying bonds makes you a debt holder. Each position has its risks and rewards. However when we bring Options into the equation we can see that the three assets, stocks, bonds, and options, have very different risk and reward profiles.For example, although stocks give you a piece of the company, and bonds offer you income, options offer you no ownership of any tangible assets but all three can lead to a total loss of investment. In the end, stocks offer indefinite holding periods, and bonds have a maturity date, whereas options have a limited life based on their expiration date.

- **Interest Rate Options**
  These are sometimes better known as *yield-based options,* as they trade on the interest rate on a specific type of bond. With this type of Option, calls (buying) become more valuable as interest rates rise, and interest rate puts (selling) become more valuable as the rates fall. Importantly, the underlying value is the interest rate and not the value of the bond itself. Because interest rates aren't securities and can't be traded or exchanged as such the settlement is in cash.

- **Miscellaneous Options**
  The way that the different options exchanges make money and compete with one another is when they develop new innovative types of contracts that capture the imagination of hedgers and speculators. As an option is just a contract, which is based on the price of another asset options can be drawn up for just about anything where someone might want to guarantee a price and someone else might want to speculate on that price. As a result, exchanges are always trying out new option types so you can find

options on different measures of market sentiment, *i.e.* whether it's optimistic or pessimistic about different economic outcomes.

- **A swap**
  This is a type of insurance contract whose terms are privately agreed upon by the participants. It is an over-the-counter style option as they are non-exchange traded options. They are often used to bet on the direction of just about anything, including the weather, that the two parties agree upon. Swaps are by design sophisticated securities and so they are not available to individual investors. This is due to the lack of regulations and the often complex financial and legal requirements required to be signed before you can trade them.

Trading in Options

As opposed to investing in stock or assets, trading Options is often a decision based upon a short term analysis. An Option having a predetermined time period, a time-to-live, will have by design an expiry date. As a result Options are renewable and can be resold many times. This makes them suitable for both trading over the short term or over longer periods delivering income when the value of the underlying stock rises, falls, or even moves sideways.

Trading Options for Profit

Now the whole purpose of trading is that you want to have more money in the future than what you have just now. Therefore, to increase your wealth you are trading Options supplied by the markets. But here is the thing, regardless of the time frame — the question will come down to whether you have a tendency to hold a position for a short or long time — your objective after all will be the same too make more money.

But here is the problem because that hunger to make a profit makes traders and especially beginners impatient. Therefore as a beginner you should consider that every time that you contemplate a new trading strategy you will also have to contemplate a new learning curve. As a result, be prepared to realize that every change in strategy or trading tactics will begin with a deep study and analysis of trade conditions. This is where paper trading or virtual trading becomes invaluable as it lets you experiment with virtual cash and practice tactics with zero risks. Always be careful that when you start to trade with real cash that losses can be amplified so always be patient and be prepared to diligently spend the time required learning how to trade safely, or you will likely lose a lot of money on worthless premiums.

Regardless of the type of financial trading that you are undertaking there are some simple steps that you should adhere to in order to trade safely. It doesn't matter if you are a beginner or an intermediary trader it is always sensible to ensure that you protect your capital. This means that even if you are experienced in other forms of trading or investing, or even have experience with options but with different assets, you should always seriously contemplate the following:

- **Check your financial health**
  This means simply to check your financial balance sheet and your disposable income. This is hugely important as before you start trading in Options or any other financial instrument you must realize how much you can afford to lose. Therefore you must go over your finances diligently, and make sure that the amount that you have as trading capital is indeed disposable income. This means reviewing your current loans, mortgages, and life and health insurances as well as school fees or college funds.

- **Draw up a financial net worth statement**
  The purpose here is to ensure that you are aware of the amount you could lose and the desire to make profits – be sure you are comfortable with the risk/reward ratio. Also try and make sure that your finances are healthy and understand why you are taking on extraordinary risk.

- **Be realistic**
  Don't chase unrealistic goals and trade beyond your experience or safe capital levels. Furthermore, never risk more than 5% of your capital on any one trade – for beginners 1%-3% is the recommended maximum.

- **Know your own risk appetite**
  If you are a typically a cautious trader or a gambler, that may indicate that you may not be a good options trader. Nonetheless, there may be many trading option tactics and strategies that will suit your risk appetite. The thing to remember is that once you understand the built-in safety nets that trading options provides then it will decrease your risk. An important caveat is that just make sure you read through the book and stick to the beginners' strategies and tactics and find the ones that make you comfortable before you jump in.

- **Analyze the Data**
  Stocks trading places a lot of emphasis on technical analysis, fundamental analysis and Charts in order to maximize your chances of trading options successfully. Option trading rides upon the underlying stock so it also places a high emphasis on improving your technical and fundamental analysis skills. Therefore, you should be a diligent analyst, especially in identifying and following the dominant trends, as well as being able to analyze charts and the behavior of the underlying assets in your options.

- **Always test your strategies before putting them into practice**
  Testing out scenarios and tactics beforehand through paper trading before you take real-life risks is essential. Testing out theories before committing them with real money is always an excellent idea that is certain to provide both practices as well as saving you a lot of money

- **Never trade with money that you aren't willing to lose**
  This might seem strange as Options are often seen as being risk management tools. But even though options are often deemed to be risk-management vehicles, you can still lose money trading them – sometimes in the case of insurance that is the whole purpose. And if you should adopt more sophisticated and riskier option strategies; your potential losses should always be identified and accepted as they could be significant if your trades – especially- sell- if they are not thoroughly investigated and analyzed beforehand.

Chapter 2 - Understanding Options

On the first day of our journey we learned about options, what they are and how they are used in financial trading both for hedging and for speculation. We also learned that Options are derivatives that derive their value from an underlying asset but they can act as financial instruments in their own right because they do have value. We also learned that an Options contract is based upon the value of another underlying asset or security such as a company's stock. Most commonly, the focus of trading options is mainly on those instruments with a value based on stocks and market indexes, although there is also a flourishing market and exchange for trading mutual funds (ETFs). In day 2, of your quest you will lift up the bonnet and take a look at what components and mechanisms make up an Option and see the different types that are available.

In This chapter you will learn:

- Under the bonnet – the components of an Option
- Options for Risk Management
- Option Contract Essentials
- Valuating Call Options
- Valuating Put Options
- Understanding Time and Time Decay
- Paper Trading
- Advantages of Option Trading

An Option's Components

There are only two basic types of options: calls (buying) and puts (selling). However, for the beginner considering entering the Options trading market they should initially restrict themselves to buying call options. This is purely a safety measure because if you stick to trading calls (buying) to start with and limit your position size you will not lose your trading fund. This is simply because when buying calls you are on the low-risk side of the deal as you own the rights. Trading puts (selling) places you on the other side of the trade with the obligations now on you and for a beginner that is no place to be.

Nonetheless as you learn more and become comfortable with the way Options work you can add the other types of options to your trading toolbox. The advantage of becoming competent in using both puts and calls is that it will add diversity to your investing and trading strategies.

This is simply because you will now have the tools and the knowledge to participate in both bull (rising) and bear (falling) markets.

Furthermore, you can learn how to use options to limit your portfolio risk i.e. to protect an individual existing position such as a stock or ETF. It is also possible to develop a strategy to generate income through specific strategies known as spreads and writes however these are not for the beginner or the faint-hearted.

Know the underlying asset

Whatever way you decide to tactically trade in Options it is imperative that you fully understand the asset on which they're based. For example in this book the focus is on stock options and so this requires a deep understanding of how stocks trade and behave in the market. This will require that you have a thorough understanding and competency in technical and fundamental analysis and detailed chart analysis. For example, you will often be speculating against a strike price being exceeded during a fixed time period so you will need to have a deep understanding of the underlying stock's price movements. This cannot be down to just guesswork you must make these decisions based upon sound data analysis.

Another interesting element that needs to be studied is stock volatility as it is also a key component of options prices. With regards volatility you will have to look at the underlying stock's market volatility as part of your analysis in order to pick the best possible option for your particular strategy.

Risk Management

However even if you are buying options as insurance or as risk-management tools your primary focus is to understand the risks associated with the use of these tools, including all of the following:

- Knowing what conditions, both in the markets and in the individual security, to consider when analyzing a trade
- Using proper trade mechanics when creating a position
- Recognizing, understanding, and following trading rules and requirements for the security
- Understanding what individual variables make any position gain and lose value

It is therefore vital that you learn the key components of options trading so as to give you a sound foundation for designing rewarding strategies, tactics and positions that ensure that any losses are limited before they become catastrophic.

Option Contract Essentials

As we learned earlier a listed stock option, a standardized option that is traded on an exchange, is a contractual agreement between two anonymous parties. All listed options are standardized contracts, which are regulated and enforced using the same set of standard rules. Therefore, when you buy or sell an option i.e. you create a new trading position then you will be initiating one of two things, either:

- You are acquiring a specific set of rights, if you are buying or
- You are acquiring a specific set of obligations should you be selling.

It is imperative that as a beginner that you understand your rights and obligations, which are dependent on the position that you take by becoming either a buyer or a seller of an Option. These rights and obligations are standardized for options trading around the globe and are guaranteed by the national or regional authorities such as in the US the Options Clearing Corporation (OCC). Therefore you do not need to worry about the legality or the enforcement of the contract or even who you are making the agreement with as of course almost all trades will be anonymous.

Another important aspect of Options which you as a beginner need to understand is the role that time plays in the process. Time is hugely important when trading in options as you are betting your position against a timeline.

Moreover, you are stating that your position will come good before or on a fixed expiry date. It's no good it coming good a day later it must come good sometime before or on that date. Therefore it is crucial that you plan your position with time being at the forefront of your thoughts. After all should Apple stock dive, it is no good thinking, ah, well Apple will definitely rise, so let's buy an option – you need to know when it will rise, will it be this week, next week, or in two months.

Understanding the Risk Components

This means that in trading Options the primary risks involved are compounded by two elements, 1) time sensitivity, which you don't need to be so aware of when trading in stocks and 2) leverage, this is the ability to generate disproportionate movement in option prices relative to your funds. Leveraging lower priced Options to control 100 stocks allows for larger percentage gains – and losses.

Time is a very important factor when buying an Option as the price of a call option will increase the longer the available time span. This is intuitive as the longer the time period that the Options remains valid the higher the probability that your position will become valid and reach the strike price. This is simply because an Options value will go up or down depending on the underlying stock's movement. However the catch is in getting not just the price movement correct it's about getting it to coincide with the time span of the Option. This is critical because even if you speculate successfully the direction of the price movement of the underlying stock should the move in the stock come about too late then the Option will expire worthless.

Therefore when you are evaluating which option to buy or later when you become more experienced and start to write Options – you must expect to pay more – effectively buy yourself time – for Options that have longer expiration periods. Typically Options will range from a few weeks to 9 months or even up to 2 years to the expiration date and obviously the price will reflect the timespan.

Placing a Value on Call Options

Nonetheless, an Option's valuation is volatile for as we have seen Time Decay does play a major role – an Option loses value every day in the countdown to the expiration date – but it also fluctuates due to the performance of the underlying stock price relative to the strike price. This is because when you own Call Options, your rights allow you to;

- Buy a specific quantity typically 100 shares of the underlying stock (exercise your rights).
- Buy the 100 shares in the stock by a certain date (expiration date).
- Buy the specific quantity of stock at a specified price (strike price).

With those points in consideration we can see that the value and the price of the Call Option rises when the underlying stock price goes up because the price of the rights you bought through the option is fixed while the underlying stock itself is fluctuating in value – hopefully trending upwards in price.

Placing a Value on Put Options

On the other hand, should you hold a Put Option then it gains value when the underlying stock falls in price. When you hold a Put Contract you have the following rights:

- Sell a specific quantity typically 100 shares of the underlying stock (exercise your rights).
- Sell the 100 shares in the stock by a certain date (expiration date).
- Sell the specific quantity of stock at a specified price (strike price).

The right to sell a specific quantity (100) of stock by a certain date at a specified price is very beneficial in a bear market when prices are going downhill. For example if you hold a Put Option with a strike price of $60 you own the rights to sell that stock at $60. Now the thing to remember here is that the contract is between you and the Option writer – so they are in effect obliged to buy the stock from you the Option holder at the strike price in this case $60. The Option writer is hoping (betting) that the price stays above $60 but stock markets can be unpredictable and volatile so events such as bad news about the company's ability to match forecasted earning may push the stock price below $60m say to $50. Should that be the case, then you will find that the Put Option you are holding has become much more valuable. This is simply because the Put Option writer will be obliged to buy the underlying stock from you at $60 even though its current market value is significantly less.

In either case whether it be a Call or a Put Option the direction of the movement in price must occur before the option contract expires. If it fails to meet the strike price regardless of whether it is a Call or Put your option will expire and unfortunately be worthless.

Understanding Time and Time Decay

Therefore we cannot stress enough that success in trading Options will depend on your ability to select suitable options. The Options must have a target strike price as well as have an optimal timespan to the expiration date, which will allow sufficient time for the anticipated stock price movement to occur.

Not all stocks have options available for trading but many do have derived options. These listed options will be available in multiple expiration dates and strike prices. Indeed, as the trading of Options requires a buyer and a seller, you may find that making a bid on a strike price will trigger another trader to write an option to accommodate you. Hence, many Options are available but many are written to meet market demand. And this is another key element which we will contemplate later – you don't need to own the underlying stock in order to write an Option and many do not. These traders are speculating on the probability that the price fluctuation on the underlying stock will stay within certain boundaries – but that's certainly not for beginners. Nonetheless, before you jump in there are two caveats around Options pricing to keep in mind:

- Options with longer time periods until the expiration date will be more expensive
- Options with strike prices closer to the current underlying stock value are more expensive

You should now understand how trading in Options differs from trading in the underlying stocks. Options represent a contract that provides— leverage, rights or obligations, as well as a locked in price whereas stocks are an asset which represents partial ownership of a company. But there is another key difference as stocks in the market are limited in numbers, which creates their value but the number of options available is unlimited as they can be created on demand – remember you don't need to own stock to write an Option. Therefore, as you can see there are several important considerations that must be taken into account when trading Options as opposed to stocks. It is these distinctions that necessitate diligent trading and decision-making, which is beyond the basic buy or sell decisions based solely on price.

Moreover for the beginner it must be considered part of the learning process, when shifting from stock trading to options trading to develop a new but complementary way of approaching trading strategy and tactics. This new way of thinking will not just focus on the price of the underlying stock, but also on other factors, such time-decay, demand for the option and the overall market conditions – whether it is bullish or bearish. You will need to monitor your Option performance with time in mind and as the trade develops, you will need to have a strategy in mind as you may want to trade the option, exercise your rights to buy or sell and pocketing the profits or simply walk away taking any losses on the chin.

At present and as a beginner this may sound way too much information and way too difficult, but it will become much clearer as you read the next few chapters. Soon it will start to make sense as it all clicks into place because successful options trading is all about giving yourself and the Option time to deliver on your expectations.

Of course, Options trading is not all new as there are some basic trading tactics and best practices that carry over from other forms of trading, such as sound fund management techniques, entry and exit planning, as well as chart and technical analysis. Of the most profound example is in planning your exit for in Options trading there are several choices in exiting a position so it is not simple but it is an essential part of any trade. Therefore having clear objectives and an exit strategy will save you money in the long term should a position not develop as hoped or starts to move against you.

Paper Trading

If you haven't traded options or for that matter any other financial instrument in the past, they always try out your trading strategies on paper. It is always best to paper trade before you take the big step in using real money. Use live data and then see how your strategy works out. Paper trading isn't perfect as it can be boring – it lacks the psychological engagement of using real money – but it can uncover weaknesses in your strategy or tactics very quickly and cheaply. Your over-riding ambition when paper trading is to learn and try out different strategies, which as a beginner is essential practice.

Ultimately, you would want to be comfortable in your option trades as well as having a deep understanding of the underlying stock. So, before you contemplate trading using a live account and risking real money, you must have experience, skill and:

- An understanding of the recent market activity and characteristics of the underlying stock in the Options you are trading.
- Be comfortable recognizing market patterns and responding by mixing specialist strategies to match particular market scenarios.
- Be clear on your objectives per Option and have exit strategies in mind that will best deliver your goals.

As you can perhaps now begin to see that trading competently in the underlying asset of the Option, whether that is in stocks or indexes, is a prerequisite for successful Option trading. You can be expert in stocks or index trading and have never heard of options trading but the reverse is simply not true. To be a successful Options trader you must have deep knowledge of the underlying asset.

The Advantages of Option Trading

We could look at Option trading as being a supplemental skill to the other types of financial trading. But the additional work required to gain those skills will be worth it. To understand why let us reiterate the advantages of Options trading:

1. Better cost efficiency through leverage – a trader can gain a similar trading position as they could with stocks but with a much lower investment (cost of the stock vs. cost of the Option premium). Similarly an Option controls 100 shares minimum so for the price of the premium you get to leverage the control and the benefits associated with 100 or more shares.

2. Lower risk – The risk in trading stock is linear and 1:1 both for-profit and loss. With Options losses are limited to the cost of the premium and no more, while potential profits remain limitless and linear (1:1)
3. Higher percentage returns – Options return huge percentage gains as opposed to direct stock trading as the cost of the trade – the premium - is miniscule in comparison to the actual stock price. The result is in most cases slightly lower dollar value as you have to subtract the cost of the premium but a much higher percentage return on investment.
4. Greater flexibility – Options allows a trader to speculate on a bull –upwards trend -, a bear – a downwards trend, and also a sideways (no-direction) moving trend. This provides for a wealth of investment alternatives which we will consider later in the book.

Considering these advantages alone and especially when you take into the equation the considerable value of risk reduction and potentially optimized profits it seems a no-brainer to trade in Options.

Chapter 3 – Putting Options to Work

On Day 2 of our journey we took a good look under the bonnet to see the components that make up a standard Put or Call Options. We saw how they comprised several elements that contributed to their valuation and how the underlying stock price, the strike price, expiry time, volatility and time-decay all play an important part in an Options Valuation. Then we learned the importance of safe trading through paper trading to test out our strategies and hone our skills and finally we recapped on the advantages of trading on Options over trading in the underlying stocks themselves.

Today in day 3 of the quest we will turn our attention to putting Options into practice in diverse market conditions and learn how Options can be deployed to take advantage of any movement in price whether that is up, down or sideways. We will learn just how flexible and useful Option strategies can be in profiting even in difficult market conditions.

In this Chapter

We will learn:

- How to deploy Put Options
- How to limit risk
- How to trade in a bear market
- How to trade in a difficult market
- How to make money in a flat market
- How to trade in EFTs
- Take a deeper dive in Option Calls and Puts
- About Option mechanisms
- About the pros and cons of Leverage

For the beginner to trading Options the transition from direct stock trading may appear to be complicated but the actual differences in trading stock and options are down to the obscure – at first – but actually pretty basic mechanics of placing the orders.

Ultimately, the advantages you will get from trading options will outweigh any disadvantages as they just provide you with a mechanism (leverage) to control the rights to the stock rather than the stock itself. This for the beginner is a big thing as it allows you to trade in options on expensive premier stocks, such as Amazon, Facebook and Apple. These stocks are very expensive but they also have big dollar moves. They are also typically out with the reach of beginners or traders of limited funds but with options they become accessible to the beginner for a fraction of the cost compared to buying and trading on the shares themselves.

Options Put to good use

Options are very flexible tools and can be deployed optimally in a number of diverse ways to maximize the risk-reward ratio. Options deployed in this manner will deliver the best mix of profit and risk reduction. A good example of this type of flexibility and out-of-the-box thinking is when an Option is deployed as insurance for an asset.

Hedging your Bets

The way the Options work as an insurance policy is what is called hedging and this is when you buy an option contract that works in the opposite direction to the asset being protected. The primary goal of a hedge is that the value of the option goes in the opposite direction of the underlying stock. This might be counter-intuitive but if we consider that you hold stock in Apple and so to protect the value of this holding and insure against any unlikely but catastrophic plunge in their value you would take out a Put Option. You would basically bet that the Apple stock will fall so that in effect should the Apple stock fall in value the Option will gain value and vice versa. The purpose of the Put Option would be to ensure that the total value of the combined position retains as much of the portfolio's value as is possible.

When using options as a way to manage risk you should be aware:

- You can manage risk for an existing position either fully or partially. With the latter you will need to monitor and adjust the hedging process based upon the market changes.
- You can also consider managing risk for a new position at a low price using a single long-term option or through deploying a combination of options.

This is typically a good use for a PUT Option and demonstrates another reason as to why there are always buyers and sellers in the Options market. After all not everyone is in trading Options for the same reasons and there will always be traders and investors as well as speculators, those looking for profit and those looking for insurance.

Trading in a Bear Market

The flexibility of Options trading is also apparent when speculating in a bear market – a downward trend with falling prices. This is because if you are bearish and are looking to capitalize from a falling market, options are a good tool for the purpose. Options will be much less expensive and have much lower risk exposure to dollar losses than the highly risky method of borrowing individual stock on a margin account to sell short.

Using Options in Challenging Markets

As we have seen Options have the flexibility to allow you to trade in bull and bear markets. Options are the perfect tool in many ways for trading in those rising or falling markets through stocks or other underlying instruments. Now that is not to say that you couldn't do the same indirect stock trading, assuming of course that you are comfortable with both owning or borrowing these securities and selling them short.

However where Options have a distinct – but risky- advantage is in the case of a sideways market, where a stock is doing nothing just fluctuating around the same price week after week and with little trade volume. With direct stock trading there isn't a lot you can do but with Options you could craft strategies for sideways markets whether you possess any underlying stock or not. These are high-risk strategies which are not suitable for beginners but we will cover them nonetheless later in the book. But for now we will just present a high-level introduction.

Making Money in Flat Markets

When you hear the term Directional bias in financial trading it refers to the link between profits and the overall direction of prices. For example, in traditional trading in order to profit when you are long – holding or buying the stock- you need prices to go up. Conversely, to profit when you're short – selling or borrowing stock - you need prices to fall. However what can be done when prices are flat and stagnating?

With options you can use combination strategies to trade in a flat market. These are crafted Options designed to let you make money when the underlying stock moves either up, down or sideways. Consider this, by cleverly combining Calls and Puts and deploying them to work in harmony you can design strategies whereby:

- You can craft Options that let you profit if the underlying rises or falls, depending on your trading strategy.
- You can also craft Options to make money in sideways moving or flat markets.

Applying options to sector investing

Recently, EFTs' has become a very popular vehicle for options trading because you can design entire diversified portfolios based upon ETFs. Then you can use options to hedge your position or the indeed ensure your entire portfolio.

One of the reasons that EFTs have become so popular is it allows investors to make sector bets without having to get too granular with individual stocks. This is because a strange tendency of the market is that individual stocks do tend to follow the overall direction of the sector's trend. This means you can bet on a sector like Technology without having to research and analyze a particular stock. Also unlike other indexes ETFs are sort of quasi-derivative that you can trade like stocks. That means EFTs can be traded at any time during market hours instead of waiting until the market closes, like you have to do in trading traditional mutual funds.

Importantly the popularity of ETFs means that they are now offered as listed options – standard options offered on the exchange. That means you can trade options on the underlying ETF just like they were stock. This allows you to diversify and lets you make index bets without using index options. There are also ETFs available that are based on commodity indexes which let you participate in trading commodities without having to trade in futures. The proliferation of EFTs has added an extra dimension to options trading which has inspired innovative trading strategies and tactics.

There are many types of options and many strategic uses for them, but this book concentrates on listed stock options which trade on exchanges. These options are used to manage your risk by limiting your losses but they also offer you the opportunity to speculate for profit when deployed using the correct strategy.

A Deeper Dive into Options

Options trading has a fearsome but ill-deserved reputation for high risk and complexity but to make the most out of options trading, it's simply necessary that you understand the Option's mechanisms and underlying asset's behavior. Having expertise in the underlying financial instrument whether that is stocks or EFTs goes a long way in mitigating most of the risks and optimizing the potential rewards.

Understanding Option Contracts

We can best consider that a financial option is simply a contractual agreement between two parties. However there are some options contracts that are considered to be over the counter, this is a term that means that they are private agreements between two parties that are not conducted via a trading exchange. This book is about standardized contracts known as listed options that trade on exchanges. Options contracts give the owner certain rights and the seller of the options specific obligations. Here are some of the important definitions and details:

- Call option: A call option provides the holder of the call option with the right but no obligation to buy a number of shares, typically 100, of the underlying stock at a specific price by a specific date. By buying a call option the holder gets the opportunity to profit from price gains in the underlying stock during the period that the option is valid at a fraction of the cost of owning the stock.
- Put option: Put options provide the holder the right to sell a specific number of shares, typically 100 of the underlying stock at a specific price by a specific date. Put options are used in bear markets where the prices are falling so Option holders are looking for the prices to fall. Option writers however can use Put options to generate income from those seeking insurance or to acquire stock at favorable prices. This is because Put Options let you profit from a decrease in the underlying stocks price much the same as selling stocks short but at a fraction of the risk.
- Rights of the owner of an options contract: A call option provides the holder the rights to buy a specific number of shares of the stock - typically a contract equates to 100 shares - at a predetermined and locked-in price known as the strike price. On the other hand the holder of a put option has the right to sell a specific number of shares of stock at a predetermined price known as the strike price.
- Obligations of an options seller: Sellers (writers) of Call options have the obligation to sell a specific number of shares, typically 100, of the underlying stock at a predetermined price also known as the strike price. Sellers (writers) of Put options have the obligation to buy a specific amount of stock, typically 100, at a predetermined price known as the strike price.

Options are extremely flexible and can be used for many purposes some of the common usages of stock options is for the following objectives:

- To benefit from bull markets and upward price moves using less money
- To profit from bear markets and their downward price slides without the risk of short selling the stock
- To protect stock or a portfolio from falling prices and sudden market downturns

But Options can have teeth and you must always be aware of the risks of trading options. In order to do so safely you must understand two key concepts:

The first is that Option contracts have a limited life as each contract will have an expiration date. What that means is that you must anticipate the timing of any market movement and not just the direction. Because, should the price-shift you have forecast in a certain stock and in a certain direction does not occur by the expiration date, the Option will be effectively worthless and you will lose your premium.

Therefore it is vital that you become comfortable in making not just directional forecasts but also predictions that are time relevant. This is not as obvious or easy as it may first seem. For example, it's not enough that you forecast and are confident that Apple stock will rise to $175 you need to anticipate when this would happen. The difference in premium prices between a one week or six-month Options will be considerable – so you need to get the timing right to both to avoid losses and optimize profits. The key to this is identifying probability – getting the percentages on your side of the deal.

You are best adjusting to this added criterion by participating in trading Options through paper trading to begin with. This point cannot be reiterated enough for beginners – before you risk your money practice strategies and get a feel for the way the market move with regards time and before you do it in live trading.

Setting your Strategy

Setting the wrong strategy can lead to poor trades and missed opportunities. This can take the form of being over-extended in any individual position or by not recognizing a good trade when you see it. A good strategy will not just help you with trade allocation of funds but in spotting good trades. No strategy can eliminate risk but you can manage risks through a sound strategy. On the contrary a risky strategy will expose you to the possibility of you losing or missing trades and ultimately losing your capital. A good strategy will dictate the principles on which your trading philosophy will be founded.

Option Pricing

A significant part of the learning process when trading Options is recognizing your risks and rewards. They come from how well you understand the value of your Option. However to do that requires that you know how an Option derives its value and what conditions will affect any movement in its price. In order to value an option, you will need to know the following:

- The type and strike price of the option (put or call)
- The price of the underlying security
- The trading volatility in that Option
- The probability of success with that Option
- The trading pattern characteristics of the underlying security for example is it trading volumes steady or volatile
- The time remaining until the option expires
- Knowing your rights and obligations as an option holder or writer

Contract Types: the Calls and Puts

There are basically only two kinds of options: calls and puts. By holding a call you have certain specific rights to buy the stock at a pre-specified price by a certain date. On the other hand, owning or holding a put gives you the holder the right to sell a certain stock at a specific price to the option writer by a certain date. The fundamental difference between a put and a call is that Put option price goes up when the price of the underlying security falls. On the other hand Call option prices go up when the underlying security's price rises. When you hold options, you can assert your rights in your own time and at your own discretion. So, anytime between buying an option and its expiration date, you can either:

- Sell the option prior to expiration.
- Manually exercise it prior to expiration.
- Let it expire for either no value (for a loss) or for value (automatic exercise on your behalf if it is in the money).

As an option writer or seller, you will be obligated to honor a specific set of requirements. What is more, your obligations are out with your control. As the Option holder can exercise their rights at any time before the expiry date. In fact, selling options will give you fewer choices, and the active choices available to you are heavily influenced by the markets. As the expiration date nears, you can either:

- Buy the option back for a profit.
- Buy it back for a loss.
- Let the option expire with no value (which will be a profit for you).

Understanding Leverage

A very attractive characteristic of Options is its inherent usage of a thing called *Leverage*. With standard stock trading you would need to buy or sell stock at the market value but that is limited by your funds. So for most beginners and retail traders with only say a $5000 trading fund this means that buying and selling premier stock such as Apple or Amazon is out of the question as it is simply too expensive.

However with Options you are not buying the stock you are buying a contract that gives you the right but not the obligation to buy hence the price and the investment is much lower. But interestingly, the fact that you do not own the stock doesn't prevent you from speculating against it. As one contract will typically consist of 100 shares this provides tremendous leverage as you can reap the benefit in trading in 100 Amazon shares for a fraction of the actual stock price.

Hence, we can say that Options contracts allows the buyers and sellers to make almost the same dollar profit for a much lower financial stake than they could by trading in the actual underlying stock. However, there is as always a big catch as increased leverage proportionately increases risk so just as it can increase profits it also significantly amplifies losses.

Here is an example of how it works in practice: If we consider the earlier Microsoft example, if you speculate that the Microsoft stock will go up in price, you have a couple of options, a) could buy some shares in their stock but if the stock is at $43 per share, it would cost $4,300 to buy 100. If you have limited funds then that might not be feasible. But you could also use plan b) whereby you buy an option to buy 100 shares with a *strike price* of $45 for a premium of $0.13 each, a total of $13.

Now we have to contemplate the potential outcomes of these actions as they are quite different. For example, should the stock increase in price from $43 to $45. Then plan A – where you invested in stock - would reap the benefits of a $200 (less the commissions) profit. But plan B, where you bought an Option with a strike price of $45 you would find that your option is out of the money it did not reach its target, so you can't exercise it as it is worthless.

However, if the stock price rises higher than $45, then the option will become much more profitable. We can demonstrate this by considering that at a stock price of $47, the stockholder has a profit of $400:

$4,700 – $4,300 = $400 but for a percentage return of $400 ÷ $4,300 = 9.3 percent

The option holder would have a profit of $200:

$4,700 – $4,500 = $200 at exercise, but the percentage return would be $200 ÷ 13 = 1,538 percent.

As can be seen the option holder received a greater percentage return on their investment on a smaller amount of initial capital.

But what if Microsoft falls in price to $40? The stockholder has lost $4,300 – $4,000 = $300. Unfortunately for the Option holder their option would expire worthlessly, so the option holder spent $13 for 100 options that are now worth nothing but their losses are fixed at $13 dollars regardless of how low the underlying stock may fall.

There are four key differences between trading using the stock position versus the option position:

- The Option strategy costs $13 upfront and the Stock position costs $4,300.
- The stock hold position can lead to larger losses if the position moves against the stock.
- The Option position is higher risk but has fixed maximum losses
- The greater potential for return comes with higher risk.
- With the options strategy, you have an increased percentage return because you earn almost the same dollar profit as you would on the stock position as you are

investing less money. Of course, that assumes your option can be exercised. Otherwise, there is no profit only the entire loss of the investment.

Options for Speculation

Leverage, makes Options a very attractive way to speculate in the market. Using this technique Traders are betting using low stakes on price changes that can generate large profits. Of course, making large profits also means taking on large risk hence Options poor reputation as being a high-risk tool for financial trading.

Nonetheless, The Options Exchange works because there are always sufficient buyers and sellers to meet the market demand of those wishing to speculate and those in the market to hedge their positions. Therefore there is always a need for those selling and those buying Options in order to make a functional market. Therefore there is always a need to bring together those looking to hedge and those looking to speculate.

Marking to Market and Margin

As we have seen an attractive feature of Options is that they have built-in leverage. The problem is though that there have to be some controls in place to ensure traders are solvent and able to meet their obligations. If not traders could merrily write Options and rake in premiums as a stream of income without any way of paying up should the market go against them. Therefore, there has to be a way for the exchange to ensure everyone can pay up if necessary when the order to exercise a position is triggered on an expiry date.

Now some of the safeguards to prevent insolvent trading are that you can't place an options trade unless you have money in your account. This is known in broker jargon as a margin. A margin account is the collateral that is used to fund your trading obligations. The amount you require to hold in your broker account will typically be a percentage of your commitments but the exact percentage vary. Also the percentage will vary depending on the type of contract in question. For example if you are writing a contract and hence have an obligation to buy a stock should an Option be exercised the amount you will need to hold in the account will be larger than a trader operating mostly on call options. But it is very complex to place a figure on the monetary value of a position as it depends on the relationship between the income received through writing the option, the inherent value of the option, and the most subjective component being the likelihood of the option being exercised. Remember the vast amount of Options will never be exercised.

Because of this complexity in working out a safe margin, the CBOE provides a margin calculator online at cboe.com/tradtool/mcalc/

The calculator will let you work out just how much cash and other collateral you must keep in your trading account to cover obligations in different trading scenarios.

However it is not just down to the brokers to police their clients' trading accounts as the options clearinghouse - which oversees the transaction between brokers and the exchange and manages the money transactions between parties on behalf of the exchange – will each evening check the value of every account relative to the value of its option position. This is a process known as marking to market.

Marking to market determines if you have enough margin to support your position. If they determine that you have sufficient margin then you are free to continue trading. However should they determine that you have the insufficient margin to cover your obligations you will receive a margin call. This is basically a demand from your broker for more funds to be deposited in your account. If you are not in a position to comply with the demand and are not able to put additional funds into the account to cover your position then your position will be sold.

Chapter 4–Getting to grips with the Jargon

In the first 3 days we have covered a lot of ground regarding Trading Options and are now well on our way to having a good solid foundation for building our trading knowledge. You have learned a lot of the theory and concepts that underpin options trading but before we move on to some of the more advanced practical stuff we have to get to grips with the trading jargon. The problem is that financial trading is steeped in jargon and unfortunately options' trading is no exception to this. Indeed, because it is much more complex than the other forms of financial trading it is possibly even more afflicted by the use of strange terms such as moneyness – yes-that is supposedly a word – and we even have a basket full of Greek terms to understand. Unfortunately, if we don't spend the time becoming familiar with the terms now it will make understanding the more advanced concepts, we will learn in the next few days almost impossible.

In this Chapter

We will learn:

- The technical terms for the Option variables
- What are the different Puts and Calls
- What are long and short positions
- Why and how do we use long or short on Calls or Puts?
- Writer and Buyers
- Setting the Strike Price
- Understanding the expiration date and process
- Understand the Option styles

Option Contract Variables

So far we have only considered Options as being a contract – but we have not considered many of the confusing terms that are associated with Options. In this section we will dive deeper into the Option contract and try to explain some of the often confusing jargon.

Here are several key terms you have to know in order to make good options trading decisions:

- **Underlying security:**The underlying stock that you buy or sell and that determines the inherent value of the option.
- **Strike price:**The price you would pay per share if you decided to exercise your rights as for call option buyer. For put option buyers it's the price you would receive for exercising and selling stock.

- **Expiration date:** The date the option and your rights disappear.
- **Option deliverable:**The number of shares and the name of the underlying security that you can call away or put to someone.
- **Market quote:**The most current price of an option that is being bid on by buyers and offered by sellers of options.
- **Multiplier:** This is the variable used to determine the value of the option and how much money you will pay it is based upon the number of shares in a single contract. Typically stock options deliver 100 shares per contract, so the multiplier of a per-share option market price and strike price quotes is 100.
- **Premium:** This is the term used to relate to the total value of the option you buy or sell. The premium is determined based on the market quote of the option and its multiplier (100)

Listed Options

In general terms a *financial option* is a contractual agreement between two parties. Options can be personalized agreements between two private individuals and these are known as over-the-counter options. However, options traded on exchanges in Options trading are standardized contracts known as *listed options.*

Option contracts have a few characteristics that we must be aware of when beginning trading. For example they have a limited lifetime determined by the expiry date. The expiry date is hugely important because once a contract expires it becomes worthless. What this means is that if you don't exercise your rights on or before the expiry date they will expire and you will lose your premium along with the entire value of the Option. This may well be what you intended as many Options are bought as insurance cover for that time period. However you would not want to lose out on a valuable Option with inherent profit just because you forgot to exercise your option on the correct date. Fortunately many online broker platforms will track and notify you well in advance of any options due to expire so that shouldn't be the problem it once was.

We use stock options for the following objectives:

- To benefit from the leverage that allows us to profit from large stock movements using less money
- To benefit and gain profit from a bear market when there are a downward trend and falling prices in stocks without the risk of short selling
- To protect the overall value of a stock portfolio against persistent falling prices or sudden market downturns

To accomplish these tasks there are fundamentally two main categories of Options - Puts and Calls.

Long and Short Puts and Calls

In general terms an option will give you the right to buy or to sell an asset. Thus there are two main types of options - *call* and *put* – whereby the call gives you the right to buy, and the put gives you the right to sell.

An important thing to understand is the difference between Buyers and Sellers as this is fundamental to the way Options work. The Rights of the owner of an options contract is dependent on the type of contract:

- A call option gives the holder (owner) the right to buy the stock before or at an agreed date at a locked in price. A put option gives the owner the right to sell a specific number of shares of stock at a locked in price.
- Option writer or seller obligations: The writer or sellers of call options have the obligation to sell shares of the underlying stock at the agreed locked in price. Sellers of put options has the obligation to buy from the option holder the pre-agreed amount of stock at the locked in price.

To see how this works in practice let us consider why traders buy call options. Traders will buy call options when they predict an upwards or bull market, i.e. they forecast that stocks will go up in price. This is because the call option gives them the right to buy the shares at a lower price than they would otherwise. Now that is straightforward enough, but why do they buy put options? Traders will buy put options when they expect the market to go down, i.e. they will be buying options when they expect a downward trend in the market.

Going long or going short

Another confusing term for beginners and especially those familiar with other stock trading methods is the trading terms, long and short. In general trading terms to take a *long* position is to buy to own it, and to take a *short* position is to sell it.

Nonetheless in Options trading these terms take on more nuanced meanings. In Options trading, the terms of *long* and *short* are more complicated because you are also dealing with whether they are related to puts or call options.

For example, to demonstrate the difference:

- If you take a long position on a call option then you are betting that the price of the underlying asset will rise.

- If you take a long position on a put you are betting on the underlying asset price going down.
- If you are short on a put, you are betting that the price of the underlying asset will be above the strike price.
- If you are short a call, you are also betting that the price of the underlying asset will be below the strike price.

Let's look at some sample transactions.

Trading Long on a Call

If a Trader speculates that a company ABC's stock will be trading above $40 at expiration, which is within a month. The best premium for each Call option with a $40 strike price is $0.85.

Now, if ABC is trading at $45 at the expiration date then all is well and the trader can exercise the option and buy shares at $40 each, for a profit of $5 less the $0.85 premium - $4.15. But if ABC's stock price has remained at or around $40 or less, then the Trader is out the $0.85 option meaning they have lost $0.85x100 =$85.

Trading short on a Call

Another use of a call can be demonstrated when a Trader thinks Company ABC stock will be trading below $50 at expiration date in a months' time. However in this scenario the premium for each call option with a $50 strike price is $2.00. What the Trader can do is writes (shorts) call options at the $50 price and they will receive $2 for each option.

If the price of Company ABC stock at expiration is $40 or below, the Trader is successful and gets to keep the $2 premium per option.

However If the price goes up to say, $54, the Trader will lose $54 – $50 = $4 per share; however the $2 premium offsets half the total loss to $2.

Trading long on a Put

In a third scenario we can see another way of using options when another Trader is confident that Company XYZ stock will be trading below $30 per share at expiration, in 3 months they use a put option.

The premium for a put option with a $30 strike price is $0.75.

If all goes as expected and the price of Company XYZ stock at expiration is $27, then the Trader will make $30 – $27 = $3 per share, less the $0.75 premium for a profit of $2.25.

However, should the price at expiration be $31 or higher, then the Trader is out of the money and the premium for a loss of $0.75.

Trading short on a Put

Another Trader thinks Company XYZ stock will be trading above $70 per share at expiration.

The premium for a put option with a $70 strike price is $1.02, so the Trader writes options at $1.02 each.

At expiration, the stock is at $72 per share, so the Trader gets to keep the $1.02 premium per share.

However, if the stock were to go to $68, then the Trader would then lose $68 – $70 per share, plus the $1.02 premium for a loss of $0.98.

The following table gives you a short summary of what happens to different types of options positions as the underlying asset's price changes.

Basic Put and Call Matrix

Option	Stock Price Goes Up	Stock Price Goes Down
Long call	Profit	Worthless
Short call	Loss	Keep the premium
Long put	Worthless	Profit
Short put	Keep the premium	Loss

Writers & Buyers

The trader who decides to short an option—in effect, sell it to someone else—is also known as the *writer*. For every trade that is made there is a writer and a buyer. Exchanges need both buyers and writers to create the market depth. This is simply because writers construct options to sell to those in the market to buy. In every trade the option writer goes short, and the buyer goes long. Nonetheless, the interesting thing is that even if every trader in the market had a common perception of a stock's behavior, there will still be those that go short when the market as a whole is going long.

The reason for this is that there are always those trading for the purpose of speculation and those looking for insurance. These traders have conflicting interests and objectives so will have to take contrary positions in order to achieve their goals.

For example, Options that are bought for insurance purposes will take the opposite perspective of the market trend. This is because an investor holding a valuable asset for example 100 Apple shares may want them to go up in price but will still need protection against their price falling. Hence the need for a put Option with a low strike price that will counter-balance any sudden decline in value.

It is this ability to mix and match long and short, puts and calls in a few different ways that are the foundation in developing options trading strategies and cycles.

Setting the Strike Price

The *strike price* of an option is the predetermined and locked-in price where the option can be exercised at any time up until expiration. For example, a call with a strike price of $70 can be exercised if the underlying price is at $70 or above. At exercise, the trader who wrote the call will receive $70 per share in exchange for a share of the stock. If the trader does not own the stock – remember they do not have to – the required stock will have to be purchased at market price. Whatever, the trader who bought the call has the right to buy the underlying for $70, whether it's worth $70.01 or $876 dollars in the market. The Option writer is obliged to sell the stock at $70 regardless of whether he has to go out to the market and buy it at $70.01 or $876 dollars in order to fulfil the contract.

Similarly, a put option with a strike price of $40 can be exercised if the underlying price is $40 or less. At exercise, the trader who wrote the put will have to buy the stock at $40 per share, whether it is worth $39.99 or $0.00. The holder of the option will receive the difference between the market price and the exercise price.

The following table shows what happens when a call or put expires in the money—that is, when the market price is above the strike price for a call or below the strike price for a put.

	Holder	**Writer**
Call	Receives cash or security	Delivers cash or security
Put	Delivers cash or security	Receives cash or security

You'll notice that the receiver and deliverer are different for puts and calls, holders and writers. This allows for the structure of many different strategies.

To exercise an option, the holder notifies their broker which then notifies the market clearinghouse, which then in turn notifies the seller that it is time to settle up.

Expiration Date

The *expiration date* is not as straightforward as you might suspect albeit it does mean the day the option is no longer valid. However the way the date is determined is by the month on the contract and the day is the third Friday of the month. Thus an Option will be dated 2019 Dec and the expiry date will be the date on the third Friday of December 2019. By the expiry date the holder must either exercise their rights and the writer has to settle up by that date, or the option will expire and become worthless.

American and European Options

There is some ambiguity between Options as there are two distinct styles an American and a European style. The only real difference but it is a significant one is that an *American option* gives the holder the right to exercise the option at any time after the sale and before the expiration date. On the other hand, a *European option* can only be exercised on the expiration date. This is a major difference in terms of trading so you must make sure you know which option style you are trading in.

To compound the problem exchanges issue both types, it is no longer the case that American exchanges only issued American style Options and European only issued European style options now there is a mixture of both. You need to know which you are trading as it can have a large effect of the Options value and ability to be traded.

Chapter 5 - Understanding and Placing Orders

The past 4 days of your journey to becoming an Options trader has been a hard slog as we have struggled to come to terms with the theory and underpinning concepts that support options trading. However, it is all downhill from here. It doesn't get any easier I'm afraid, but it does become more practically orientated as we finally learn how to trade in Options. So in this chapter on our 5th day we will start to pore over and study quote reports and option chains.

The option quote reports and the option chains we use in this section can be accessed at http://www.cboe.com/delayedquote/detailed-quotes?

In This Chapter

We will learn

- How to read option quotes
- To decipher option chains
- Understand option premiums
- learn how to make orders
- Learn the different types of order and when to use them
- Managing margin through the mark to market
- How to open and close an order
- About all the different types of orders and when to use them

Now that you have learned all about the trading concepts behind Options, as well as all the basic terminology, what they are, how they work and why we use them, it's time to get into the details of how options work in an exchange environment. After all Listed Options are sold around the world on exchanges, which may have different rules. Also the Option contracts may have different specifications; they may be American or European style. Therefore, it is very important for you to check the style format and the specific rules for trading in each contract with your broker or the exchange. Most modern broker platforms automatically furnish you with the relevant information as well as track Option expiry dates – as last trading days may differ – but if you are not sure check with the exchange as that at least ensures you won't be unpleasantly surprised.

Nonetheless, despite there being some difference from region to region there is a still far more common ground between exchanges. This is because trading has become electronic and global so there has essentially been a harmonization of different options, trading rules across the different exchanges.

Reading the Quotes

The first thing as a beginner trader that you will need to become familiar with is the confusing and somewhat intimidating dashboard of your online trading app. The broker app that you subscribe to will present you with a digest of the current Options quotes available presented in what is termed quote tables. These tables display a list of option price quotes but they are also crammed with other supporting information. For example they will list the time to expiry, the strike price and the price of the option including the bid-ask spread. These quote tables as they are known will also include information on indicators for the current open interest and the implied volatility.

These price quote tables list what is known in trading as the *options chain* or *options series,* which is the technical term for a list of all of the options currently available for a particular expiration date. However, they are not quite the same thing, as an options chain is a list of all the options available on a specific stock whereas an options series is a list of all the puts and calls on a specific stock that have the same strike price and expiration date.

Nonetheless the terms do appear to be used interchangeably depending on the broker application.

In the following screenshot you can see a quote table with an option chain with the same expiration date but a variety of available strike price.

Calls — 03/15/2019

Last	Net	Bid	Ask	Vol	IV	Delta	Gamma	Int	Strike
3.85	+1.27	3.8	3.95	11,655	0.1951	0.8643	0.0677	16975	AAPL 177.500
1.91	+0.745	1.91	1.99	61,903	0.1956	0.6227	0.1178	45939	AAPL 180.000
0.75	+0.345	0.73	0.75	58,877	0.1997	0.3258	0.1094	15035	AAPL 182.500
0.25	+0.125	0.25	0.27	53,371	0.2177	0.136	0.0608	18670	AAPL 185.000

Reading the Quote Table

If we look at the table and read it from left to right we can consider each column in turn:

- Last: This is the price of the last transaction i.e. the latest successful bid price
- Net: This is the change in price between the latest and the price at closing the previous day.
- Bid: This is the highest bid price, which is the highest available price bid by someone to buy the stock.
- Ask: This is the lowest ask price, the best available offer of a price that someone has made to sell the stock
- Bid-Ask spread: Although not shown in our table – we have to calculate it ourselves – this is the difference between the two prices i.e. the lowest ask and the highest bid. The

spread is a good indicator or volatility and marker depth as a stock being aggressively traded by many participants will have a smaller spread. Conversely a stock that has low trading volatility and volume with only a few people actively trading will have a higher spread. The bid-ask spread is an important indicator for setting entry and exit price strategies and what type of order to use – i.e. don't use market orders on high spreads use a limit order. The reverse strategy holds true for small spreads. Typically avoid stock with spreads higher than 5-10% as you will likely be overpaying and risk not finding a buyer when it comes to selling.

- Volume: This is the number of trades carried out on the option during the current trading session and this total is reset at the end of every trading day– the higher the volume the more liquid the stock and the better for trading.
- Open Interest: In the option chain this is an indicator – not a live metric - of the number of open options available as it is tallied up at the end of each trading day – higher open interest is an indicator of high trading interests as options are created and retires due to market supply and demand.
- IV: This is termed Implied Volatility (IV) and is an estimate of the trading volatility on that option. You want to buy options when implied volatility is low as options are likely to be at their cheapest due to lower demand and be an option seller of options when implied volatility is high when options are likely to be more expensive due to higher market demand.
- Delta: Delta is an indicator of the option's sensitivity to changes in the underlying stock price. It provides an estimate of the price change of the option given a $1 change in the underlying stock. So if an option has a delta of 0.2 then for every $1 move in the price of the stock the option price will move $0.20 in the same direction.
- Gamma: This is a measure of how much the delta will change given a $1 move in the underlying stock. Gammas can be thought of as an indicator of the rate of change in delta, so an option with a gamma figure of for example, +0.05 will see its delta indicator value also increase by 0.05 for every $1 movement in the underlying stock price. Gamma is at its highest with at-the-money options and for short-dated options i.e. in the final week. Sellers will want low gamma as they want the prices to stay relatively stable whereas buyers want large gamma as they want prices to rise quickly.
- INT: This is the measure of the Open Interest in that option – in contrast to trading volume – this figure is derived from the previous day's trading

If we drill down on a quote say for the strike price of $185 we get the detailed price data table shown below:

AAPL190315C00185000 LAST 0.25 CHANGE +0.125 (0%)

Chart

Price Data Table
Mar 12, 2019 @ 22:01 ET (DELAYED)

Last Sale	0.25	Tick	No_change
Time of Last Sale		Underlying Symbol	AAPL
Net Change	+0.125	Percent Change	0
Previous Close	0.115	Open	0.16
High	0.8	Low	0.15
Bid	0.25	Ask	0.27
Bid Size	1	Ask Size	506
Volume	53,371	Security Type	Option
Open Interest	18670	Expiration Date	03/15/2019

Contract Naming Conventions

Prior to 2010 the standard naming convention for US options was based upon a format where each contract name was made up of the stock's *ticker symbol,* followed by the date of expiration in year/month format, then the type of option – Call or Put, followed by the strike price.

For example: AAPL19MarCall185 was a representation of an option expiring in March 2019 on a Call order for a strike price of $185 and it was very readable but not scalable to the new market volumes. So after 2010 the naming convention and format changed to accommodate scale.

An example of a modern contract name post-2010 would be: "AAPL190315C00185000"

Now let us break this down to show how this equates to March 15th, 2019 $185.00 Call Option on Apple stock.

The new format is 21-bytes long and comprises a (the ticker symbol that indicates the company name) + the Year of expiry (yy) + the Month of expiration (mm) + the actual Day of expiry (dd) + they type of transaction, the Call/Put Indicator (C or P) + Strike Price:

For Example, a March 15th, 2019 $185.00 Call Option on Apple would be listed as "APPL190315C00185000"

What it means:

Component	Value	Location in symbol
Root Symbol	AAPL	**AAPL**150416C00030000
Expiration Year	2019	YHOO**19**0416C00030000

Expiration Month	03	YHOO150316C00030000
Expiration Day	15	YHOO150415C00030000
Call or Put	Call	YHOO150416C00030000
Strike Price*	$182.00	YHOO150416C00185000

Basics of Orders

Once you decide on a favorable stock and strike price you can browse through the options chain, which will list all the available contracts and their price quotes that meet your criteria. You can choose:

- The contract type
- Transaction type
- Expiry date
- Strike price

You can scan through the list to find a particular put or a call with a strike price and expiration that you like or you can usually filter only contracts that meet your criteria. Once you have found a contract that matches your requirements you can then place the order.

As we said earlier there is additional support information that is available with each Option. The information will detail such things as the open interest, which will be shown in a column in the quote report showing how many of these contracts are outstanding. Another column of interest indicates the *implied volatility* and this shows the volatility of the price of the underlying asset. If you remember volatility is one of the six factors that determine the valuation of an Option and it is based on the current price of the option.

Option Transactions

There are four basic transactions that make up all Option trading. Even the most advanced trading strategies come down to initiating these four basic transactions to open and close positions. So you must understand their terminology as most transaction will be referred to as one of the following:

- A *buy-to-open* transaction - this gets you a contract to establish a new long position in a put or a call.

- A *sell-to-close* order – this is used to close out or end a position in an existing long contract.
- A *sell-to-open* order – this order is used to write a put or a call and to establish a new short position.
- A *buy-to-close* transaction – this is used to end an existing short position.

Opening and Closing a Position

When you open or enter a position you are actually submitting your order to buy an option. However, when you make your bid there may not be an available option on the market with anyone willing to take the other side of the trade. But you won't know that, because your demand will create a contract if one isn't already in existence with a counterparty willing to take the other side of the trade. Therefore an important factor is in knowing the correct protocol to use when you go about entering and exiting positions.

For example: To buy a call option, the correct protocol for you to use can be seen in the following order:

Buy to Open, 1 APPL March 15 185.00 Strike Call Option

Now to exit that open position, you would then have to submit the following order:

Sell to Close, 1 AAPL March 15 185.00 Strike Call Option

You will use the same type of order and protocol when opening a position in an option with underlying stock that you don't own. This is because the simplicity of the order process only requires that you specify the stock of the option you are selling. Therefore you would use the same protocol and order format when opening and closing an option that you don't own:

Sell to Open, 1 APPL March 15 185.00 Strike Call Option

Buy to Close, 1 APPL March 15 185.00 Strike Call Option

The underlying importance of ensuring a strict protocol is to enable the exchange and clearinghouse to match and tally up the number of transactions at the end of each day. This also allows them to determine the number of open contracts, which is also known as the open interest.

Selling an option you don't own

When you take up a position by writing or selling a call option as an opening transaction, you are now on the opposite side of the deal so you become obligated by market rules to sell a stock at the strike price at any time until the option expires. For the time you sell the option if a call option holder goes in the money and decides to exercise their rights, you the option writer will have to meet your obligation. In trading terms this is called *being assigned* the option. When you are assigned on a call option contract, you will have only a couple of alternatives:

- If you are covered and you own sufficient shares then you must sell the shares to close the position.
- If you are in a naked position then you will need to buy the shares regardless of the cost.

If you own shares when you sell a call option, it is known as a *covered* transaction, because you have the underlying shares to *cover* your short position. However, if you don't own the shares to cover the position when you sell the call, this is known as a *naked call*. You should never as a beginner open a naked call as the losses can be *unlimited* given the market potential of stock to continue to rise indefinitely.

On the other hand if you sell a put option as an opening transaction, you are putting yourself into the position of holding an obligation to buy the stock at the locked in strike price at any point until the option expires. Should anyone exercise their rights you will be assigned the option, and this typically happens on a short put when the underlying stock has fallen. If assigned, you will be obliged to buy stock buying stock at a higher price than the current market value. As with the call option your short put position can be covered if you hold the stock or naked if you have no stock.

Selling puts is a risky transaction not for beginners or the fainthearted, the reason for that is when you sell an option, you are creating a short position on a stock option contract and are effectively out of the active decision-making process. This means you are at risk of assignment from the time you create the position all the way through to the expiration of the contract. The only way you can get out of the obligation is to exit the position. To exit the position means entering a Buy to close order for the option.

Understanding option orders

Options are made on demand by the market and are not limited in the way stock is by its float, which is the term used to describe the number of shares outstanding and available in the market to trade for stock.

Contracts are different in there is no physical limit as they are created on-demand when two traders create a new position, or open a trade. This increases the metric that is known as open interest for that specific option. Open interest is a measurement of market sentiment for that option and it decreases when traders close existing positions.

Open interest is typically done on a market-wide basis and doesn't get updated trade-by-trade. It's more an end-of-day reconciliation by the Options Clearing Corporation (OCC) as they need to keep the accounting straight and control all that leverage. It also means you'll have to communicate a little more information when placing option orders than trading in stocks.

Knowing basic option order rules

Buying or selling options can be done on any order. However, you cannot just create orders haphazardly as the ability to go long (buy) or short (sell) a contract depends on your brokers' permission. The broker is likely to make their decision based upon your history, experience, trading strategy and the option approval level for your account. This is to prevent beginners or the inexperienced from creating unlimited-risk, short-option positions, which could be calamitous until their broker approves the transaction.

Because contracts are created and retired based on market demand, you must enter orders in a way that supports this end-of-day reconciliation by the options markets. This requires the use of a specific language. For example:

- A new position you're creating is an opening order.
- An existing position you're exiting is a closing order.

Using a call option as an example, the following table provides you with the transactions required to enter and exit a long call or short call position.

Position	Entry	Also Known As	Exit	Also Known As
Long Call	Buy Call to Open	BCO	Sell Call to Close	SCC
Short Call	Sell Call to Open	SCO	Buy Call to Close	BCC

When exercising or getting assigned on an option contract, there is no closing transaction. The same holds true for options expiring worthless. In each case, the appropriate number of contracts is removed from your account after the transaction completes or expiration weekend comes to an end.

Basic Order Types

Before you place an order however you need to understand what type of order you wish to make. You will find that you have a variety of different order types available, some orders are designed to guarantee to fill an order but not necessarily at the price you desired (such as market order) whereas others are configured to guarantee price but not necessarily to fill the order (such as limit orders). Although there are some other unique parameters and considerations for options orders, the fill-versus-price conundrum remains the most common reason for selecting an order type.

By managing the orders behavior means that you have greater control as to how the order is executed as well as the price. When in doubt, consider what limits your risk.

There are several types of orders that have certain parameters that affect the way they are carried out. These parameters are selectable which allows you to fine control the behavior of the order.

An options transaction can be configured to be executed in a particular way by using parameters the trader sets when the order is placed. Almost all brokerage applications that support the handling and trading of options will allow traders to set these basic parameters. These configurable orders are essential today as market prices fluctuate rapidly due to high volume electronic trading. Therefore as prices change quicker than a human can respond traders need to try and automate the trading processes. By having a good understanding of the types of orders available to you can greatly reduce the stress and the losses associated with financial trading.

Many of these parameters change the order type and its behavior and are required by an average trader as several of the order types are based on prices:

Market orders

Market orders are standard trading orders used to buy and sell at the best price on the exchange when the order is placed. The issue with a market order is it does just that it trades at the best price available which is not always the price you want. Therefore you use a market order when you are more concerned with obtaining or ridding yourself of the stock rather than the price. Market orders are the most common type of orders.

Limit orders

Limit orders are a type of order used to selectively buy or sell only at a specific price or better (higher for a sell order, lower for a buy order). A limit order works just like a market order except that it will only match a trade if the best match also matches the pre-determined price. The broker can only execute the order if the price meets your pre-set price criteria. But limit orders can also work against you if you are not careful. For example, you place a limit order on a call option to buy at $10 when the option is trading at $12, and the price falls to $10.01, your order would not be executed. This behavior may be what you want as the use of Limit orders does make trading more predictable, but they might also lead to missed opportunities.

Generally, limit orders are good for entering a position; this is because you only want to establish positions that are within your desired trading allocations. However, if you need to guarantee an exit, only a market order will guarantee that for you. Effectively managing order execution means knowing when it's more important to get the order executed versus the price where it's executed. When in doubt, consider what limits your risk.

Stop orders

Stop orders are very important and you need to know how they work and practice setting them by paper trading. A stop order is designed to trigger and to buy or sell once an option hits a specific price. Stop orders are typically used to automate trading as they limit losses by closing a position if a particular price is hit. However stop orders should not be confused with limit orders because stop orders are used very differently than limit orders as they continue to be executed if the stop is hit. For example, if you place a stop order of $10 to close out a call position at $10.50, i.e. to limit any losses and lock in the $10 profit. In this scenario the stop order will be executed as soon as the price hits $10. But here is the problem as a stop order reverts then to working as a market order and fills the order with the best available price and that may be $9 so it ends up filling the order at a worse price.

Stop-limit orders

The solution to the fallibility of a standard stop order is to use a stop-limit order, which is a combination of a stop and a limit order. This aggregate order is only executed when the stop price is hit but the order only executes at the limit price or better. The stop-limit order does enforce a level of discipline on the trade but it is however still restricted to only making a trade should there be a matching trade available – which means you might miss the opportunity to abandon a position which can lead to even greater losses.

Placing a stop order is similar to monitoring security and placing a market order when certain market conditions are met. A sell-stop order gets triggered when either the option trades at or below your stop price or if the asking price reaches your stop. On the other hand a buy-stop order gets triggered when the option trades at or above your stop or when the bid price reaches your stop. Because you sell on the bid and buy on the ask prices you will need to account for the bid-ask spread when you are determining an appropriate option stop level. Another issue with option stop orders is duration. The option contract you're trading may only allow day-stop orders so you'll need to enter a new stop order each evening after the market closes.

Stops are superior to stop-limit orders for managing risk because they guarantee an execution if the stop condition is met. Some systems will allow you to have two standing orders for the same underlying stock. If that is the case then include a stop-loss order for the purpose of risk management and a limit order configured for profit-taking. If your platform allows a "one cancels other" trade type, then you can enter both orders that way.

A system that supports a one cancels other order will allow you to enter two different orders that are both active on the same stock in the market. The way it works is that if or when one of those orders is executed, the system will automatically cancel the other order. But be aware if the system doesn't support one cancels other, then having two live orders against the same stock position is dangerous as it would only take a strong swing in the position to cause both orders to trigger and be filled. This could result in you holding an unlimited risk position. Too often beginner traders who fail to grasp the nuances of options stop trades and pay the price for not being diligent in selecting their order types.

In terms of duration, the two primary periods of time your order will be in place are as follows:

- The current trading session or the following session if the markets closed.
- Until the the broker clears the order or the order is cancelled by you
- Order duration is identified by adding day or good 'til cancelled (GTC).
- Market orders guarantee execution, so they are good for the day only.

If you want to cancel an active order, you need to submit a Cancel Order. After the instructions are completed, you receive a report back notifying you that the order was successfully cancelled. It is possible for the order to already have been executed, in which case you receive a report back indicating that it is too late to cancel. One thing to be aware of is that you cannot cancel a market order. This is because it is guaranteed to be filled at the best available price.

You will also find that the way you go about changing an order is a little different from the way that you cancel one. This is because there are two ways to change an order:

- Cancel the original order, wait for confirmation of the cancellation, and then enter a new order.
- Submit a Cancel/Change or Replace Order

Even though the electronic order process is very fast, when replacing an order it's better to use the Change/Cancel approach. Otherwise, you must wait for the cancellation confirmation report before you can make your new order so as to avoid duplicating an executed order.

There are other, special purpose order types available that are less used that we will discuss in the next section as it is important to know all the choices you have to hand. This is simply because it is your responsibility to select the correct order type. So it is crucial that you understand all the order types available and how they behave and are handled in the market. What you will find is that the order type when using trading options online, will appear in the order drop-down menu. Here will be all the pertinent choices, and the order ticket will have all the required boxes. Nonetheless you must still read the order ticket carefully before hitting the Execute button. Also read the confirmation ticket that you will receive because if you have accidentally filled in the wrong box you could have committed to a very risky trade.

Type of Order	Guarantees
Market Order	Order will be executed (filled)
Limit Order	Order will get fixed price
Stop Order or Stop-Loss Order	Order will be executed (filled)
Stop Limit Order	Order will get fixed price

Specialist Types of Order

Price is not the only parameter that can be used to tune the behavior of an order as traders can also set time limits on their orders:

- *Day orders* will be executed and filled if possible the same day they are received and are always cancelled at the end of the day if they cannot be filled Day orders are standard orders in day trading
- *Good 'til date (GTD) orders* work in a similar manner but they are good until the end date specified, if they cannot be filled earlier they always terminate on the expiry date.
- *Good 'til cancelled (GTC) orders* are not date dependent and will remain valid until they are filled or until the trader cancels the order.

These are additional parameters that determine stock so in addition to price and time a trader can request All *or* None for the order. How this works is that if a trader makes an order for 3 Options at a defined price they can also set the all or none parameter. This determines how the order will be filled. Without that parameter being set, the trader might receive only one Option i.e. a partial fill, which might not be desirable.

Advanced Order Types

Traders are always on the lookout for more control over their orders. That's especially true in options trading so many brokerage firms will offer additional types of useful orders:

Contingent orders

This type of order can trigger two transactions at the same time. A contingency order can be executed if the underlying or another security reaches a target price. They are sometimes used for placing stop-loss points, as they don't show up in in the order book. This is especially helpful for options traders

Trailing stop orders

These are orders to buy or sell once an option hits a specific price. Unlike stop orders, they are set as a percentage above or below the option's current market price. This means they can be set to move with the market. This prevents the order being triggered when it is no longer advantageous. Further, if the price moves back in a favorable direction, the stop will be automatically reset.

One cancels other (OCO) orders

OCO orders are actually two orders that are placed at the same time with the understanding that if one order's stop price is hit and it is triggered, then the other order will be cancelled automatically. That means they can be used to automatically close positions when either a target profit or loss target is hit.

One triggers other (OTO) orders

OTO orders are another type of combination order whereby two separate orders are placed simultaneously. The goal here is that if one of the orders is triggered then that will cause the other to execute. For example, an OTO can be used as a stop order, which will close one position but also causes another order to be opened automatically.

Chapter 6 – Being in the Money

At the end of day 5 you reached a point whereby you understand all about option theory and how to read a quote table. You know what the parameters and metrics are and how to use them to select attractive options from the options chain. Using this knowledge can assist you in selecting good options that match your specific trading intentions. Furthermore you will now know what type of orders to use and in what scenario. This will enable you to control the price you pay/receive on a transaction or guarantee an entry or exit from a position in a hurry. You will also know how to combine orders to blend custom actions to suit any trading scenario. Now on day 6 we will move on to consider the financial position of an option and whether it is financially attractive, we will also turn to consider entry and exit strategies based upon the financial status of an option.

IN THIS CHAPTER

You will learn:

- All about moneyness
- How to judge whether an option is in, at, or out of the money
- How to choose good entry and exit point in a trade
- How to exercise your right at expiry
- How to evaluate an Option (intrinsic vs. extrinsic value)
- How to gauge the effects of volatility
- How to use the Greeks

The concept of moneyness

The term moneyness is used in Options trading to describe the financial status of an Option. An option is said to be *in the money*– or profitable to exercise if its strike price is lower than the price of the underlying asset. For example it would be in the money if you could exercise your rights to buy the underlying stock at the strike price to immediately sell on the market for a profit.

However, the concept of moneyness has a few different aspects to it.

Remember that the strike price is the locked-in price that the underlying stock can be bought or sold for, if exercised. Therefore the strike price is an important factor in determining the Options value as we can compare the Options strike price with the actual market price of the stock. This relationship between the strike and actual market price determines the intrinsic value of the Option and will be a determining factor:

- At the money: This is when the strike price and the stock price is the same and so it applies to both calls and puts
- Near the money: As it is unlikely for the strike and actual price to exactly match any close to equality is termed near the money
- In the money: This is when the strike price in a call option is below the price of the actual stock. On the other hand with a put option the strike price is in the money when it is above the stock price
- Out of the money: This is when a call option strike price is above the stock price. With a put option the strike price will be out of the money when it is below the stock price

As you start to practice and gain experience working with quote tables and orders, you will become very familiar with these terms. This is because you will soon become accustomed to using the relationship between the stock price and the strike price to determine if there is any intrinsic value in the Option. A thing to remember is that only options that are "in the money" will have any intrinsic value.

Indeed, an option will be said to be *in the money* only if it is profitable to exercise. It is *out of the money* if it is not profitable. This means that just because the strike price is above or below the actual price doesn't automatically make it in the money as we must always consider the cost of the premium. Also, the relationship of the underlying price to the strike price depends on the type of option involved.

In other words, a long call is in the money if the strike price is less than the underlying stock price. Therefore you would make a profit if you to exercise your rights under the option, by buying the underlying asset, and then selling it at the higher market price. On the other hand, if the underlying stock price is less than the strike price, then the option is out of the money.

Conversely for the writer of the option, the trader that is obliged to fulfil the holder's rights whether that is to buy or to sell, then they will have the opposite point of view. For the writer of the Option has taken a short position and will be out of the money when the price of the underlying asset is greater than the strike price and in the money when the price of the underlying asset is less than the exercise.

Similarly, the positions are reversed when we consider relative perspectives of the holder and writer of the put option. For example, if the holder of a put option has a strike price of $35 and if the underlying stock is trading at more than $35, then they would be out of the money as it would not be profitable to exercise, so the long put position would be out of the money. However the holders long put would be in the money if the underlying were to trade at less than $35.

But conversely, if we consider the short put position, we will find that an underlying price of more than $35 would mean the option would not be exercised by the holder, so the writer could keep the premium and be in the money. But, if the underlying stock price were to fall below $35, then the option would be in the money from the holder's perspective as it could be exercised at a profit and the writer's short position would now be out of the money.

The following table offers a neat summary of it all.

The Moneyness of an Option

Position	In the Money	Out of the Money
Long call	Stock > Strike	Stock < Strike
Short call	Stock < Strike	Stock > Strike
Long put	Stock < Strike	Stock > Strike
Short put	Stock > Strike	Stock < Strike

Stock = current market price of the underlying stock (variable)
Strike = the locked-in strike price of the Option (fixed)

As we can see the holder and the writer of the Options always have an opposite position except when the strike price and the underlying price are the same, then the option is *at the money or near the money.* This is regardless of the type of option whether it is a put or a call, or whether you are going long or short.

Furthermore, the moneyness of an option is not affected by the style of the option. What this means is that even with a European option, which can only be exercised at the expiry time, it can still transition many times during that period often jumping between being in, out, or at the money at any given time.

Open Interest

An interesting metric that is often included in quote tables for Option contracts is an indicator depicting Open interest, which is the total number of outstanding options contracts. Open interest is tallied at the end of each day. Open interest is used as a metric for the measurement of market sentiment. It should not be misinterpreted as the number of options traded because it is not the same thing as volume as many options are traded to close out existing positions.

However if you are speculating in short term trading of options then Open Interest is an important metric as you will want as much market interest as you can get on your option. This will make it easier to trade when you choose to exit the position as there will likely be many potential buyers.

Expiration and Exercise

Options expire at regular intervals determined by the expiration date, which is the date the option expires. Most options expire on the third Friday of a given month. However, some high-volume weekly options have expiration dates every Friday. The last time to trade the option is at the close of the market immediately before the option expires. Some European options close earlier (sometimes on a Thursday but the closing time would be specified for the option, and most broker apps track the options expiry dates and send a notification so you'd know):

The option period is the term used to denote the valid time **until** expiration and it starts the moment the option is made (written) and ends on the expiry day. However, there are ways to stay in the position if you want to beyond the expiry date. If you want to maintain the position you can *roll* by closing your current – soon to expire - open position and simultaneously make a new position at a different strike price or expiration.

Exercising your Rights

To *exercise* is the term used to cash in an option but the vast majority of options are never exercised. But should you want to and you have a call option giving you the right to buy shares of ABC at $100 per share, and the stock is trading at $105, all you have to do is notify your broker that you want to exercise the Option.

When exercising your option to buy the stock you will need to have the funds in your account. Almost all brokers will require that you buy – pay for the stock – before you sell. This means that you will need sufficient funds in your account before you can exercise your position. Some brokers allow you to turn around and sell the stock immediately and you may get away with selling the stock before you pay the broker, but that type of free-riding - is frowned up.

Delivery and Settlement

When a call option on a stock is exercised, the writer has to transfer the shares to the option buyer's account at the strike price. If the writer is not covered by already owning the stock they must go and buy the shares in the open market.

However, if there is an option for *cash settlement,* then the person whose option is profitable receives a cash transfer payment. This is more commonly used in trading in index options.

Extrinsic and Intrinsic Value

Options have two primary sources of value. The *intrinsic value* is the option's strike price in relation to the price of the underlying asset. An option has intrinsic value only if it is in the money. If it is not in the money then there is no profit so no value.

Time value, on the other hand is known as *extrinsic value.* This value is the difference between the option's price and the amount of intrinsic value - the amount it is in the money. The logic behind this is that the amount that an option is in the money is its intrinsic value, the profit should you claim it today.

But the option can be worth more today than the profit you would realize if you exercised it. This is an important consideration when you are hedging as you do not want to exercise the option – take the profit. Instead you value the time remaining on the insurance value of the option. This additional time value cannot be ignored as it explains why people will often hold onto options when they are profitable to exercise. Of course they may just be riding a trend and hoping to end up with a larger profit.

Nonetheless, it is important to realize that Options do have both extrinsic value and intrinsic value. The more you understand the components of an option's price, the better you can value the option relative to your needs.

One additional concept of Option value that we must know about is *parity.* When we refer to Parity with regards to an Options value we mean the point where an option is in the money but has no time value. Options generally don't reach parity until just before expiration.

Weighing Option Costs and Benefits

There are many advantages to trading using options, but you don't get all those benefits without taking on-board some element of risk. A notable risk that you have to accept is that options have a limited lifespan as they are limited by an expiry date. Now there are clear strategies that you must have in place when handling this risk such as having an exit strategy. For example your choices are, trade the option during the timespan of the option, expire the option on or before the expiry date or simply let the option expire.

However, there can be a big problem with just leaving options to expire. For example, if the option is in-the-money at expiration, your broker may well automatically exercise/assign the option. The problem here is that by exercising the valuable option they have effectively converted a low-cost option position into a high-cost stock position, which you may not want or be able to afford. Consequently, you need to carefully monitor your options and check for notifications from the broker platform regarding any in-the-money option positions, which are nearing the expiration date. You need to do this in anticipation of this likely change in your margin requirement. Alternatively you want to make sure you have sufficient time to trade the option or make other adjustments such as rolling over a trade in order to avoid buying the stock.

Risk of Leverage

Another significant risk to be aware of is that of leverage. Because Options don't cost much as stock as they are simply a contract, this means that they experience disproportionately larger percentage price gains in reaction to the far more expensive underlying stock's very small price movements. The huge benefit of this is that it results in large percentage gains when the underlying stock moves in the anticipated direction by even a small amount. The downside though is that it also results in a 100% wipe-out of the investment if the stock moves by even the smallest amount in the wrong direction. This is not necessarily an issue with beginners or at least it shouldn't be as the risk manifests itself mainly through trading too large a position size. However, you need to be aware that as beneficial as leverage clearly is, it can also be a double edge sword, so be aware that leverage is a risk that needs to be addressed. One simple way to nullify or minimize this level of risk is to keep your position size small.

Lastly, Options as we know possess a time value (extrinsic value) in addition to their inherent intrinsic value (in the money value), which is also another double-edged sword. For option buyers, time-decay acts as a headwind because it is continually decreasing the value of the option. By doing so this increases the dependency on greater stock price movement to break even on the trade. For option writers, it acts as a tailwind because it allows a profit to be generated through steady premium incomes regardless of whether the stock moves or not.

Two other option cost factors should be considered:

1. Costs associated with the trading process
2. Cost of exercising the stock

By understanding the basic cost structure for an option, you can see how options also add through leverage an element of risk, despite the fact that options also provide leverage at a reduced risk.

To complicate the matter a little is the fact that Option prices are partially based on probabilities. For stock options, you want to consider the likelihood that a particular option will be in-the-money before or at expiration given the type of price movements the underlying stock has recently undergone. The way an Option is valued takes into consideration 6 factors; Stock price, strike price, time to expiration, interest rates and dividends but there is a wildcard factor – volatility.

Understand the role of Volatility

Volatility is often considered to be a wildcard because it is difficult to gauge in real time as it is constantly changing throughout each hour of every trading day. As a result to determine the level of volatility mathematicians have come up with a model that indicates an implied value and it does this by working backwards. How it does this is to use the other known inputs listed above and then subtracts that figure from the current option price being quoted to arrive at the up to date volatility figure.

An interesting thing about options is that although they derive their value from the underlying asset the price is not a fixed 1:1 ratio. For example a $1 dollar movement in the price of a stock does not necessarily result in a similar $1 price move on the option. This is because as we have seen that the option price is determined by several factors such a strike, price, expiry time, volatility, etc. However, the largest single factor in an option's value is the underlying stock's price, so there is a relationship between the two.

In order to work out the relationship mathematicians have developed a set of variables, which traders call the Greeks – delta, gamma, theta, and rho. The Greeks are used to try and understand the relationships and the dynamics between the option and stock prices. These variables are considered to be very important to traders as they need to predict how an option's price may change in response to changes in a stock's price.

Using "Greeks" for Options Trading

The Greeks provide an easy way for traders to predict changes in an options price in response to a price change in the underlying stock. The downside is however that they also add a level of complexity and confusion that is disproportional to the benefit they provide. This is because overwhelmingly the most important factor affecting the value of an option is the difference between the stock price and strike price and the time left before expiry. The other components do affect the option price but to an almost negligible level in comparison. So when using the Greeks try and not get too wrapped up in this fine analysis that you lose sight of what is really important.

The Greeks in Brief

The Greeks are valuable variables that can be helpful to traders and analysts so we provide an overview of what each one aims to measure. In brief, as we have seen already when reading option quote tables, Delta measures how sensitive an option's price is to changes in the underlying stock's price. Gamma is a measure of the rate of change of delta. These two variables are the most commonly used Greeks but there are others. Theta, for example, is a measure of the value decay in an option as it approaches its expiration date. Then there is Vega, which is an indicator of the sensitivity of an option's price to volatility in the stock's price. There is also, Rho which is one of the Greek variables that indicates how an option's price be affected by a change in interest rates.

The Greeks are very important if you wish to take a deeply scientific approach to options trading but for most traders and especially beginners they are more a distraction that can trigger analysis paralysis.

Chapter 7 - Trading like a Pro

In this the seventh and final day we will wrap up with a chapter dedicated to helping you take a professional approach to trade in options. We will show you how to run your trading operation as a business by observing the best practices and procedures that the professionals use. We will also set out a good trading strategy that will provide income and profits regardless of the market conditions as well as some specialist strategies that you can use when trading under specific market conditions.

IN THIS CHAPTER

You will learn:

- To Develop a reliable business/trading plan
- Identifying business costs
- Minimizing learning curve costs
- Understanding order execution
- Design a small business strategy
- How to use risk defined or risk capped strategies
- Different types of beginner strategies
- When to use the trading strategies to best effect

Treating Option Trading as a Business

In this chapter we will move on to the management and business skills that you will need to adapt to become a successful Option trader. This is simply because trading options is a business albeit with unique situations but it does require its own management style. No matter what you trade, you are a business manager running a financial trading business. Therefore you must become comfortable understanding the costs associated with operating the business as this help you budget accordingly. In business a simple equation of Profits = Cash Income – Operating Expenses, will dictate how profitable a business is being run. Therefore your goal as a business manager will be to maximize profits and an easy way to do that is control or minimize operating expenses.

Now as a beginner, operating expenses may be high as initially certain costs will be unavoidably higher. This is because you will likely be paying more for a broker platform, education and your trading losses. But that's all part of the learning curve that any beginner must expect when they start trading. However, as you become more experienced and your trading skills and strategies evolve, many of those starter costs will go down. However as you get more experienced you will start to realize the need for more complex strategies and market analysis tools so subscriptions to analysis platforms and data services will likely go up.

Nonetheless, always keep in mind that Option trading for you is a business and that some early losses are part of those operating expenses. The goal of course should be to manage the risk and thereby minimize it but the nature of trading makes it impossible to eliminate risk. Managing risk is very doable and is done by disciplines fund management through determining proper trade allocation amounts and setting maximum loss per trade.

Starting out you should never be risking more than 1%-3% of your fund on any one trade. Options trading is far more flexible than most other types of financial trading in allowing this due of course to the lower prices and the power of leverage. And although effectively executing trades is one way of minimizing losses, designing reliable fund management and a trading plan is the foundation of a successful trading career, which will be judged on longevity.

Controlling your emotions

It one thing being keen and wager to start trading but it's quite another to start to trade without a deep understanding of what you are actually doing. If for example you just jump in with little market knowledge you will be gambling using your limited knowledge. This can lead to emotional trading whereby you can start reacting to price movements in an irrational manner. Humans are after all irrational creatures and we tend to stick with something long after we should have chucked it as a bad deal. This is a form of what is called cognitive bias which leads us to continue to throw good money after bad because we think we must turn around our losses. The problem is that emotional trading is usually the path to even bigger losses. That's why we have to understand the rules about sunk costs – went it's lost it is lost, forget it and move on. When we have strict rules that free us from chasing losses and allow us to let go we can then start to consider each trade as a separate entity with no correlation or connection with anything that has gone before. Then we can start to trade rationally and logically. And this is why you need to design an anticipatory trading plan.

A suitable trading plan should have these basic ingredients:

- That you have the technology that you need to trade efficiently such as a computer, fast internet and mobile devices that will allow you to work anywhere
- Time Management: You need to plan your working hours so that you can commit time to trading. Short term positions will require more of your time so allocate the hours necessary to monitor your trading position
- Good Communication: Build up and have to hand a collection of reliable and trusted real-time quote table and option chain services.

- Reliable Trade Execution: Work with an online broker that has a good reputation for efficiently and accurately executing trades.
- Education: A trading plan must take into account provisions for developing your skills. This should include working on enhancing your technical and fundamental analysis skills. You will also need to develop good option chain and chart reading skills in order to find appropriate options and opportunities.

Managing Your Costs

There will be a variety of start-up and operational costs that you will need to consider when starting your trading business. But after saying that there will be expense categories that will persist throughout your trading career:

- Education: Training expenses will include materials, courses, and of course the unavoidable learning curve losses when trying new strategies and tactics as well as when entering new stocks in the market. Some of the learning costs will hopefully decrease as you hone your skills and find the strategies and tactics that work for you, but other will persist as you will need to stay abreast of developing market conditions. One of the most enduring costs of trading will be supporting your learning curve. This would hopefully decline as your experience and knowledge grow but you will need to come to terms with the following:
    - Trade in the best conditions for each type of option, stock and strategy.
    - Select options with the appropriate liquidity.
    - Develop your paper-trading and chart reading skills.
    - Manage your fund by allocating the appropriate amount to each trade.
    - Effectively enter orders for the best exit.
    - Take profits.
- Analysis costs: As you progress from a beginner concentrating primarily on long call options and your skills progress you will naturally become more adventurous. Further, as your trading generates regular profits, you may start to migrate to more advanced and risky strategies. To successfully manage this trading transition will place a heavy emphasis on adding analytical tools to your business costs. Analytical tools for deep technical analysis are one of the few costs that may increase as your skills develop.
- Trading costs: One of the most easily forgotten or commonly overlooked costs is brokerage fees for handling the transaction or exercising the option. You need to calculate them into all calculations when determining if the position is in the money or not. Many beginners remember and account for the commission but forget to consider for slippage. Slippage is the cost associated with the market spread — it is the difference

between the bid and the ask prices and that is where the broker makes their profit. A good exercise to get you familiar with your broker's charges is to paper trade using commission and slippage percentages for different size option positions. Soon you will have a feel for what the charges will likely be for different price points such as $1, $5, and $10.

- Taxes are another consideration and you can get the full information from the Internal Revenue Service (IRS) (www.irs.gov).
- If you open a margin account whereby you borrow from your broker you need to add that monthly margin interest fees into the calculation. As a beginner you should not need to do this but as you get more skilled you may start to use short option positions, which will have margin requirements. If you decide to write short option strategies that will be requiring margin, be sure you fully understand all of the associated fees and account charges.
- Losses are another trading cost you could say it is an occupational hazard. Nonetheless losses have to be considered part of doing business. They are certainly likely to be higher at first, but can be reduced but never eliminated altogether through diligent paper trading and experience.

As you spend more time trading and get sufficient time and experience under your belt you will find that sticking to your trading plan will help keep these initial costs to a minimum. Some important factors to bear in mind are:

- Determining the trading allocations: The term trading allocation means the safe amount relative to your capital fund that you can risk on a single trade. Hence a crucial element of a trading plan should identify both your total trading capital as well as your maximum amount, the allocation, that you are willing to risk per trade. Of course if you are experienced in other forms of financial trading such as direct stock and ETF trading you will know that they will require larger risk or per trade funding than when trading positions in options. If you are trading on limited funds then you may if you are risk averse set a maximum allocation amount for every new strategy, say 1% to 3% of capital funds. However that should be based on your paper-trading results and you should always avoid over-committing funds to a single trade.
- Calculate the trade size: You must also determine guidelines for maximum position size prior to entering any trade. It is important to always identify beforehand the maximum number of contracts you can take on a position. The way to do this is to divide the option price by the allocation amount that you are comfortable with and ensure it is below your maximum limit. It is best not to try to use the max allocation as that can be very risky should the trade turn against you.
- Identify the maximum acceptable loss on a trade: When you contemplate this figure it is essential that you control your greed or fear. Consequently, you should set the maximum acceptable loss that you are comfortable with at either a pre-defined dollar

value or an as a percentage or the return on investment (ROI). The latter metric may be preferable because a fixed dollar amount can be significant only if you are trading with larger allocations than on smaller trades in less liquid stocks. Of course success in percentage gains does not put food on the table or bolster your trading account only dollar gains does that. Either way you should regularly check your trading performance through an analysis on your trade results. This is essential in determining if your strategy is correct and that your losses remain at acceptable and ultimately sustainable levels. Even a brief periodic review of your trading results should be enough to let you know how well you are doing. After all you must know how much money you are gaining or more importantly if there is sufficient capital left in your trading account and whether the strategy is working.

- Focus on entry and exit rules: The decisions to enter into an Option position come about by spotting trending market conditions but they may also be based around a scheduled event. In which case the Option exits will tend to be after the scheduled event has passed. The may also be triggered by a change around in a market trend. Regardless, of the reason why you enter or exit a position they must be consistent with your overall risk management strategy that determines the maximum acceptable loss per trade.
- Exiting a position based on technical indicators alone will not enable you to take an acceptable loss metric into the equation. Therefore you will need to come up with your own figure for an acceptable loss and set your stop loss orders to match
- It is always a good business model to segregate your brokerage account used just for options trading from other trading interests. This could make your record keeping and your life much simpler.

Optimizing Order Execution

Successfully trading options means gaining proficiency with order execution. A variety of factors come into the mix here:

- Understanding order placement rules unique to options
- Knowing how different order types work
- Learning how to use combination orders for multi-leg positions
- Gaining skill while using the underlying to identify option exists
- Recognizing your broker's role in execution quality

There is also a learning curve for executing options trades, but for the most part these are mechanical steps that can be easily mastered with some practice. You can get a leg up on this with your paper trading, but it's never the same as the real-time action. This will go a long way toward successful strategy implementation.

Trading rules you should know

Whenever you begin trading a new market, you'll need to become acquainted very quickly with the trading rules. Usually your broker or their trading platform will prevent you from going wrong but you shouldn't need to rely on them to keep you right. In this section we provide a short list of common basic rules for trading Options that will hopefully help you through your initial trading executions and throughout your trading career:

- Contract pricing: In general Options trade in increments of $0.01, $0.05, and $0.10.
- Option premium: The price of the premium that you pay for an option is obtained by multiplying the option price offered by the multiplier. When trading in stocks the multiplier value is usually based upon 100 shares of the underlying stock. Therefore, when you purchase one option that is quoted at $2.80, you are actually going to have to pay $2,80 x 100 = $280 for the option, plus any broker commission.
- Market conditions: There are different market conditions that impact both the stock and options markets. These include the following:
- Trading halts for a security or entire market: If you find yourself holding an option for a halted stock, them the any options based on the stock will also be halted. This does not affect your rights or prevent you from exercising your contract rights. However be aware that when this occurs before expiration it may be difficult to trade the options but will not prevent you from exercising the option on or before the expiry date.
- Fast trading conditions: In fast-moving markets stock prices can change rapidly and you are likely to see quotes changing quickly. As a result when you are placing an order you might find that there are significant delays. This can simply be because your bid is not falling out with the bid-ask spread so is being ignored. Therefore you need to check and if necessary to edit your order to make it more acceptable. Also in fast moving market conditions make sure to use limit orders that are price focused rather than market orders as you may end up paying more than you wanted.
- Booked order: In the case of a booked order – one that a market maker places that improve the current market quote. You may encounter problems filling these types of orders for Options greater than 1 contract and you are likely to only get a partial fill of the order. Be aware of this if using ALL or No parameters on your order.
- Best-execution: Execution quality is a measure of a broker's ability to fill orders at, or better than, the current market for the security. Options exchanges are required to monitor and send a daily exception report to your broker whenever a trade is executed at a price other than at the NBBO, referred to as traded-through. If you are unhappy with the price on transactions or are finding it hard to make a trade on what appears to be competitive prices you will need to contact your Broker for an explanation.

Finding a Broker and a Platform

Finding a suitable Brokerage account is a critical activity for any serious investor looking to trade Option in the market. Not all online brokers are suited to options trading however and some have very strict rules, which are serious constraints on a beginner's activities. Interestingly, as options are becoming more main-stream and are finally being seen as a way to manage risk and use leverage rather than a field for reckless speculation things are improving. Indeed many brokers are beginning to welcome beginners in options trading as they now view them as serious risk-aware traders that are diversifying into options to boost their profits.

However for the investor it is still a problem finding a suitable brokerage because it is true that any broker can buy and sell stocks, but not all of them have the skills, knowledge and the online tools to help their clients in establishing and executing options-based transactions and strategies. Nonetheless, each year more brokerages are stepping up to the plate with improved portfolios of services aimed at the options trader. So, here are some of the things that you'll want to be looking out for when you're searching for an options broker.

1. **Tools to assess options strategies**

Evaluating and selecting appropriate options involves different analysis and information than picking the underlying stocks. Picking options on that stock will require looking at measures of market conditions, bid-ask spread, implied volatility, probability, and open interest, and trading behavior in order to come up with successful strategies.

The best online options brokers will have the specialist tools and analysis charts to help you evaluate which options are a good match with your trading strategy. They will also be able to provide access to trading simulators, historical and current market data, analytical platforms, and easy to navigate quote and order functions.

2. **A trading platform that works with your strategy**

Trading options can be very complicated especially when you advance into using risk-defined combination strategies to manage and risk and limit losses. Most beginners will start out simply buying or selling single Call or Put options on a particular stock. However, as their skills and experience develop they will gravitate towards using more advanced options strategies, which requires building a trading strategy by buying or selling combinations of different types of options. Constructing and coordinating the deployment of these strategies is very difficult unless your options broker's trading platform support these types of strategies. Ideally, they should be available as a turn-key option and selectable from a menu whereby the platform will do all the heavy-lifting in constructing these multi-leg combination orders.

The best trading platforms will have simple interfaces that make it easy to navigate and are intuitive to use so that you know exactly what you're doing. To most traders the platform is the broker so if you are comfortable with the trading experience then you will be happy with your options broker.

3. Make sure your broker's customer service agents know options

Although the vast amount of transactions will go solely through the broker's online trading platform, there will inevitably come a time when something goes wrong. This is when customer support becomes important as you will probably need to talk directly to a customer service agent in order to resolve your issue. This is when it becomes imperative that you speak to an experienced agent who can help resolve your issue quickly and efficiently.

Unfortunately, for many brokerage firms, options are a new service that they are entering into, and regular customer service agents aren't well trained or are not experienced enough in options to communicate and resolve issues effectively. The problem is that you cannot really evaluate a brokerage firm's customer service until you need their help and by that time it could be too late. However if you go with a broker that specializes in options, they are more likely to have options specialists working in the customer service department that you can communicate with when you need them. It is also a very good sign if the brokerage has invested in omnichannel communication support and technology like bots and robot-advisors as that can greatly speed up the issue resolution process.

4. Check Commissions are Competitive

Commissions on options trading can be a thorny issue as they are often obscure and for a good reason as often they are a lot higher than standard stock commissions. So it's important not to assume that broker that has a good reputation for low-prices with stocks will be so generous with options. This is down to the economics as most options markets are a lot less liquid than the markets for individual stocks so there isn't the same economy of scale.

Sometimes, you'll have to work with standard stock commissions and then add on an additional commission for the option. Others thankfully will just charge a one-off fee for each option transaction (2-leg). However there are several other fees you need to be aware of with options, such as margin charges and exercise transaction fees so you will need to dig through the fine print as sometimes the fees to exercise an option can be excessive.

Nonetheless, it is certainly true, that often you get what you pay for and in some cases, paying higher commissions will be worth the price if it equates to high-quality service.

5. Get trained on options

It is actually in the broker's interest to educate you in options trading or any financial trading for that matter. As not only will you use those services you will likely be more competent and take up less of their time trying to resolve your mistakes. However, some brokers are better than others and go a lot further than is strictly required to educate their clients in strategies, tactics and transaction processes. Most brokers will have freely available educational materials mainly online videos about options trading and these are often comprehensive catalogues covering just about every technical aspect of the business. This is in the broker's interest as it provides promotional material as well as a form of lock-in as all the demos have been performed on their own platform. Hence it may be considered a red-flag if a broker has little in the way of educational material or free demos/accounts. However at the very minimum every brokerage is required to give you disclosure documents from the Options Clearing Commission.

Education, guidance and technical support on options trading can take place on many types of media. A good combination of online videos, webinars, online FAQ and accessible customer service specialists through voice, chat and email is probably a gold standard. But remember you get what you are willing to pay for – after all a brokerage is a business as well and they cannot be expected to provide a Rolls-Royce service yet charge rock-bottom commissions. If you are willing to accept the trade-off you can get you what you need to be a more effective options investor at the price you are willing to pay.

Spend time evaluating brokerages, try out their demo platforms if you can and be diligent in finding the best broker that matches your needs as getting it wrong could cost you serious money.

To trade options well, you will need to have a good options broker. Then you will make the most of the opportunities that arise and that trading in options gives you.

There are many online brokers that beginners can use for trading options and several of the top ones don't even require you to fund an account. This makes them very attractive for testing and practicing on when experimenting with order types and paper trading. The most notable is in no particular order:

- **Interactive Brokers** – Cheapest around with no per-leg base fee, lowest margin rates are and dozens of options-oriented lessons - Account Minimum: $0 Fees: $0.005 per share

- **TD Ameritrade** (think or swim)- High-quality educational tool, which has live content on TDAmeritradeNetwork.com, it also has a trading simulator for practicing options trading strategies, the platform also has many tools for selecting options strategies, as well as streaming data available on all platforms - Account Minimum: $0 Fees: $6.95 for stock and ETF trades, $6.95 per leg plus $0.75 for options
- **Charles Schwab** (StreetSmart platforms) – very good beginner Options-oriented trading lessons, with a wide array of asset classes that can be traded on any of the available platforms - Account Minimum: $0 Fees: $4.95 per stock and ETF trade, $0 for Schwab ETFs and $4.95 plus $0.65 per contract for options
- **Tastyworks** - Very stable platform, All the tools are accessible from a single page, The platform is focused on derivatives trading Account Minimum: $0 Fees: $5.00 stock trades $1.00 options trades

All of the online brokers suggested above have a variety of features and tools, some are better than others and some are a lot cheaper than others so it is something of a trade-off. The most important thing is to try some out and find one that matches your own budget and requirements.

Understanding Transaction Fees and Slippage

Broker fees across the trading world vary greatly as can be seen from the sample listed above. However saying that they do all tend to charge fees based upon per transactions or leg (2 legs per transaction a buy and a sell) and something that they call slippage.

Slippage is the term used to account for the difference between a quoted price and the actual price you pay or are paid for a stock. In today's fast markets slippage has become unavoidable as prices change so rapidly. The amount of price slippage is determined by the difference between the bid and the asking price - the spread. The larger the spread the more likely there will be significant slippage, as it's a sign of low liquidity and volume.

There are two ways to approach minimizing slippage:

1. Use limit orders instead of market orders – Limit orders will only execute at the price you set, market orders on the other hand will always fill the order at the best available price and that is the primary cause of slippage.
2. Consider slippage to be a cost of doing business – If using limit orders is unsuitable – in many cases they are as there will be times that you must guarantee opening or closing a position – then you must calculate the likely cost of slippage into the financials.

The ways to calculate slippage - as a cost of doing business, just like all the other fees and commissions - is to use the following formula:

Amount of bid-ask spread in dollars x 100 (shares) x 1 (contract) x 2 (legs (open/close)) = slippage

Develop a Small Account Trading Strategy

Beginners always want to know how much money they need in their fund to be able to trade successfully. The truth of the matter is that you can trade happily with a small fund of 5,000 dollars it is just with a small account you have to be very sensitive to risk. That means making small percentage trades on high probability, high volatility options and always ensuring that your positions are risk defined and covered. Therefore a simple trading strategy for a small beginner account would be to adhere to the following pointers:

- Trade using small allocations for each trade
- Trade using risk defined strategies (always covered and never naked)
- Trade those high probability Options (pick the low hanging fruit)
- Trade in high Implied Volatility (IV) Options
- Build long term consistency – use the big numbers

When you first start out trading it is imperative that you protect your capital fund and that means only making a small allocation for each trade. A general rule of thumb on an account of around $5,000 would be to limit your allocation to 1%-2% per trade. You can later when you become more experienced start to look to 2%-3% allocation but you should never need to go higher. It is always better to make several small allocations per trade than being over-committed on a single trade.

Another reason for having a small account trading strategy is that trading at the end of the day is driven by probability and percentages (returns on investment) rather than purely on dollar returns. There is no reason at all why you cannot trade on a $5,000 account if you remember that it's more about managing the risk rather than the dollar stakes. For example, with a $5000 fund and you take allocations of 1% ($50) per trade and you have a run of trades that go against you that will be bad but not catastrophic. However if you start out taking 5% allocation ($250) or worse 10% ($500) allocations things go wrong exponentially quicker and leave you cleaned out in no time.

Placing too large allocations per trade is a path to ruin so bear in mind to keep it low. This may be frustrating at first as there will be some attractive trades that you will want to make but simply you cannot risk. In these cases you must be disciplined and not make the trade - never trade over your allocation or your account size as that is the surest way to get cleaned out.

After all as you can build up your fund using small allocations on high probability trades over time and then you can start to allocate more dollars but the percentages should stay the same regardless of the equity fund size.

The second point in our strategy is to always have a risk defined position as with small accounts we do need to guard against excessive or unlimited risk. Therefore we want to be using well-defined trading strategies which limit our risk exposure. The one thing you must never do is go naked as that is inviting unlimited risk and to be cleaned out should the trade go against you. There are many safe risk defined strategies that we can use even with small accounts to make small profits. And the thing is if we concentrate our efforts on high probability trades and making more consistent and frequent trades whereby we are winning more often than we lose. This is why sticking to consistently making small frequent high probability trades is so important for small accounts.

Gradually that account will soon start to build up as we will have the law of big numbers and the percentages firmly on our side, which makes things a lot more predictable and profitable.

Deploying Risk-Defined Techniques

In the strategy that we have just looked at for Options trading with a small fund there was a recommendation to use risk-defined trades. In this section we will look at how we make these risk defined or risk-capped trades such as Credit Spreads, Iron Condors and Butterfly Spreads.

Now the first thing that often springs to mind is that in Options trading we are working with limited risk trades anyway as if setup correctly we should only we at risk of losing our premium. But the beauty of combining Calls and Puts in sophisticated ways means that we can construct some really elegant risk-defined strategies. A good example is in the classic credit spread strategy.

Credit Spread Strategy

A Credit Spread is a risk-defined strategy that involves combining two Call orders. The way it works is that you will need to buy a call with one strike price, and then sell (write) a call with a lower strike price.

Now, if we look at the differences between the call Options, one was bought with a strike price of let's say $39 for $0.15. But if you then write a call Option with a strike price of $32 for $1.27. You now have a net credit position of $1.27 – $0.15 = $1.12. Now, your overall position is out-of-the-money but that means it is profitable to you the writer and will remain so as long as the underlying price is below $32.

Should the price reach $32 dollar the option may well be exercised. That would mean getting assigned the option and you would have to buy the underlying asset at market value. In this case your loss would be the market price less $32. However, if the underlying price were at $39 or above, you could exercise your long call to limit your loss. Hence, your maximum loss would be $39.00 – $32.00 – $1.12 = $5.88.

However, with the technique of combining different types of orders we can construct sophisticated trading strategies that tightly define-risk or even cap risk. For example let's look at the Iron Condor, which is a great beginner strategy because it is both non-directional and also range bound.

Iron Condor

An Iron Condor is a suitable beginner strategy for selling a range-bound stock position for a steady income. The way it works is that it requires you to make several Calls and Puts that define the upper and lower ranger boundaries. So for example we need to:

- Sell a Put and then Buy a Put at a lower strike price – basically create a Put spread
- Sell a Call and then Buy a Call at a higher strike price – basically create a Call spread

The logic behind the Iron Condor is that the strategy creates range-boundaries between the two sold points. So long as the traffic, which can move in any direction, stays within the range-boundaries, the strategy will earn money – premiums.

The Iron Condor strategy will only lose money should the trade move out with the bounded range formed by the two spreads.

Covered Calls

These are another good beginner strategy as they can provide profit when a stock is flat, moving sideways or falling just slightly. To be covered is essential in the risk-defined strategy so you need to buy 100 shares in stock then sell a Call option for the 100 shares. The trade will then make money so long as the stock goes up, remains flat or even if it dips slightly.

The way this works is that the money collected through the premiums not only provided some protection against a fall in price but also enhances the returns when the stock stays flat.

Married Put Strategy

This is a rather sophisticated strategy that is suited to beginners due to its risk definition. The married Put works because like in the covered stock you have to combine an Option with a physical stock. In this case you would buy 100 shares in a stock. Then the key is to buy long put options for the equivalent number of shares. As a result the married put strategy works like an insurance policy against short-term losses. Then you need to buy long call options with a specific strike price. At the same time, you'll sell the same number of call options at a higher strike price. This makes the Married Put profits tied to the underlying stocks price performance, as you will need it to rise to make a profit but the added benefit is any downside is completely covered.

Protective Collar Strategy

This is another risk-defined trading strategy that like the covered spread is based upon the trader holding shares of the underlying stock. The trader can then buy protective puts and then sell call options against the stock holding. The puts and the calls are both chosen to be out-of-the-money options but they must have the same expiration date. Another caveat is that the stock must be equal in number to the options. For example 100 shares against 1 contract OTM Put, 1 contract OTM Call.

The way that it works will be that the investor will buy an out-of-the-money put option and simultaneously write an out-of-the-money call option for the same stock. The protected collar is a good strategy to use to protect the price of the underlying security whilst also providing a source of income via premium for the covered calls.

Long Straddle Strategy

With the long straddle strategy the trader will buy a call option and a put option at the same time. The way that it works is that both options must have the same strike price and the same expiration date. The strike price is at-the-money or as close to it as possible. The strategy is to make a profit from a significant shift in the price of the underlying stock regardless of the direction. The long straddle strategy is deployed when it is expected that a stock will move from a low volatility state to a much higher one and it is geared to benefit if the price moves in either direction. Typically a trader will set up along straddle just before an important news event is about to break to capture the sudden burst in trading volatility. The long straddle strategy has limited risk and unlimited potential for profit.

Long Strangle Strategy

Another form of unlimited profit but limited risk strategy is to use the long strangle strategy. In this case the investor will buy an out-of-the-money call option and an out of money put option at the same time. The two options will need to have the same expiration date but they will have different strike prices. The put strike price should always be lower than the call strike price. Large gains can be made using the long strangle if there is sufficient change in volatility before the expiry date but it is a debit spread at setup.

Putting it all together

Throughout this book, we have strived to teach you how to start successfully trading options. In the course of your studies you have learned much of the theory and concepts behind options as financial instruments and how they are traded. You have also learned how to read an options table and an options chain to find those elusive options that meet your trading ambitions. You now know how to open and close positions using a number of orders that are suited to specific trading conditions and markets. Finally, and very importantly you have learned how to run your trading operations as a business and to trade like a professional. Crucially, you will have learned and understood the importance of having a trading strategy. To this purpose we proposed an advanced trading strategy that is suitable for beginners. The five-point strategy is designed to provide tracing longevity and make profits even in the most difficult markets. However, it is not a pick and mix list, you must adhere to all five principles to be successful. This is because it is not a bundle of trading tactics, it's a mindset, a philosophy, which if you develop it early in your trading career and stick with it, then you will greatly increase your chances of surviving long term. Successful traders are measured by their longevity and not their short term gains as luck can distort that picture immensely. And luck doesn't last forever but a good strategy, which enforces best practices and risk management does make you a better trader.

After reading this book you now have all the knowledge necessary to trade in options and a sound strategy on which to base your trading career. But this should be only the start of your education as in options trading – every day's a school day. It has taken you 7 days or less to learn how to make money trading options – now it's time to step up and start trading.

Good Luck and Healthy Profits!

Thank you

Before you go, I just wanted to say thank you for purchasing my book.

You could have picked from dozens of other books on the same topic but you took a chance and chose this one.

So, a HUGE thanks to you for getting this book and for reading all the way to the end.

Now I wanted to ask you for a small favor. **Could you please consider posting a review on the platform? Reviews are one of the easiest ways to support the work of authors.**

This feedback will help me continue to write the type of books that will help you get the results you want. So if you enjoyed it, please let me know.

www.ingramcontent.com/pod-product-compliance
Lightning Source LLC
Chambersburg PA
CBHW051750200326
41597CB00025B/4504
* 9 7 8 1 9 5 3 0 3 6 1 6 2 *